Acoustic Guitar

Acoustic Guitar

An Historical Look at the Composition, Construction, and
Evolution of One of the World's Most Beloved Instruments

Teja Gerken
Michael Simmons
Frank Ford
Richard Johnston

HAL•LEONARD®
C O R P O R A T I O N

7777 W. BLUEMOUND RD. P.O. BOX 13819 MILWAUKEE, WI 53213

Akustische Gitarren—Alles über Konstruktion und Historie
© 2003 GC Carstensen Verlag.
This edition is published by arrangement with GC Carstensen Verlag, Munich, Germany.

Published by Hal Leonard Corporation
7777 W. Bluemound Road
P.O. Box 13819
Milwaukee, WI 53213

ISBN 0-634-07920-4

AUSTRALIAN CONTACT INFO:
In Australia Contact:
Hal Leonard Australia Pty. Ltd.
22 Taunton Drive P.O. Box 5130
Cheltenham East, 3192 Victoria, Australia
Email: ausadmin@halleonard.com

Library of Congress Cataloging-in-Publication Data

Gerken, Teja.
  Acoustic guitar : an historical look at the composition, construction, and evolution of one of the world's most beloved instruments / Teja Gerken ... [et al.].-- 1st ed.
    p. cm.
  Originally written in English; translated and first published in German by Carstensen Verlag, 2003 with title: Akustische Gitarren-Alles über Konstruktion und Historie.
  Includes bibliographical references (p.   ) and index.
  ISBN 0-634-07920-4 (alk. paper)
  1. Guitar. 2. Guitar--Construction. I. Title.
ML1015.G9G52 2005
787.87'1923--dc22
                              2004029367

Printed in the U.S.A.

First Edition

Visit Hal Leonard online at
www.halleonard.com

JUL 1 0 2007

Contents

Chapter 2: The Neck   25

Chapter 12: A Look into the Future — **353**

Foreword

I grew up in a family steeped in guitar history, but even with my background, I continue to be amazed at how the acoustic guitar has managed to evolve into so many different varieties. It is hard to believe that classical guitars of Spain, the archtops of American builders like Gibson and D'Angelico, the Gypsy jazz guitars of Selmer, the 12-string guitars of Stella, and the flattop steel strings designed and built by my own ancestors all share a common history.

One of the things this book does is explain how these various styles of guitars differ, and paradoxically show how much these different kinds of guitar really have in common. The book also covers topics like what to look for when buying a guitar, how to take care of it when you do choose one, how different types of wood affect the tone, and what the various option for amplification are.

No matter whether you're new to the acoustic guitar or have been involved with it for years, this book will help you find the answers to your questions, and perhaps even teach you a few things you hadn't considered before. Whether you're a player, collector, retailer, or manufacturer, give it a read, and then grab your favorite guitar and make some music of your own.

C.F. Martin IV

Introduction

It is difficult to imagine today's musical landscape without the acoustic guitar. Whether the instrument is used to strum a simple folk song, play a flamenco *compas*, swing the night away, or interpret classical music's most revered composers, its unique versatility has made it a cultural ambassador and a link between musical styles.

Nobody knows for sure where the guitar originated, but its popularity may go back as far as 1400 B.C.—the origination date of a Hittite stone carving that features a guitar-like stringed instrument with an hourglass-shaped body and a fretted neck. At about the same time, the Egyptians tomb walls were decorated with paintings of people playing an instrument called the *nefer*. The name *guitar* may derive from the ancient Greek word *kithara*—a lap-held, harp-like instrument to which the modern-day guitar bears little resemblance. Instead, the 10th-century, guitar-like Persian *rebab* (which is still played in Iran and throughout central Asia) is more likely the oldest actual ancestor of the guitar as we know it today.

The guitar is also a descendent of a 13th-century European instrument known as the *gittern*. Although no actual gitterns survived the ages intact, we are familiar with the instrument through its depiction in numerous church carvings and paintings of the period. In fact, in three of his *Canterbury Tales*, Chaucer describes the gittern as an instrument commonly heard in taverns and in accompaniment to love songs. In the 15th century, a small-bodied, four-course (i.e., double-strung, like a mandolin) instrument called the *guitarra*—officially the earliest version of what would eventually evolve into the modern-day guitar—began replacing the gittern. In response to the time's changing musical demands and the popularity of additional strings, luthiers began to progressively increase the size of the guitarra's body. By the 18th century, the guitar, as it was now finally called, had five or six courses of strings and a much larger body than its predecessors. Then, sometime in the late-18th century, French and Italian luthiers guitar makers began building their guitars with six strings, which, by the early 19th century, had become the standard throughout Europe. The most famous guitar makers of this time were Italians like Gennaro Fabricatore, Austrians like Johann Stauffer (who would later serve as a mentor to Christian Frederick Martin before he set sail for America), and Frenchmen like François René Lacote.

Finally, the mid-1800s saw the development of the guitar that today's players would recognize. In Spain, Antonio de Torres developed what has come to be regarded as the modern nylon-string classical guitar, while C.F. Martin quickly broke from his German roots by designing an X-braced instrument that would eventually become the quintessential American steel-string guitar. In the late nineteenth century, American luthier Orville Gibson started carving the tops and backs of his guitars and mandolins to arch like those of a violin. While countless others contributed to the advancement of the modern-day guitar, it was clearly these three innovators that set the stage for the guitar to become what it is today.

The guitar has always had a raffish reputation. Paintings by Watteau, Goya, Velázquez, Picasso, and Eakins all show the guitar as the center of the party, making it an even more prominent subject than the ubiquitously depicted glass of beer or wine. Even allegorical paintings, like Brueghel's *The Fight Between Carnival and Lent*, employ the guitar's symbolic qualities to signify the struggle between probity and licentiousness. But even though it was the preferred instrument of society's fringe, the guitar nonetheless found a place in the royal courts of Europe and the parlors of the middle class. And, from the 17th century on, the guitar was the instrument of choice for well-born ladies, or those who aspired to be.

Throughout the 16th and 17th centuries, the lute was considered the more "refined" of the fretted instruments, relegating the guitar—the most popular choice of the dedicated amateur—to an almost second-class status within "serious" or classical music circles. However, the beginning of the nineteenth century saw the emergence of a number of guitar "virtuosos"—Fernando Sor, Napoleon Coste, Francisco Tárrega, and Dionisio Aguado—who developed new playing techniques and incorporated greater musical complexity to their compositions, helping to elevate the guitar's social standing and making them the predecessors of the contemporary guitar hero.

In the 1920s, a player named Andrés Segovia managed to earn the guitar a grudging acceptance in concert halls. With his stunning technique and likable repertoire, Segovia found his way into critics' hearts—and his impact is still felt today. However, it was through its use in popular music that the guitar achieved its standing as the most embraced instrument in the world. Practically all of the major musical styles developed in the 20th century were guitar-driven; in particular, blues, country, folk, pop, and rock.

Because it is inexpensive, portable, and its basics are easy to learn, the guitar has become a true instrument of the people; as such, it became the favored musical accompaniment for cultural icons such as Woody Guthrie, Bob Dylan, Victor Jara, and countless others. These artists, whose songs defined their generations, paved the way for rock and pop music to serve as the voice of an era's sentiments. And while screaming electric guitars are often considered the definitive rock 'n' roll tool, it is the acoustic variety that provides the signature sound for artists such as Neil Young, Bruce Springsteen, and Tracy Chapman, as well as Generation X stars such as Beck and the Dave Matthews Band.

While many acoustic guitarists are content to do nothing more than pick out simple chords and melodies, others are continuously searching for ways to expand the capabilities of their instrument. Those who think that the acoustic is limited to campfire sing-alongs are encouraged to listen to legends such as Eddie Lang, Django Reinhardt, Andrés Segovia, Leo Kottke, Baden Powel, Tony Rice, or Paco de Lucía, as well as the constant stream of new talent that keeps the acoustic scene interesting and innovative.

Perhaps more than other musicians, guitarists tend to develop a keen interest in their instruments. Many people start perusing guitar catalogs and magazines long before they ever learn to play, while other beginners find themselves unable to walk past a guitar shop without sampling the wares. In extreme cases, guitar aficionados and collectors get so caught up in discussing the merits of a guitar's minutiae, they lose sight of its fundamental purpose.

Perhaps the reason that the guitar has instigated such an instrument-centered culture is that it is difficult for enthusiasts to resist the enticing variety of instruments that belong to the guitar family. For example, the differences between various violins, saxophones, or pianos are nothing compared to the structural variances between the steel-string dreadnought, flamenco, and archtop styles of guitars. You don't need to be an expert to spot the differences between the various styles of guitars, but the more you learn, the more fascinating the story becomes.

Therefore, in looking at this popular instrument from headstock to tailblock, this book seeks to cover just about every kind of acoustic guitar that is commonly found. Divided into chapters that cover each individual part of the instrument's construction, it dissects the guitar's often confusing construction details, and explains how different models and styles vary from one another.

Due to the fact that the steel-string flattop guitar offers the greatest amount of variations of any acoustic guitar, it is upon this instrument type that this book is centered. However, we also recognize the importance of covering the equally popular nylon-string classical guitar, as well as the acoustic archtop—which, while not currently used as frequently as the instruments mentioned above, has seen a renaissance in popularity, and represents an important step in the guitar's history. Let's take a brief look at the major distinguishing features of these main instrument types:

> **Steel-string flattop:** The quintessential guitar used in folk music, this is also the acoustic guitar of choice in pop and rock music. The steel-string flattop is also very popular with instrumental fingerstyle players, and represents virtually the only type of guitar used by bluegrass flatpickers. Steel-string flattops offer an extremely broad frequency spectrum (which is somewhat dependent on their body size), excellent sustain, and the ability to accommodate both a delicate touch and aggressive strum. The majority of these instruments are more or less variations of the guitars designed by North America's C.F. Martin and Gibson companies during the first half of the twentieth century.

> **Nylon-string guitar:** Primarily associated with classical music (and often referred to as a "classical" guitar), these guitars feature a warm tone with an incredibly large dynamic range. The nylon string is also virtually the only kind of guitar used in South American music, and many jazz players also prefer its sound. Another type of nylon-string guitar, the flamenco, features a brighter sound with less sustain than many other guitars of this type—a quality that's achieved primarily by the kinds of woods that are used in its construction. The construction of most

nylon-string guitars are based on a mid-19th–century Spanish design, but over the last twenty years, this instrument style has also served as the template for some of the most radical developmental changes in luthiery.

Archtop guitars: Closely associated with jazz music (and therefore sometimes called "jazz" guitars), these instruments are a uniquely American phenomenon. Though largely replaced by electric guitars (many of which happen to feature a hollow body), the acoustic archtop guitar is *the* instrument of choice for playing swing rhythm guitar. As such, it has an incredibly punchy sound with a quick attack and short sustain. Its somewhat limited frequency range (which often emphasizes the mid-range) makes it the loudest type of acoustic guitar when strung with heavy strings and played with the appropriate technique. The instrument had its heyday from the 1920s to the 1950s, but a new generation of luthiers has recently elevated this guitar type to new heights. As its name implies, the archtop guitar features a curved top similar to that of a violin or a cello; and further similarities to bowed instruments are found in the frequent incorporation of *f*-holes and tailpieces.

While these three categories encapsulate the main instrument types covered in this book, information on a variety of other styles is also included. When appropriate, we also discussed such important instruments as 12-string guitars, Selmer/Maccaferri "gypsy jazz" instruments, and acoustic-electric guitars of all styles. Additionally, we included niche instruments like travel, baritone, and tenor guitars.

Because almost any type of guitar is available within a wide range of prices, most beginning guitarists are wondering what kind is best to for getting started. That answer is almost always dependent on the type of music the new guitarist wants to play. Although certain kinds of guitars are quite versatile, it would be a mistake to show up at your first classical lesson with a steel-string guitar made for playing gypsy jazz, just as a traditional Spanish guitar will be rather out of place at a bluegrass jam. Many advanced players use the non-versatility factor as an excuse to own more than one instrument; and for many professionals, it's absolutely essential that they're able to produce a variety of sounds and play many musical styles. So, whether you're a beginner trying to determine what your first guitar should be, or a seasoned pro who wants to fill a certain stylistic niche, it helps to understand how the different guitar designs differ from one another, how they sound, and even what their origins are.

This is exactly what we consider the purpose of this book to be. We hope that by explaining the construction, materials, shapes, and styles of the various available acoustic guitars, you will become educated enough to determine on your own whether or not a guitar is a good value and right for you. We have tried to infuse each of the chapters with a sufficient historical perspective without boring the reader with endless lists of dates and minutiae. When it seemed appropriate, we included information on some of the prominent musicians associated with certain guitars.

In order to take advantage of each this book's contributing authors' fields of expertise, the organization of this book is as follows:

> Michael John Simmons took charge of the chapters on the headstock, neck, strings, and the back and sides of the instrument; and, as an admitted fan of any guitar with a non-conventional and unique appearance, Simmons also contributed to the "Variations" section of the chapter on body styles. He also helped considerably with this introduction.

> Richard Johnston penned the chapter about the top of the guitar, and also put his encyclopedic knowledge of the acoustic guitar to use by proofreading all the chapters and making myriad suggestions and additions.

> As one of the most respected guitar repairmen on the scene, Frank Ford was the ideal candidate for writing about glues and finishes, and also contributed the material on the care and repair of the instrument.

> Finally, besides coordinating the team's efforts, I also wrote the chapters covering body styles, body hardware, pickups and electronics, and "What to Look for When Buying an Acoustic Guitar"; I also made an attempt to peer into the crystal ball for some insight and predictions regarding the acoustic guitar's future.

The authors would like to thank the staff at *Acoustic Guitar* magazine, Gryphon Stringed Instruments, Rick Turner, Geoff Stewart, and Dan Erlewine for their input and suggestions. Additionally, a special thank you goes to Heather Gould, Leanne Simmons, and Joy Imai for their patience and support throughout this project.

Teja Gerken

Headstock

To the practiced eye, the headstock contains a wealth of information about a guitar. If you know what to look for, a distinctive silhouette can declare who the builder is, a subtle curve can reveal when the guitar was made, and the very shape announces what style of music the guitar was designed for. Headstocks are sometimes called "pegheads," a word that recalls the time when the strings were tightened with a friction peg made of bone, ivory, or wood instead of the geared metal tuning machine that is almost universally used by contemporary luthiers. Although both terms are in common use, "headstock" is the preferred word for guitars with mechanical tuning machines and "peghead" is more correct for 19th-century guitars or traditional flamenco guitars with friction pegs.

Shape

Headstocks come in a bewildering array of shapes, including the simple squared-off Martin design, the fancy art deco inspired contours of D'Angelico, and the subtle curves of Antonio de Torres. The variety is partially created by aesthetic concerns—luthiers want their instruments to stand out in a crowded marketplace—but even the wildest designs have to be functional.

Clockwise, from top left: The square Martin shape, Breedlove's modern, pointed asymmetrical design, the classical Torres shape, and Johann Stauffer's shape from 1840.

The Maker's Mark (Trademarks, Logos, Etc.)

In the 1800s, it was rare for luthiers to inlay their names or other marks on the headstock as they do today, so each builder developed a distinctive shape to help aficionados identify the makers' instruments. The most striking shape in those early days was probably Stauffer's scroll, which featured six-in-a-line tuning machines. Other early 19th-century builders who developed immediately recognizable headstocks include Panormo, with his "half-moon" shape, and Antonio de Torres, who used a triple-lobe shape. The tradition of builders creating unique headstock shapes has continued to this day.

Sometime in the beginning of the 20th century, builders such as Martin and Gibson began inlaying their names in the headstock, and it has since become the fashion for steel-strings builders to use inlays or decals along with a distinctive shape to identify their instruments. Classical guitar makers for the most part retain the 19th-century practice of leaving the headstock blank.

In the last few years, it has become common for modern builders making replicas of famous makers' vintage guitars to duplicate the headstock shape—even if they have their own trademark shape. So when Bill Collings or Richard Hoover of the Santa Cruz Guitar Company makes a replica of a circa 1937 Martin D-28, he will copy the peghead shape, just as classical builders like Kenny Hill or Gary Southwell reproduce the Panormo shape on their replicas.

Acoustic guitar headstocks are almost always built symmetrically with the tuning machines arranged in a three-on-a-side pattern. The only significant exceptions are the guitars with six-in-a-line tuning machines made by Johann Stauffer in Vienna in the early part of the 19th century, the very first guitars made by C. F. Martin in the 1830s (a style they have revived on a few new models), and the acoustic guitars made by the Fender company in the late 1960s.

Martin recently revived the Stauffer headstock shape on a limited basis. A few builders like Steve Klein and Jeff Traugott and the Canadian company Seagull have been making guitars with headstocks that have an almost pointed shape. They feel that this shape puts the strings in a straight line and helps keep them from binding in the nut.

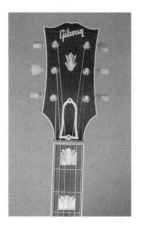 

Gibson and Ovation both have easily distinguished headstock shapes.

You would think that after 200 years of guitar evolution all of the good headstock shapes would have been used up, but luthiers are still coming up with distinctive designs. So to the classic shapes of builders like Torres, Ramirez, Selmer, Martin, Gibson, and D'Angelico, we can add the triple cut shape of Taylor, the carved curves of Ovation, and the elegant line of D'Aquisto.

Solid vs. Slotted

Headstocks can be either solid or slotted. *Solid* headstocks with right angle tuning machines are found on most flattop steel-strings and practically all archtops. Traditional flamenco guitars also have solid headstocks, but they use wooden friction pegs rather than geared tuning machines. *Slotted* headstocks, which always have geared tuning machines, are found on classical guitars, many steel-string guitars made before 1920, and instruments made in the Selmer/Maccaferri style. In the last few years, modern builders have been building a few guitars in the old "parlor" style with slotted headstocks.

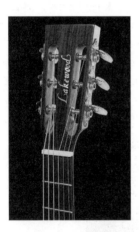 

A slotted headstock on a Lakewood steel-string, and Hopf Guitar's distinctive cutout headstock.

There is almost no functional difference between the two headstock styles, but the slotted version is a little more difficult to restring, particularly if you need to change a string onstage in a hurry. Steel-string guitars with slotted headstocks often have wider fingerboards and necks that join the body at the 12th, rather than the 14th, fret—a style that recalls the instruments roots in the 19th century. Because the strings angle quite sharply over the nut on a steel-string guitar with a slotted headstock, some players and builders feel that this gives the instrument a slightly brighter sound. A few modern luthiers like Rick Turner, Taylor, Froggy Bottom, and Gallagher build guitars with modern designs and slotted headstocks to take advantage of this effect. Jimmy D'Aquisto, the great archtop guitar builder, felt that lighter headstocks sounded better, so he cut slots into the headstocks of some of the last guitars he built, but he used the right-angle-style tuning machines found on guitars with solid headstocks.

The slotted headstock of an acoustic-electric Turner Renaissance guitar.

One-Piece vs. Grafted

During the 19th century, it was common practice for luthiers to make the neck and headstock out of two separate pieces of a lightweight wood (like cedar) and to attach them together at the nut. This construction technique is known as *grafting*, and was used to strengthen the area behind the nut where the headstock angled back. In the late 19th and early 20th century, guitar makers began to switch to mahogany for the neck, which is stiffer than cedar and less likely to warp or twist. Because mahogany is stronger, it is possible to carve the neck and headstock out of a single piece of wood, which has become the standard construction technique for many classical and almost all steel strings in the 20th century.

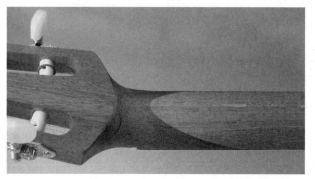

The grafted headstock on the same Turner Renaissance.

A large number of modern classical guitar builders use a technique where they carve the neck and headstock as a single piece and then cut the headstock and graft it back on for extra strength. In 1996, Taylor began using a complex finger joint to graft the headstocks on their Baby model. They initially did it as a cost-cutting measure, but they found the new joint was stronger than expected, and have since gone to grafted headstocks on their complete line of guitars.

Headstock Overlay

Traditionally, the headstock overlay is made of ebony or rosewood and is matched to the wood used on the fingerboard or the back and sides. Occasionally, builders will use plastic—either in a tortoise-shell color to match the binding on the body—or perhaps use a contrasting material such as a pearloid "mother-of-toilet-seat" pattern. The headstock overlay is purely ornamental, but is such a recognized tradition that even the cheapest guitars will have an overlay of some sort, or the headstock will be painted to make it appear as if it had an overlay.

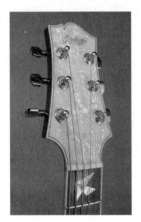 

For an extravagant look, "mother of toilet seat" plastic can be used for the headstock overlay. Dale Unger of American Archtops uses ebony for his headstock overlay.

Binding

Headstock binding is very rare on nylon string guitars; and even on steel strings, it's only found on the fanciest models. Headstock binding usually replicates the pattern and materials—usually celluloid, although wood is sometimes used as well— found on the neck binding to create a seamless appearance.

Triple binding on a Collings, and five-layer binding on a Guild Artist Award archtop.

Headstock binding is perhaps most common on archtops—particularly the Art Deco–influenced instruments by Gibson, Epiphone, and D'Angelico, as well as those by modern builders working in the same tradition. The only reason a luthier uses headstock binding is for aesthetic purposes, as it serves no structural purpose.

Volute

The *volute* is the small bump carved into the neck behind the nut on some guitars. The volute helps strengthen the weak area where the headstock changes angles. On some 19th-century guitars, the grafted headstock was reinforced with a piece of wood shaped like a pyramid, which was sometimes called a *dart*. Although Martin switched to a one-piece neck and headstock—a building technique that made the dart superfluous— they still retained it on certain models such as the style 28 and the style 45 for purely cosmetic reasons. Now, when builders such as Collings or Santa Cruz build a guitar in the style of an old Martin, they also reproduce the dart.

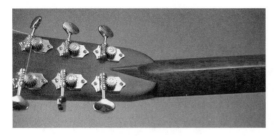

The dart-shaped volute was originally part of a grafted joint, but today it's often more of a decorative element.

In the 1960s, Guild started incorporating volutes; and even though doing so resulted in a stronger headstock, players objected to the shape and it was discontinued around 1970. Coincidentally, around the time Guild was dropping volutes, Gibson started using them on their guitars. As with Guild, players objected to the shape, and by the end of the1980s, Gibson discontinued the practice of putting volutes on their instruments. So now, volutes, in the dart form, are only found on a few models made by Martin and guitars made in the style of Martin.

Truss Rod Access

The adjustable truss rod was invented by Gibson in 1921, at a time when all of their instruments were made with carved arched tops. Gibson opted to make the truss rod accessible at the headstock end of the neck, rather than down by the soundhole. This required carving a channel in the face of the peghead just in front of the nut, which was then hidden by a small truss rod cover. Builders soon began to use the functional truss rod cover as a decorative element, and over the years, used them also as mini-billboards and carved the model name of the guitar into the plastic (a common practice for Gibson), or occasionally, the name of the owner of the guitar. The truss rod cover can be made out of wood (generally matching the material in the headstock overlay), or contrasting material (like pearl or abalone), but by far the most common material is black plastic.

Access to the adjustable truss-rod on the headstock of a Taylor.

Size

For a luthier, choosing size of the headstock is more than an aesthetic decision. The mass of the headstock can affect the tone and sustain of the guitar; and if the headstock is too heavy for the body and causes the guitar to overbalance, it can affect playability as well. This isn't much of a problem on large steel-string guitars and archtops. In fact, the large size of some big archtops like D'Angelico's New Yorker and Gibson's Super 400 seems to have inspired the builders to come up with excessively large headstocks to help visually balance out the guitar's appearance.

Two extremes: The small headstock of a Larrivée Parlor, and the gigantic variation on a D'Angelico New Yorker.

Weight and Sound

Most players and builders feel that the heavier the headstock, the more sustain the instrument will have. The trade-off is that guitars with heavier headstocks may lose some treble response and perhaps some volume as well. This is not a problem on large archtops like the Super 400 or the New Yorker—which have huge headstocks—because they have more than enough treble response to start with.

Nylon-string builders try to make the headstocks as light as possible—on traditional flamenco guitars builders use friction pegs and on classical guitars they use slotted headstocks—to bring out more volume. One problem with making the headstock too heavy is that it may be more likely to break at the nut if the guitar falls or is subjected to whiplash inside its case.

Angle

The headstocks on all acoustic guitars are cocked back at different angles, depending on the style of instrument. The angle on solid headstocks ranges from 12–17 degrees, while slotted headstocks are usually angled back between 8–15 degrees. Angling the headstock creates more downward pressure on the nut, which helps the strings stay seated in the slots.

Affect on Sound

Some players and luthiers feel that a steeper headstock angle increases the clarity of tone and the sustain. While this is true to a certain extent, too much angle can cause the strings to wear out the nut prematurely.

Examples of Angles Used by a Variety of Guitars

D'Angelico	14°
Gibson before 1966 and after 1973	17°
Gibson between 1966 and 1973	14°
Martin solid headstock	16°
Martin slotted headstock	12°
Taylor	16°
Torres jumbo headstock	17°
Torres slotted headstock	12°

Tuning Machines

A *tuning machine* (also called *tuning peg*, *machine head*, *geared peg*, *gear*, and *tuner*) is a device attached to the headstock of the guitar that allows the player to tighten and loosen the strings. Practically every guitar made these days uses a mechanical tuning machine of some sort. The only exception are some traditional flamenco guitars and reproductions of guitars from the very early part of the 18th century, which both use friction pegs.

Different approaches to tuning pegs: Violin-style friction pegs on an old Martin guitar (top), and modern mechanical gears on a Garrison steel-string.

Steel-String vs. Nylon-String

Tuning machines for steel- and nylon-string guitars work in the same way, and their parts are similar. Both styles of tuning machines consist of a *capstan*, sometimes called a *roller* or a *post*, which is attached to a cog by a screw or rivet. This cog meshes with a worm gear, which is part of a shaft that terminates in a button. The tuning machines for a nylon-string guitar are designed to be used in a slotted headstock and usually have large rollers—which used to be made of a bone sleeve over a metal shaft but are now more commonly made with a plastic or nylon sleeve. Steel-string tuning machines can be used on either a slotted or solid headstock, but in either case, the rollers are of a much smaller diameter, and consist of just a metal shaft.

Close-up of the open gears on a classical guitar, and a typical arrangement of individual tuning machines on a steel-string.

The very first tuning machines made in the early part of the 19th century had small metal rollers, but players soon discovered that the gut strings that were used at the time broke quite easily when wrapped around a small diameter post. The larger rollers became common by about 1870 and have remained standard ever since.

Single vs. Three-on-a-Plate

Tuning machines are available with all three gears for one side of the headstock mounted on a single plate, a style commonly called *three-on-a-plate*, or as single units. The three-on-plate style is commonly found on guitars with slotted head-stocks, both steel- and nylon-string, and on some less expensive guitars with solid headstocks. The vast majority of guitars with solid headstocks are fitted with six single tuning machines. In the past, manufactures of three-on-a-plate tuning machines would use their own ideas of what the spacing should be, which meant that if you wanted to change your gears, you would have to use a set made by the same maker. Now the spacing has been standardized ($1^3/8$" or 35mm) so the tuning machines from one maker will most likely fit the holes in the headstock of an already-built guitar. There is no inherent mechanical advantage to one style over the other, and builders usually follow tradition and put three-on-a-plate tuning machines on slotted headstocks and single tuning machines on solid headstocks.

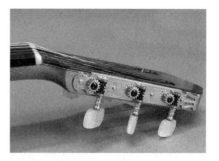

Three-on-a-plate tuning machines with custom engraving on a Santa Cruz, and a set of classical machines by Schaller.

Open vs. Closed Designs

Tuning machines can have exposed parts, sometimes called *open gears*, or feature gears enclosed in a housing of some sort. Open gears are used almost universally on instruments with slotted headstocks such as parlor guitars—both the vintage models and modern reproductions—and classical guitars. Open gears are also common on guitars with solid headstocks made before 1950, as well as on many modern, inexpensive instruments.

As with any other manufactured item, the quality of open tuning machines varies widely. With the inexpensive models, the parts fit together poorly, and the units barely do the job of getting the guitar in tune. But well-made tuning machines can last decades, if not centuries. There are a few companies like Waverly in

These individual open-back Waverly machines are based on vintage Grover G-98s.

America and Gotoh in Japan who make excellent reproductions of the tuning machines used in the 1920s and 1930s. A particularly popular repro is of the Grover G-98 or Sta-Tite unit that was used on the best guitars made by Martin and Gibson. Modern builders, particularly those making guitars in the vintage style, have been using these reproduction tuning machines.

In the early 1930s, Mario Maccaferri invented the first enclosed tuning machine for guitar. His tuning machines were used exclusively on the guitars made by Selmer from 1932 to 1953. Other makers, such as Kluson and Grover, began making enclosed single-unit tuning machines in the 1930s, but as these were very expensive and quite fancy, they were only used on top-of-the-line models made by companies such as Gibson, D'Angelico, and Epiphone. In the 1960s, Grover began offering the Rotomatic, and the German company Schaller came out with the M-6; and by the end of the decade, most medium- to high-end guitars came with enclosed tuning machines as a standard feature.

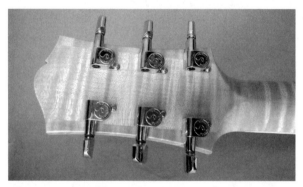

Enclosed housings on a set of Schaller machines.

Enclosed tuning machines come in two sizes: standard and mini. The mini gear is about 25% smaller and is generally used on instruments where headstock space is at a premium, such as 12-strings. There is little difference in operation between open and enclosed tuning machines, but the open style machines do require regular lubrication to keep working smoothly. Enclosed tuning machines are usually packed with grease before they are sealed; and since the worm and gear aren't exposed to the elements, they are unlikely to attract the dirt and grime that can cause them to wear out prematurely. Some builders feel the lighter weight of the open tuning machines improve the tone of the guitar, while others say that guitars with the heavier enclosed tuning machines have greater sustain.

Mini tuners such as these Grovers are often used on 12-strings.

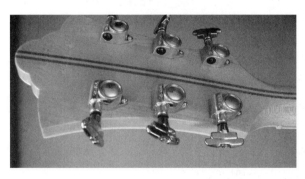

Art Deco–style Grover Imperials are a popular choice with archtops.

Schaller, Gotoh, and Grover all make tuning machines for classical guitars, but many of the finest builders prefer to use machines designed by small manufacturers such as John Gilbert and Irving Sloane. These ultra high-end tuning machines are built to exacting tolerances and work extremely smoothly. Some of them, such as the sets made by Rogers, allow the player to adjust how tightly the button turns.

Cast or Stamped Metal

The housings on all of the better enclosed tuning machines—such as those made by Schaller, Gotoh, or Grover—are made using a casting process. This increases the strength of the unit, but it also increases the weight. Some inexpensive tuning machines use a cover stamped out of thin metal to make it look like they were made using the more expansive casting method.

In the 1950s the most popular tuning machine on American guitars was the Deluxe made by Kluson. This tuning machine featured a stamped metal housing that was shaped to cover the worm and gear. The Deluxe was not a particularly good tuning machine, but because it was standard on some of the most popular guitars ever made—particularly the solid-body electrics made by Gibson and Fender—they are also being reproduced. Some players want the Kluson look without the tuning machine's problems, so now Schaller offers a version of the old tuning machine that has a cast shell that resembles the stamped metal housing of the original.

Vintage Keystone-design Gibson tuners stamped out of sheet metal.

Locking Designs

Some tuning machines are designed to lock the string in place with a screw mechanism instead of the more common tied-on method. Locking tuning machines were designed for solid-body electric guitars with tremolo systems as a way to help keep the strings from slipping and going out of tune. String slippage at the tuning machine is not a problem on acoustic guitars; and even though manufactures such as Sperzel and Schaller do make them for acoustic guitars, most players feel the tiny advantage of not having to tie the string on is outweighed by the extra mass added by the locking mechanism.

Planet Waves' Auto-Trim tuning machine.

Planet Waves Auto-Trim

The Planet Waves Auto-Trim tuning machines, which were designed by Ned Steinberger, combine a locking mechanism along with a hardened steel blade that automatically cuts off the dangling string end. As with other locking tuning machines, these are useful for electric guitars with tremolo systems; but most acoustic guitarists feel that the extra locking and string cutting features add little value to their instruments.

Mounting

To operate correctly, tuning machines must be properly mounted. It's important to make sure the holes for the posts are drilled evenly apart. This is particularly vital on guitars with slotted headstocks, where a misdrilled hole can cause the post to bind. It's also important to have tuning machines that have the proper bushings to keep the post from binding. Die-cast tuning machines, like those from Schaller or Grover, come with bushings that thread into the housing. Open-geared tunings machine usually come with a bushing that is pressed into the top of the headstock, which gives a bearing surface to keep the post from binding.

Buttons

The buttons on tuning machines can be made out of just about any durable material, but metal, plastic, and wood are the most common. Classical guitars usually have plastic buttons, although very expensive instruments may have buttons made from mother-of-pearl or ebony. In the 19th century, it was common to find buttons made of bone or ivory, but these proved to be too brittle, and were liable to break even if they were lightly knocked against a tabletop or a music stand.

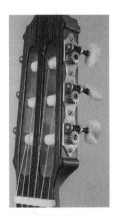 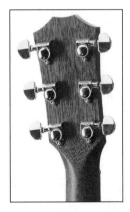

Plastic tuner buttons on an Albert & Müller classical guitar, and Grover machines with metal buttons on a Taylor 514.

The tuning machines on most steel-string guitars are made of metal, although plastic and ebony are fairly common as well. Many vintage steel-strings were fitted with tuning machines with celluloid buttons—a material that proved to be unstable over the years. On many of these guitars, the buttons have decomposed, but it's possible to get new replacement buttons that can be fitted to the old shaft.

Banjo Tuners (On Vintage Guitars and Keith–Style Tuners)

In the 1920s, the guitar began to overtake the banjo in popularity. In an attempt to ease banjo pickers onto guitar, some builders like Martin and Gibson experimented with putting banjo tuners on their guitars. But even though a few early Gibson L-5s and the entire first-year models of Martin's OM line had banjo tuners, guitarists pretty much rejected the whole idea. Very occasionally, builders like Eric Schoenberg will build a new OM with banjo tuners, and Martin has used them on some OM vintage reissues, but they're very scarce.

Banjo tuners on a four-string Martin tenor guitar.

There is one banjo tuner that some guitarists like: the so-called Keith-Scruggs pegs—a tuning machine that come with two set screws so you can oscillate between two set pitches. Some guitarists will put a Keith tuner on the first string, and sometimes the second as well, which allows the player to quickly change the tuning or get pedal-steel-style effects. Adrian Legg carries the idea to an absurd degree, and has replaced all six of his tuning machines with Keith tuners.

D-Tuners

It's very common for guitarists to tune the E string down one step to D. A *D-tuner* is a device attached to the E-string tuner to allow the player to drop the string down one step with just the flip of a switch. Hipshot makes a D-tuner called the X-Tender that is built around a Grover Rotomatic or a Schaller M-6 Mini, which, if your guitar is set up with these gears can be installed simply. Because the shifting mechanism is mounted on a plate that is larger than a standard tuning machine housing, D-tuners won't fit on headstocks with volutes such as those found on some Gibsons, Lowdens, and Guilds. D-tuners will also not fit on Martins with the dart on the back of the headstock.

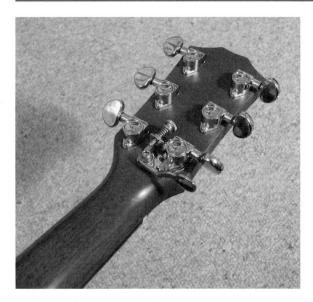

Hipshot's X-Tender allows quick and precise re-tuning of the low E-string.

Tuning Ratio

The tuning ratio refers to how many times you need to turn the button to get the shaft attached to the string to rotate once. Most modern tuning machines have ratios of 12:1, 14:1, or 18:1. On a set with a 12:1 ratio, you need to turn the button twelve times to get the string shaft to rotate once. The higher the ratio, the finer the tuning adjustments you can make; but also, the more turns you'll have to make when you restring your guitar. Tuning machines for steel strings and classical guitars have similar ratios.

Friction Pegs

Friction pegs (which are similar to those found on violins) were the only tuning mechanisms available for guitars until the introduction of the geared tuning machine in the mid-18th century. Players greatly preferred the convenience and precision of the geared tuning machines; and by the end of the 19th century, the friction peg had become extinct on all guitars except those used by traditional flamenco players and a few South American and Portuguese folk guitarists. It's more difficult to keep a guitar in tune with friction pegs, but flamenco players feel that the lighter weight at the headstock increases the volume and treble response, so they are willing to put up with the difficulties.

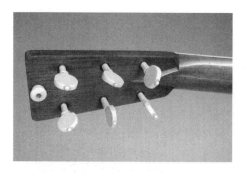 

Ivory tuning pegs on a 19th Century Martin guitar (left), ebony pegs on a flamenco guitar by Klaus Röder.

Nut

The nut, sometimes called the *topnut*, is a piece of dense material set at the headstock-end of the fretboard with six equidistant slots cut into it for the strings to ride in.

Function

The nut, along with the *saddle*, which is set in the bridge, defines the string's vibrating length. The width of the fretboard is also measured at the nut, even though the neck tapers outward as it approaches the body. Although it is possible to make a nut, and hence the fretboard, in dozens of different widths, players and builders have settled on just a few. The two most common widths for steel strings are $1^{11}/_{16}$ inches—which is favored by flatpickers and is used on dreadnoughts and most archtops—and the slightly wider $1^3/_4$ inches, which is found on many modern OMs and grand concert sized guitars. In general flatpickers like to have the strings close together to make it easier to move the pick from one string to the other, while fingerpickers like a wider nut, which allows them to get their right hand fingers in between the strings. The wider nut spacing also allows the fretting hand to move around more easily without bumping into adjacent strings.

The nut of a Selmer guitar (left), and that of a modern steel-string by Albert & Müller.

Other common sizes include $1^{13}/_{16}$ inches, which is used on many 12-fret parlor guitars, and $1^{7}/_{8}$ inches, which is used on some 12-fret dreadnoughts and the occasional grand concert designed for fingerpickers. Classical guitars usually have a wide nut spacing of about two inches. Classical guitarists, being fingerpickers, need the wide spacing. Also, nylon strings vibrate in a much wider arc than steel strings, particularly when played loudly, and the wider spacing allows them ample room to move.

Natural Materials

In the past, nuts have been made from a variety of natural materials, including ivory, mother-of-pearl, cow bone, and occasionally woods like ebony and rosewood. The ideal nut material is strong (it has to support the tension of the strings without splitting or cracking), durable (it has to be able to resist the filing action of the strings as they are tuned up and down), dense (a soft material can absorb string vibrations and deaden the sound), and good-looking. Although most of the natural materials mentioned do fulfill these requirements to a greater or lesser degree, the scarcity of some (such as ivory) or the cost of others (such as mother-of-pearl), preclude their use on a large scale.

Some high-end hand builders have been experimenting with fossilized walrus tusks, which are dug up in Alaska. Walrus ivory can vary in color from off-white to dark brown. It's very dense and it wears quite well. Many players insist that it improves the tone of their guitars; and even though it's very expensive, they pay what it takes to have their nut, saddle, and bridge pins carved from the same tusk.

Synthetic Materials

The first synthetic material used in making guitar nuts was probably *galalith*, a plastic like substance made from milk protein. Selmer was one of the first companies to use galalith for the nuts on their guitars. (They also used galalith for the buttons on their tuners.) Galalith proved to be too brittle, so most builders stuck to bone or ivory until synthetic plastics became widely available in the 1950s.

Plastic never became popular with builders because, although it was easy to mold into shape, once it was formed it was difficult to work with. Also, many players felt it wasn't dense enough and didn't sound as good as other materials. In the 1970s builders began experimenting with various materials made from high-tech resins such as micarta and Corian.

These new materials proved to be easy to work with, and more importantly, they were of uniform density unlike natural materials, which sometimes had soft spots that adversely affected tone. One of the most popular of these new materials is *Tusq*, a synthetic substance that looks and sounds very much like bone or ivory.

Zero-fret

A *zero-fret* is a fret that is set right next to the nut. On a guitar with a zero-fret, the string height is set by the height of the fret and the nut is just used as a spacer. Advocates of the zero-fret feel that because the strings are riding over a metal fret instead of a bone nut, that the fretted and unfretted strings will sound more alike. Zero-frets are very rare on guitars built in America, but many luthiers in Europe, particularly in France, Germany, and Italy, use them. Mario Maccaferri designed his Selmer guitars to work with a zero-fret, and most of the luthiers working in that tradition use a zero-fret.

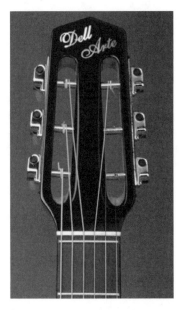 

Zero-frets on a Dell' Arte (left) and on a Steve Klein flattop

Compensated Nuts

Nuts can be compensated in two different ways to help improve the intonation of the guitar. The first is to make a nut that has different length slots that give a different scale for each string. This can be done by cutting away part of the nut to give the string a longer vibrating length, or by adding small pieces of material to shorten the vibrating length.

The more common method, which was been popularized by Buzz Feiten, is to cut away part of the fretboard to move the entire nut forward. This method works well if it is built into a new guitar, or if it's done to a recent vintage used guitar. Shortening the fretboard on an older vintage guitar will cause its value to decrease.

2 The Neck

The neck is the most important part of the guitar when it comes to playability, and in a way, it defines whether or not a guitar is good or bad. Think about it: no matter how good the guitar sounds, if the neck is poorly shaped and uncomfortable to play, musicians won't want to play that particular instrument. The trick for luthiers is to make a neck that somehow appeals to the widest number of players without compromising structural stability. If the builder makes a large neck, it will be more stable, but many players will reject it as being too clunky and "slow." If the luthier makes the neck too slender, it may appeal to a wider range of players— particularly electric guitarists who are looking for a "fast" neck similar to those found on Fender Stratocasters or Gibson Les Pauls—but if it's too thin, it will be more likely to twist or warp.

Types of Necks

In the acoustic guitar world, necks almost always consist of three parts: a fretboard; the neck itself, which includes the heel and can be carved from a single piece of wood or laminated from multiple pieces; and an internal reinforcement of some sort, which can be metal, a stiff wood like ebony, or a space-age material like carbon fiber. Even though the necks of steel-string flattops, steel-string archtops, and nylon-string guitars share these parts, each type of instrument fashions and utilizes them in slightly different ways. One big difference is that because nylon strings exert much less tension on the neck, many luthiers who build nylon-string guitars omit the neck reinforcement.

The narrow neck of a Taylor 414ce steel-string.

Flattop Steel-String

On a flattop steel-string neck, the fretboard extends over and is glued to the top. This helps stabilizes the neck and keeps it from wiggling from side to side. Some modern builders like Taylor and Dana Bourgeois bolt the fretboard on from underneath the top. This offers the same stability as the glued-on fretboard, along with making it easier to remove the neck when performing a major repair, like a neck reset. The necks on steel string guitars are usually carved from a single piece of wood, although some builders such as Taylor use a grafted-on headstock and stacked heel.

Nylon-String

On classical guitars built during the late 1700s, the fretboard stopped at the body and the higher frets were actually set into the top itself—as they were on lutes. By the early 1800s, this style of construction was replaced by a fretboard that extended over and was glued to the top. This method of building was not only easier, it also offered more side-to-side stability. Classical guitar makers have been using this method ever since. The necks of many nylon-string guitars have grafted-on headstocks and stacked heels, but a significant minority of builders carves the neck, heel, and headstock from a single piece of wood.

Classical guitars like this Hirade H8SS (left) and Hopf F314B8 have wider necks.

Archtop

On the first archtop guitars built by Orville Gibson in the late 1800s, the end of the fretboard was glued to the top as it was on steel-string and classical guitars. This construction method held sway until 1923, when the acoustical engineer Lloyd Loar redesigned the archtop and came up with the L5, on which the fretboard extended over the body without touching it. This cantilevered style of neck construction allowed more of the top to vibrate than was possible on a guitar with the fretboard glued to the top, which increased the volume of the instrument. Most archtops built after the L5 have cantilevered necks, but a few builders stayed with the older, glued fretboard style of building, particularly on their cheaper instruments.

Archtops such as this Epiphone Triumph (left) and Gibson L-5 have fingerboards that "float" above the body.

Resonator

On resonator guitars, the fretboard extends over the body, where it is attached to the top by four screws. The screw heads are usually covered by pearl or plastic dots.

12- vs. 14-Fret

Guitar necks generally join the body at the 12th or 14th fret. Classical guitars are defined as 12-fret guitars. In fact, when a maker does make a 14-fret, nylon-string guitar, as Takamine did with the NP-65C, people usually redefine it as a guitar for playing jazz or Latin American pop music. Most contemporary steel-string guitars are built with fourteen frets clear of the body, but there are a number of 12-fret steel strings being built as well.

The first steel-string guitars built in the early 20th century by companies like Martin and Washburn had 12-fret necks. This style of guitar fell into disfavor after the introduction of 14-fret guitars in the 1920s. But extending the neck two frets

Martin dreadnoughts with neck joints at the 12th (left) and 14th frets (D-28VS and D-28).

required changing the body shape and moving the bridge closer to the soundhole. These changes allowed greater access to the higher frets; but because the bodies were shorter and the bridge was moved closer to the soundhole, which is a stiffer portion of the top, the guitars had a tighter, brighter sound.

Starting in the 1950s, players began to seek out old 12-fret models because they wanted the warmer, richer sound of the earlier guitars. In the 1990s, contemporary luthiers began making new versions of the 12-fret guitars, either as reproductions like the 000-2H from Collings or the Martin 000-28S, or as newly designed guitars like the Goodall Parlor or the McCollum Skyforest. But even though there has been a renewed interest in 12-fret steel-string guitars, the 14-fret neck style is still the most popular by an overwhelming margin.

Archtop guitars made after 1924 are almost always 14-fret guitars, but the instruments made by Gibson prior to that had 12-fret necks. The guitars designed by Mario Maccaferri for Selmer initially had 12-fret necks, but after he left the company, the neck was elongated to fourteen frets. Almost all of the 12-fret

Selmers had the large D-shaped soundhole, and most of the 14-fret guitars have the small oval soundhole. But during the transition from twelve to fourteen frets Selmer made 12-fret guitars with oval and round soundholes.

Although builders have settled on 12- and 14-fret necks as the two standards, there have been other versions as well. In the 1920s, the roundneck version of the National Tricone had an 11-fret neck. Around the same time, Gibson experimented with a 13-fret neck version of the Nick Lucas model, and in the 1950s, they made the J-160E with a 15-fret neck. More recently, the first version of the Santa Cruz Guitar Company Model H had a 13-fret neck, emulating the Nick Lucas model from Gibson.

Shapes

The contour or shape, of the back of the neck, varies depending on the style of guitar. Classical guitars tend to have a fairly flat contour without a lot of curve. This is because classical guitar technique requires the thumb of the fretting hand to be planted squarely in the back of the neck and the flat shape helps keep the thumb from slipping. In contrast, modern steel-string necks, particularly those that measure $1^{11}/_{16}$ inches at the nut, have a rounder shape. This allows players to use a variety of different grips, including some that allow the thumb to reach around and fret the sixth and sometimes the fifth string.

Prior to the invention of the adjustable truss rod by Gibson in 1921, steel-string necks tended to be quite bulky with a pronounced V shape. The shape and mass made for a stiffer neck that resisted the tension of the steel strings. Some players feel that the mass of the larger V-shaped neck improves the tone of the guitar, and so a few modern builders have resurrected the shape, including Martin, who uses it on some of their vintage reissues. In the 1970s, Taylor began making necks with a very low profile that replicated the feel of the necks of electric guitars. These necks proved to be very popular with players who switched between acoustic and electric guitars; and over the next few years, other companies began slimming their necks down as well.

Materials

Luthiers have a wide range of materials that they can use in the top and bodies of the guitars they build, but they are fairly restricted in the wood they can use for the necks. The wood for a neck has to be strong (to support the pull of the strings), light (so it doesn't over balance the guitar), and attractive.

What Type of Wood?

There are a few exceptions, but generally, flattop guitars have mahogany necks, nylon strings have cedar or mahogany necks, and archtops have maple necks. Most luthiers in the 19th century used cedar for their guitar necks because it was light, but still quite strong for its weight. But towards the end of that century, builders began making larger guitars that required a higher string tension. The cedar necks couldn't support the higher tensions, particularly on the steel-string guitars being made by companies like Martin in America, so an alternative had to be found. The first choice was mahogany, which was fairly light but quite strong. It was also very stable and didn't twist under the tension of heavier strings. By the early 1920s, almost every maker in America was using mahogany, although some classical builders continued to use cedar. Some builders began using maple for their necks of guitars with maple bodies, such as archtops or jumbo flattops like the Gibson SJ-200 or the Guild F-50. Mario Maccaferri specified that walnut should be used for the necks on the guitars he designed for Selmer. A year or two before Selmer stopped making guitars in the early 1950s, they switched to making necks out of solid Brazilian rosewood. Most builders working in the Selmer tradition use walnut for their necks.

Two typical necks by Martin and Gibson: Mahogany (dark wood on top) and maple (light-colored wood, bottom).

In recent years, builders and players have become aware of the growing scarcity of tropical hardwoods like mahogany, and various builders have been experimenting with different neck woods. Martin has used Spanish cedar on some guitars in their 16-Series, and Seagull uses cherrywood necks on some their instruments.

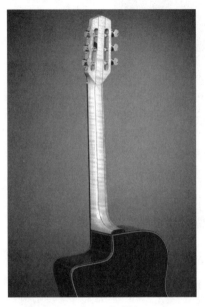

A multi-piece neck on a Dell' Arte guitar.

One Piece or Multiple Pieces?

Because it ensures stability, mahogany necks are almost always carved from a single piece of wood. The only common exception are the necks on some classical guitars that are made with one or two strips of ebony or rosewood to help stiffen the neck without adding the extra weight of a metal truss rod. But maple, which sometimes has the tendency to twist on its own, even without the pull of strings, is commonly made into necks with alternating pieces of ebony, rosewood, or some other dense wood. By gluing the pieces together with the grain going in opposite directions, luthiers can make a neck that is more stable and less prone to warping than a plain maple neck.

The laminates are always done in an odd number of layers, generally of three, five, or seven. Some flattop builders including Ovation, Lowden, Fylde, James Olson, and Lance McCollum make mahogany necks with alternating pieces of denser woods in a similar fashion to the maple necks of archtop makers. Along with being more stable, some builders feel the stiffer neck improves tone and clarity.

A few builders will split the neck down the middle and then reglue the two pieces back together. This process relives some of the tension in the neck, particularly those made of maple, and helps keep it from twisting. Framus occasionally makes necks out of dozens of pieces of thin strips of wood, which they claim makes for the most stable neck of all. But even though the multi-laminate necks are quite strong, other builders have been slow to adopt the practice. One significant exception is Martin, which uses a multi-laminate they call Stratobond for the necks on their X-Series of instruments.

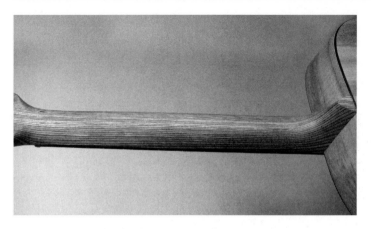

The laminated Stratobond neck on an X-Series Martin.

Direction of Wood Grain (Flatsawn vs. Quartersawn)

Wood that is quartersawn is less likely to twist than wood that is flatsawn, so it is the first choice of builders for necks. (For a description of

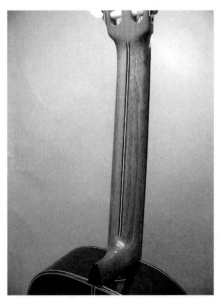

the differences between quartersawn and flatsawn wood, please see chapter 6, entitled "Slab-Cut, Quarter-sawn, Veneers.")

Graphite and Metal Reinforcements

For centuries, luthiers have been trying to come up with a way to reinforce a neck and to keep it from warping or twisting from the tension of the strings without adding excess weight. In the 19th century, builders would inlay a strip of ebony or some other dense hardwood in the neck under the fretboard. Many modern

An ebony neck-reinforcement on a classical guitar. classical builders continue to use ebony in this way. In the 1930s,

Maccaferri experimented with stiffening the necks of his guitars with aluminum blades. Modern builders including Taylor and Collings have started using a similar stiffening system in their own guitars.

In the 1980s, builders began to experiment with graphite stiffening rods. Graphite is very light and very stiff and keeps the neck straight without adding mass. This form of stiffening has become popular with some of the more progressive classical guitar builders like Greg Smallman and Thomas Humphrey. Some builders extend the graphite rod through the headstock, which strengthens the weak area behind the nut. This method also reduces some of the flex in the headstock, which can slightly improve the clarity of tone.

Finish

Necks are usually finished with the same lacquer or varnish as the back and sides. On classical guitars, the tradition is to use a gloss finish that matches the body. Some players prefer the feel of bare wood, and so a very few guitars are made with unfinished necks. It is common for some steel-string builders to finish the neck with a satin or semi-gloss lacquer, even though the body is finished in full-gloss. Archtop guitars are almost always finished with full-gloss necks. Ebony and rosewood fretboards are never finished.

Neck Joint

The neck-to-body joint is subject to incredible stress and consequently needs to be very strong and stable. Luthiers have been experimenting with various ways of attaching the neck to the body and have come up with a handful of designs that work. All of these designs are collectively referred to as the *neck joint*.

Dovetail

One of the most common neck joints featured on steel-string guitars is the tapered *dovetail*: a complex version of the mortise-and-tenon joint, from which the dovetail gets its name (the *tenon*, the part that sticks out, resembles the shape of a fanned-out dove's tail). Dovetail joints require a great deal of skill to cut accurately, but if they are done correctly, the neck-to-body connection is very strong. The tenon is widest at the fingerboard end and tapers towards the heelcap. This is fitted into a slot cut into the neckblock, which is called the *mortise*. The *neckblock*, sometimes called the *headblock*, is almost always made of mahogany. Because of the tapered tenon, the joint is self-locking; and the more carefully it is cut, the tighter it sits in the mortise. In fact, it's possible to fit a neck with a well-cut dovetail joint and string it up without gluing it.

The disassembled dovetail neck joint of a Martin D-28.

Because the joint is covered by the fretboard when it's finally assembled, it's difficult to take apart should you need to remove the neck. The current method of taking apart a dovetail requires injecting steam into the joint to soften the glue, which can damage the finish if not done carefully.

Larrivée also uses dovetail neck joints:

Some players claim that because the dovetail is so strong, it improves the tone of the guitar, but this is still a minority opinion. Martin, Gibson, and Guild use dovetail neck joints almost exclusively, although Martin has been experimenting with other designs on some of their less expensive models. Dovetail neck joints are used primarily on steel-string guitars, flattops, and archtops, but they are rarer on nylon-string guitars—particularly those made in Spain.

A neck is being glued to the body at Martin.

Bolt-on

Bolt-on necks have been around since the 1830s—some Stauffers and a few early Martins had a complex clock-key mechanism to hold the neck on, but it wasn't until the 1970s, when Bob Taylor introduced a bolted-on neck capable of supporting the tension of steel strings, that more builders began using bolts in favor of the traditional dovetail joint. Taylor used to set the neck with a butt joint, with the heel set flush against the body. The heel had two threaded metal inserts that accepted two bolts that went through the neckblock. The tongue of the fretboard was then glued to the top, and the bolt heads were covered with a label that included the model number and serial number.

Recently, Taylor patented a bolt-on neck attachment called the "New Technology" (NT) neck design. This neck joint still has two threaded neck inserts in the heel and two bolts that go through the neckblock, but the heel is slightly inlaid into the side instead of butting up against it. Also, the tongue of the fretboard is slightly inlaid into the top and is held in place with small Allen bolts that attach from under the top.

Taylor's NT neck is completely bolted on, and offers easy adjustability.

Prior to Taylor's use of the bolt-on neck, most builders shied away from the idea, but now more builders are beginning to use bolts of some sort. Bolt-on necks are easier to build that those with dovetails, and are much easier to take apart if the neck has to be removed. It's now common to find guitars built with bolt-on necks, especially from new companies such as Lakewood and Seagull, who don't have a tradition of using a dovetail joint.

Mortise-and-Tenon

Mortise-and-tenon neck joints used to be quite scarce, but they have become more common in the last few years. Because it lacks the self-tightening shape of the dovetail, the standard mortise-and-tenon joint is not quite strong enough to support the tension of a steel-string guitar on its own. To make it more stable, some builders, such as Collings and Cumpiano, combine the mortise-and-tenon with bolts to make it stronger. Collings screws two hanger bolts into the heel, which is reinforced with a maple dowel. The hanger bolts stick through the neckblock where they are secured with nuts. The Cumpiano system is similar, but it has two threaded inserts set into the heel, much like Taylor's method.

Mortise-and-tenon neck joints, when combined with bolts, are perhaps the strongest neck joints of all. Martin now uses a combined mortise-and-tenon/bolt neck joint on everything up to their 16 Series guitars. (You can still detect the stigma against bolt-on necks in Martin's claim that the bolts aren't there to hold the neck on, but are instead designed to draw the neck to the body and do away with the need for clamping the joint.)

Spanish-Foot

On classical guitars, particularly those built in the Spanish tradition, the neck and neckblock are built as an integrated unit, then the sides, back and top are built around it. If you look inside a guitar made in this manner, you will notice that the bottom of the neckblock—the part attached to the back—extends a short way into the body. This extension is known as the *Spanish-foot* or sometimes the *Spanish-boot*. Although it is harder to see, there is a similar extension under the top that helps support the fretboard. This style of construction works well with guitars that are strung with light-tension nylon strings, but because the neck, neckblock, top, back, and sides are integral, it is nearly impossible to remove the neck if necessary. Although the Spanish-foot method of constructing guitars is used primarily by classical guitar builders, a few European steel-string builders such as Stefan Sobell and the German builders Albert & Müller use it as well.

The Spanish Foot (shown here on a Pimentel cutaway guitar) involves gluing the guitar's sides into slots in the neckblock.

Variations (Fender-Style Bolt-on, Turner/Howe-Orme, Etc.)

There are other, less common, methods of attaching necks that show up from time to time. In the late 1960s, Fender introduced a line of acoustic guitars that had necks that bolted on from the back, much like their solid-body electric guitars. This style turned out to be unstable, and the massive neckblock necessary to make it work added too much weight. Even though some builders, like the Italian Company EKO and Japan's Epiphone tried it, the Fender-style bolt-on neck is essentially extinct on acoustic guitars. Taylor has developed a neck joint for their Baby and Big Baby models in which the neck has a heelless design like the old Fenders, but the neck

39

The neck on Taylor's Big Baby is attached with two screws through the fingerboard.

is attached by screws to the body through the top of the fretboard. In an effort to keep costs down, the screw heads are left visible; but because they are black, they blend in with the fretboard.

California luthier Rick Turner has been experimenting with an unusual neck joint where the heel rests on three adjustable pivot screws. The neck is attached to the body with one large bolt. This unconventional method was inspired by the instruments made by the Howe-Orme Company in the early part of the 20th century. This method of neck attachment allows for instant neck-angle adjustment and a fretboard that floats over the body. On some inexpensive guitars, the neck is held on with dowels, which is not particularly stable in the long run. But as most people move on from these cheap instruments to better guitars, this is not much of a problem with new instruments. But it does mean you have to be careful when buying older, cheaply built guitars, and to make sure the neck is firmly attached.

Neck Heel

The *heel* is the part of the neck that extends in a curve and attaches to the body. The heel is designed to give a larger gluing surface for the neck, and to help set the proper neck angle. Although the heel is essentially a functional part of the neck, some builders approach it as a design element, and will use it to express their aesthetic sense.

Heelcap

Because the end of the heel usually has exposed end grain, which is prone to absorb moisture, luthiers usually cover it with a *heelcap*. On classical guitars, it's common to extend part of the back to cover the heel. On steel-string guitars, builders usually use a small piece of plastic that matches the binding, or wood that generally matches the wood used for the back and sides. On very fancy guitars, the heelcap will be engraved, or in some cases, it will even be inlaid. Sometimes builders will use metal or mother-of-pearl for a heelcap, but this is extremely rare.

Engraved heelcap on a Froggy Bottom guitar.

This multi-piece neck heel is made out of four segments.

One Piece or Stacked

Heels are either carved from the same piece of wood as the neck, or they're made of two or more pieces of stacked wood. Generally, guitars with grafted-on headstocks will have stacked heels, and guitars with one-piece headstocks will have one-piece heels. There is no functional difference between the styles. Stacked heels are most common on classical guitars, although the steel strings from Taylor now have stacked heels. Many of the guitars made by Selmer in the 1930s and 1940s have stacked heels as well, as do many of the less-expensive guitars made in Asia.

Flat or Pointed

Heels can be either flat or pointed. Because they allow easier access to the higher frets, flat heels are usually found on guitars with cutaways, particularly archtops and guitars made in the Selmer style. Flat heels aren't as common on steel-string flattops, or even cutaway models. Guild is one of the very few flattop builders to commonly use a flat heel on their instruments. Classical guitars almost always have pointed heels. There is no structural or functional difference between flat and pointed heels.

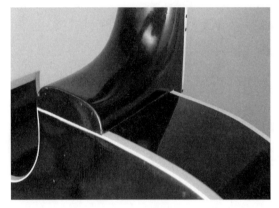

The flat heel on a Gibson L-4C archtop.

Martin uses a pointed heel.

Neck Angle

The geometric relationship of the neck to the top of the guitar is called the *neck angle*, the *neck set*, or the *neck pitch*.

Steel-String Flattop

On steel-string flattop guitars, the neck is cocked back at a very shallow angle of between $1/2$ and $3/4$ of a degree. As a rule, the taller the bridge and saddle on a flattop, the more leverage put on the top, which increases the volume and power of the guitar. But if the neck angle is too steep, the excessive pressure can cause a lightly braced top to warp or bow. Some builders of dreadnought guitars, particularly those destined for bluegrass flatpickers who want as much volume as possible, will cock the neck back a bit more steeply than they would with a smaller guitar, like an OM.

Because the angle is so small, even tiny changes can affect the playability of the guitar. Over time, the constant tension of the strings causes the body to change shape at the neck joint. When this happens, the neck has to be removed and reset at the original angle. Steel-string guitars usually need neck resets after twenty to thirty years.

Classical and Flamenco

Classical guitars are usually built with the same neck angle as a steel-string guitar: between $1/2$ and $3/4$ of a degree. Because of the lower tension of the nylon strings, classical guitars rarely need neck resets—which is a good thing, because the Spanish-boot style of construction makes the job extremely difficult.

Flamenco guitars are commonly set with a shallower neck angle than a classical guitar. This is because the tops of flamencos are much more lightly braced, and the lower bridge and saddle are less likely to cause the top to warp. Also, the lower bridge puts the strings closer to the top, which allows the player to more easily play the various percussive taps on the top that are part of the flamenco style.

Luthier Thomas Humphrey has developed the Millennium Model, a guitar with a "negative neck angle." On the Millennium, the sides narrow as they approach the neckblock, giving the top a pronounced slope. The neck is set high on the body with the fret resting on an extension over the top. The neck points at the top of the guitar, and the strings pull on the bridge in a manner that is more like a harp. The raised fretboard also allows easier access to the higher frets.

The negative neck-angle on a Cervantes copy of a Humphrey Millennium.

Archtop

On archtop guitars, the strings drive the top by pushing down, rather than pulling up, as they do on a flattop. Because it takes more pressure to drive a top by pushing on it, archtop guitars have neck angles around 2^1/$_2$ degrees, which, when combined with the tall bridge and trapeze tailpiece, gives plenty of downward pressure.

Fretboard

Although the terms *fretboard* and *fingerboard* are sometimes used interchangeably, when talking about guitars "fretboard" is the more accurate and therefore preferred word (instruments in the violin family, for example, all have fingerboards, but they rarely, if ever have frets). Fretboards are wider at the body and taper as the get closer to the nut. On some guitars, like the 12-fret Selmer/Maccaferri, the fretboard is longer on the treble side as it goes over the body. This fretboard extension allows the guitarist to reach a few higher notes than is possible with a standard fretboard.

Materials

African ebony, sometimes called Gabon ebony, is the preferred choice for fretboards because it is very stiff, which helps keep the neck straight, and very dense, which means that it is very good at resisting wear. Most ebony is black with brown streaks, so many builders stain it to give it a uniform appearance. Indian rosewood, which is quite a bit cheaper, is the second choice of builders. Rosewood is also quite stiff and dense, but it does wear a little more quickly than ebony. Builders almost never stain a rosewood fretboard, opting instead to leave its natural, dark brown color. Some players claim that guitars with ebony fretboards have a slightly brighter, crisper tone than other similarly built guitars, but if it does make a difference, it's too subtle for most people to hear. It's common for the builders of very cheap guitars to use fairly soft, cheap wood for the fretboards and to stain them black to look like ebony.

The fretboards on acoustic guitars are never finished. African ebony (botanical name: *diospyros crassiflora*) shouldn't be confused with Macassar ebony (botanical name: *diospyros celebica*), a less dense wood from Indonesia, which is used occasionally for making guitar bodies.

Martin has started using a synthetic material called *micarta* for the fretboards on their 16-Series guitars. Micarta is an excellent choice since it's strong, stiff, and smooth, but time will tell if players will accept this non-traditional material. Ovation has been using a fretboard made of black walnut impregnated with a polymerized acrylic resin, which they feel greatly reduces wear.

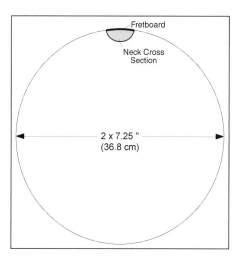

Measuring a fingerboard's radius.

Radius

The fretboards of almost all contemporary steel-string guitars have a slight arch or curve to them. This arch is calculated as a section of a circle, usually somewhere between 10–17 inches in diameter. The smaller the radius, the more curve the fretboard will have. The feeling among players is that, the more curved the fretboards is, the easier it will be to make barre chords, while the flatter fretboards make it less likely for bent strings to fret out. Steel-string builders began using arched

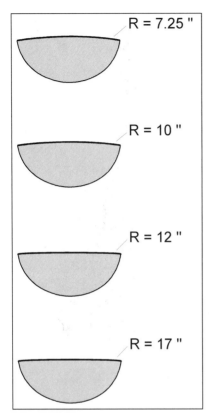

R = 7.25 "

R = 10 "

R = 12 "

R = 17 "

Four different fingerboard radii.

fretboards in the 1920s, but many older guitars, particularly those with 12-fret necks, have flat fretboards. Blues guitarists who play bottleneck-style prefer flat fretboards because the strings are all in the same plane, which makes it easier to use a slide. Builders, like National or Beltona, who are making new resophonic guitars , which are the instruments of choice for many blues players, still put flat fretboards on their guitars. Classical and flamenco guitars traditionally have flat fretboards, although some nylon-string guitars made for playing jazz have arched fretboards. A few of the more progressive classical guitar builders like Thomas Humphrey have been building instruments with arched fretboards.

Position Markers

Fretboard inlays can range from a simple dot to the most intricate tree-of-life pattern. As beautiful as a fancy inlay can be, it fails in its main purpose if it does not let guitarists know where they are on the neck. Inlays designed to orient the guitarist are called *position markers*, and are usually placed at the fifth, seventh, ninth, twelfth, fifteenth, and seventeenth frets. It's also common to find position markers at the first and third frets as well. Some builders put a double inlay at the seventh fret to mark the location of the dominant or fifth scale degree on an open string, and at the twelfth fret to mark the octave. Selmer guitars put a dot at the tenth fret instead of the ninth, although many contemporary builders working in the tradition put the inlay at the ninth fret.

For many years, builders of flattop guitars tended to use plain pearl dots or small diamond-shaped inlays, but recently, advances in CNC (computer numeric control) technology have allowed makers to start offering more fanciful shapes at cheaper prices. Builders of archtop guitars tend to use large, rectangular-shaped inlays, called *blocks*, rather than dots.

Rectangular position markers made of out of abalone on a Guild D-55 (left), and simple pearl dots on a Taylor 414ce.

The edge of the fretboard that faces the player is almost always inlaid with small dots, called *edge dots*, which correspond to the inlays on the fretted side. Classical and flamenco guitars almost never have fretboard inlays, but many do have edge dots at the fifth and seventh frets.

Inlay Material

The most common material used in fretboard inlays is mother-of-pearl because it wears well and its white color stands out against the dark fretboard. Mother-of-pearl, which is sometimes abbreviated as MOP, comes from the interior shell lining of the pearl oyster. Although white is the most common color for mother-of-pearl, it can come with a golden tint or in a smoky gray color. Another common shell used in inlay is abalone, which comes in a wide variety of colors including red, green, blue, and purple. The most desirable part of the abalone shell is the section where the muscle attaches. This section, called the *heart*, has a very colorful burl pattern.

Fingerboard inlay can be very elaborate, such as on this custom Goodall KJKC and a Presentation Series Taylor.

The white binding on this Gibson J-200 is made out of plastic.

Less expensive guitars will sometimes use a pearlescent plastic for inlays. This plastic is commonly used for many other products, a fact that is reflected in the irreverent names like "mother-of-toilet-seat" and "mother-of-dinette-set" that some luthiers use.

In the last few years, many builders have been using a material called *AbaLam*, a laminate made of abalone and epoxy. AbaLam comes in much larger pieces than is possible with natural abalone, which makes it popular for inlay artists who want to work on a larger scale. Some luthiers, such as Grit Laskin or the inlay artist Larry Robinson, will work with a variety of inlay materials, including stones (jade, lapis lazuli, and agate), different woods, precious metals (gold and silver), and even synthetic materials like Corian.

Binding

There are three different ways of binding a guitar fretboard. The oldest method is to bind the edges of the fretboard with a matching strip of wood. This method, which is used primarily on nylon-string guitars, hides the fret ends and gives the fretboard a clean appearance. The other two binding styles are found on steel-string guitars.

The first is the Gibson style, in which the fret stops at the binding, which has a little nub that covers the fret end. Most other guitar builders use a style in which part of the fret tang is cut away from each fret end, which then overhangs the binding. When Gibson frets are replaced, they are almost always done in the Martin style and the little nubs are sanded off.

On steel-string guitars, the fretboard binding usually matches that of the body and headstock.

Elaborate binding on a vintage archtop.

Truss Rod

A *truss rod* is a form of reinforcement that is set into the neck to counteract the string tension, and can be made out of metal, carbon fiber, or a dense wood like ebony. Truss rods can be *passive*, as is the case with an ebony or carbon fiber insert, or *active*, such as the adjustable metal rods found in almost all steel-string guitars.

History

Luthiers have been experimenting with various types of neck reinforcement since the early 1800s. The first truss rods were nothing more than a strip of ebony, which, because the tension of the gut strings was so light, was all that was required. Many luthiers then, as well as many classical and flamenco builders today, used no form of neck reinforcement at all.

But when American luthiers started building guitars in the early 1900s, the ebony truss rods proved to be too flexible to counteract the heavier string tension. At first, companies just beefed up the necks to counter the string tension, but that made them too bulky to be easily playable. Sometime in the early 1920s, a Gibson employee named Ted McHugh invented an adjustable steel truss rod that allowed Gibson to make their necks with a more slender profile than they had been using. In the early 1930s, Epiphone came up with their own truss rod design, which they called a "thrust rod," but generally, guitar builders used non-adjustable rods of some sort.

But when Gibson's patent expired in the early 1950s, just about every guitar company started using the adjustable models except for Martin. (Martin was always slow to change and were still using ebony truss rods until the early 1930s, when they switched to a non-adjustable T-shape metal rod). They used the T-shaped rod until 1967, when they changed over to a square, box-shaped rod. In 1985 Martin finally started making guitars with an adjustable truss rod.

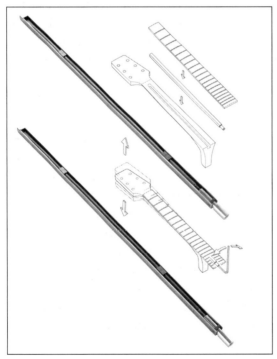

A modern truss-rod.

Also in the 1980s, builders began experimenting with space-age materials like carbon fiber and graphite, which are not adjustable, but do add stiffness. These materials are still rare in guitars built by the larger companies, but individual builders like Rick Turner and Thomas Humphrey have found them to be useful.

Sometimes, very cheap guitars have a sticker on the headstock claiming that they have steel-reinforced necks, but that can mean they only feature a simple metal reinforcement, not an adjustable truss rod.

Function

Most adjustable truss rods work in the same basic way. One end of the rod is anchored either in the heel or up near the headstock, while the other end terminates in a nut or a screw of some sort. The rod, which has a slight curve to it, is set into a channel carved into the neck. Loosening the rod causes the strings to pull the neck into a slight forward curve. This curve is called the *relief*. Tightening the nut causes the curve in the rod to compress, which straightens the neck and reduces the amount of relief.

Truss rods are not designed to adjust the neck angle or the action. Action adjustments are done by raising or lowering the saddle and nut. But occasionally, when you change string gauges, the truss rod will need to be adjusted to account for the change in tension. Over-tightening a truss rod can break it or strip the threads of the adjusting nut, which can lead to a very expensive repair job.

Various Designs

On the Gibson-style truss rod system, one end of the truss rod anchors in the heel and the adjustable end terminates at the nut. A small channel is carved in the headstock to access the nut, which is hidden under a truss-rod cover. Because Gibson had a patent on this type of truss rod, other companies had to come up with their own versions. In the 1930s, Epiphone invented a truss rod that they called a "thrust rod," which was anchored at the nut end of the neck and adjusted at the body end of the fretboard. In 1952, Epiphone switched to a truss rod that adjusted at the headstock. In the late 1970s, Ovation revived the idea of having the truss rod adjustment located at the body-end of the fretboard. They came up with a rod that was encased in a square aluminum channel, which they named the "Kaman Bar" (later shortened to "K-Bar"), after the founder of the company.

Sometime in the early 1980s, Japanese companies such as Takamine began using a similar truss rod that was seated in a U-shaped aluminum channel. Because the truss rod is adjusted through the soundhole, the builder doesn't have to carve out part of the headstock to access the adjusting nut, which means the area behind the nut is a bit stronger. In 1985, Martin started putting similar truss rods into their own guitars. Although they didn't invent the idea of a truss rod that adjusted through the soundhole, this style of rod is almost universally referred to as a Martin-style truss rod.

Martin and many other companies provide access to the truss-rod through the soundhole.

Some small builders like Collings, Ted Thompson, and the Santa Cruz Guitar Company use a modified version of the Martin system. On their guitars, the truss rod adjustment is actually in the neckblock, and is only reachable through the soundhole by using a specially designed wrench. There are a couple of reasons builders use this variation. The first is that the standard Martin system cuts a small hole through the brace under the fretboard, making it a little weaker. The second is that truss rod adjustments are usually a very subtle process, and by making it difficult to reach the adjustment screw, the builders feel that players are more likely to bring the instrument to a qualified repair person rather than attempt the job themselves which could possibly ruin the guitar neck. Both systems work well, and there is no real advantage to one over the other in function.

In the 1960s, Guild started putting two adjustable truss rods side by side in their 12-string models, which allowed the neck to be adjusted for the extra tension on the bass side of the neck. Some builders have been experimenting with a "double action" truss rod, which is active in both directions.

Non-Adjustable Necks

Prior to the invention of the adjustable truss rod in the early 1920s, all guitars that had neck reinforcements had non-adjustable rods. Classical guitars made since the early 1900s usually have an ebony insert in the neck, but the light tension of the nylon strings doesn't really require it. Some contemporary classical guitar builders like Greg Smallman and Thomas Humphrey use one or two carbon fiber rods to add stiffness to the neck. In 1985, Martin was the last major steel-string builder to switch to an adjustable truss rod, but they still make a handful of D-28s every year with the box-style, non-adjustable rod on custom order for players who want an accurate reproduction of their earlier guitars.

In the 1930s, Mario Maccaferri designed a system that used two non-adjustable aluminum plates for the guitars built by Selmer. Selmer stopped using these plates in the mid-1940s, opting instead to make the neck out of solid rosewood. Most luthiers working in the Selmer tradition now use adjustable truss rods that adjust through the soundhole.

Frets

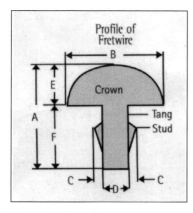

Cross-section of a fret.

Frets are the small strips of metal inlaid into the fingerboard that you press the string against to get a particular pitch. In the 1600s, frets were made of strips of gut that were tied on to the fretboard. By the early 1700s, these gut ligatures were replaced with small pieces of bone or ivory, which were then replaced by metal frets in the late 1700s, which have been the standard ever since.

Acoustic guitars generally have 21 frets, although some models with cutaways may have one or two more. A modern fret has two parts: the *tang*, which is the section that fits into the slot on the fretboard and has small nipples or bumps to help it grip the wood. the *crown*, the part that you press the string against, which is sometimes also called the *bead*.

Martin uses a pneumatic machine to press frets into the fretboard.

The extended fretboard on this classical Hernandez guitar allows access to a couple of additional frets.

Material

Modern frets are made of a mixture of nickel and steel that is called "nickel silver" or sometimes "German silver," even though the alloy has no silver content at all. Nickel silver is fairly pliable so it is easy to work with, but it is also quite durable, so the frets last awhile before they develop enough string wear to warrant replacement. Some very inexpensive guitars have brass frets, which wear out very quickly. Brass frets are easy to recognize because of their golden color. Some electric guitars like those made by Parker have stainless steel frets, but because they have to be glued onto the fretboard, they are still rare on acoustics.

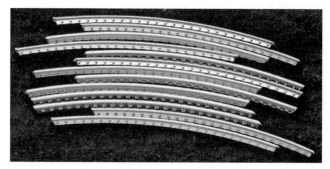

Fretwire ready for installation.

Luthier Boaz Elkayam has been experimenting with frets made of *Delrin*, a nylon derivative. He feels that this material cuts down on the noise that comes from the string hitting the fret, as well as increasing the life of both the string and the fret. Elkayam learned about Delrin frets from luthier Richard Schneider, who used them on the guitars he built in the Kasha style.

Size

The *crown* of the fret comes in a wide variety of heights and widths to suits a range of playing styles. As with everything in life, choosing frets is a series of trade-offs. Generally taller frets have a little brighter, more ringing tone, while lower frets have a slightly duller sound but a faster feel. Narrow frets can have slightly better intonation, while wider frets make it a bit easier to bend strings. Most acoustic steel-strings tend to use a fret of medium height and width. Classical guitars tend to use slightly wider frets, while archtops, particularly those with pickups, tend to use wider, taller frets.

Modern Frets with "Tang" vs. Vintage Bar-Frets

The earliest metal frets were just a very thin piece of metal set into a slot in the fingerboard. These frets are known as *bar stock frets*, and almost every guitar made before about 1900 had them. Sometime in the 1890s, someone (nobody knows who) invented the modern fret with a *tang*. Bar stock frets required a great deal of skill to install. The slots had to be cut to the exact depth, otherwise the frets would sit too high or too low; and the slots had to be the correct width, otherwise the frets would sit too loose and fall out or not fit at all.

The fret with the tang solved these two problems. Because the fret was T-shaped, it was impossible to set it at the wrong height, so all the builder had to do was tap it until it was properly seated. And the little studs on the tang gripped the wood, making it a simple matter to install it. Also, the rounded tops of the T-shaped fret had a smoother feel than the squarer edges of the bar stock fret.

But even though the T-shaped fret is easier to install and the vast majority of players prefer the feel, bar frets have two advantages. The first is that if the bar frets are properly installed, they make the neck very stiff. The second is that bar frets are made of a much harder alloy than T-frets. Martin didn't switch to T-frets until 1934—almost a quarter century after all of their competitors. That meant that the first few years of Martin's fabled 14-fret OMs were made using bar stock frets. The necks on those guitars were so stiff that they didn't need metal truss rods, and the material was so hard that many of them have been played for decades without needing a refret. Eric Schoenberg is one of the few modern builders who still make guitars with bar stock frets, which you can get on any of his guitars as a custom order.

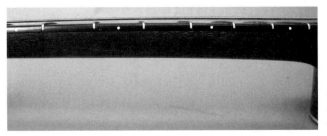

This vintage Martin is equipped with bar-frets.

Scale Length

Scale length is the distance between the nut and saddle, or the effective vibrating length of the string. Generally speaking, the longer the scale length, the louder the guitar will sound. The higher tension drives the top more efficiently, but the guitar will be harder to play, because of the higher tension and the fact the frets will be more widely spaced apart.

The scale length is measured from the leading edge of the nut and, because steel-string guitars have slanted saddles, to the center of the saddle between the third and fourth strings. You can get a more accurate measurement by measuring the distance from the nut to the 12th fret—the middle point between the nut and saddle—and doubling it. Because steel-string guitars were developed in America, the scale length on them is usually expressed in inches. By the same token, the scale lengths of classical guitars, which were developed in Europe, are expressed in centimeters.

24 in = 609.6 mm	650 mm = 25.59 in
24.75 in = 628.7 mm	660 mm = 25.98 in
25.5 in = 647.7 mm	664 mm = 26.14 in

Some Standards

Although it's theoretically possible to build a guitar with any scale length, builders and players have settled on a few standard lengths. In the steel-string world, larger guitars like the dreadnought and the jumbo have a scale length of 25.4 inches, which is known as a "long scale." Some builders like Collings goose this to 25.5 to give their instruments a slightly brighter tone. A few smaller-bodied instruments, like the OM and the 12-fret 000, also have 25.4-inch scale lengths. Many smaller bodied guitars like the concert and grand concert have a short scale of 24.9 inches, as do many Gibson dreadnoughts. A few companies like Taylor build grand concerts with the long, 25.4-inch scale length. Twelve-fret Selmers have a scale length of 25.4 inches, while the 14-fret models have an ultra-long scale length of 26.5 inches.

In the classical guitar world, the scale lengths have been growing longer since the 1830s. Back in the early part of the 19th century, builders like Stauffer and Panormo built guitars with a scale length between 600 and 620 millimeters. In the 1850s, Torres began building guitars with a scale length between 635 and 650 millimeters. This scale length held sway for a century or so, when José Ramirez, in an attempt to build a guitar that could fill a large concert hall, introduced a scale length of 664 millimeters. Although this long scale was popular for a time with concert guitarists, many player and builders have since reverted to a scale of around 650 millimeters.

Fanned Frets (Novax, Etc.)

Many players like the feel of a short-scale guitar because it's easier to fret and to its bend strings, but they like the powerful bass response of the long scale. California luthier Ralph Novak came up with the fanned-fret design to try and reconcile those two needs. On his fretboards, the treble side frets are closer together and fan out towards the bass side. The saddle and nut are also angled effectively giving a guitar with two scale lengths—shorter on the treble to help ease string bending, and longer on the bass side to give a fuller low end. Although the fanned frets look a little odd at first, they are very easy to get used to. While Novak himself doesn't make acoustic guitars as such, he has licensed the fanned fret design to various individual luthiers like Rick Turner, Michael Greenfield, and Jeff Traugott.

Intonation

Intonation is the term used to describe a guitar's ability to play in tune along the entire length of the neck. In the West, we use a system known as *equal tempered tuning*, which divides the octave into a scale of twelve equal semitones.

Fingerboards with special frets for microtonal music.

Intonation is a complex subject, and a luthier setting up a guitar to play in tune needs to take numerous variables into account, including string gauges, scale length, action, neck angle, and saddle height. Luthiers use a number of different techniques to set the guitar up to play in equal tempered tuning. The most important step to achieving good intonation is to make sure the frets are in the correct position. This is rarely a problem on modern guitars, although some very cheap guitars may not have the frets spaced correctly. Because each string is a different diameter, each would ideally be set to a slightly different scale length.

On many steel-string guitars, the saddle is set at an angle, pulling the sixth string back and moving the first string forward, in a simple attempt at setting the intonation. More sophisticated builders will carefully carve the top of the saddle to move the third string forward and the second string back to make the guitar in even better tune. Archtop guitars have always had compensated bridges. Classical guitars almost always have a straight saddle. This is because the nylon strings don't vary in diameter as much as steel strings do, and therefore they don't need as much compensation.

Buzz Feiten System

Perhaps the most sophisticated system for intonating a guitar has been developed by Buzz Feiten, a studio guitarist who felt the intonation on his guitars wasn't as good as it could be. Feiten has worked out a series of calculations based on string gauge and scale length that tell the luthier exactly how far forward or back to move the string at the saddle. The saddle is also ramped rather than rounded, which gives a more defined intonation point. Feiten's system also requires cutting away part of the fretboard and moving the nut a bit closer to the first fret. Along with the mechanical changes, Feiten advocates a slightly different temperament when tuning the guitar. Rather than using a strict equal tempered tuning, he will tune some strings slightly sharp or flat depending on the gauge and scale length. Korg offers an electronic tuner set to the Buzz Feiten tuning system to be used in conjunction with the setup. The Buzz Feiten system is available on only a handful of new guitars, like Washburn and Garrison, but any guitar can be retrofitted by one of his authorized repair people. Because the system requires an irreversible change to the fretboard, you should be aware that having this procedure done to a vintage guitar would probably devalue it.

3   Strings

Types of Strings

Strings usually get short shrift in discussions on guitars, but musicians ignore them at their own peril. Strings, after all, are the part you actually touch, pluck, strum, fret, bend, and even caress to make the guitar sing. A guitar without strings is just an oddly shaped box. Strings are so important that the material they're made of defines the two classes of acoustic guitar: those instruments built for steel strings and those built for nylon strings.

String nomenclature can be a bit confusing for beginners, and even trips up some advanced players. Strings are defined by the material used for the plain strings and the core of the wound strings, not the wire used to wrap the core. Because the core of the three bass strings on a standard classical set is made from nylon floss, and the three treble strings are made of nylon monofilament, they are referred to as "nylon strings." And because the core of brass- or bronze-wrapped strings is steel, as are the two treble strings, they are known as "steel strings."

Steel Strings

Although luthiers were experimenting with wire-strung instruments as early as the 16th century—the cittern (also known as the English guitar), the bandora, and the orpharion are all early guitar relatives that were strung with metal strings—the modern steel-string guitar is a product of the 20th century. Steel-string acoustic guitars can be divided into three categories: archtop guitars, flattop guitars (like the Dreadnought and the OM), and guitars built in the style of

Selmer/Maccaferri, which are sometimes known as Gypsy jazz guitars. Specialty instruments like the 12-string, the harp guitar, and the tenor guitar are almost always strung with steel strings, as are the resophonic instruments from National and Dobro. These guitars are quite different from each other structurally, but the strings they use are all essentially identical.

Plain Strings, Core Wire, and Winding Material

Steel-string sets almost always contain a combination of *plain*, or *unwrapped*, strings and *wrapped*, or *wound*, strings, as they are often called. The unwrapped string is just a piece of plain, high-carbon steel wire, which is sometimes tin-plated to resist corrosion. C.F. Martin's SP series and D'Addario's EXP series feature brass-plated trebles. Most steel-strings have a metal ferrule, called a *ball-end*, attached to one end.

Raw string wire arrives on spools at Martin.

The wound strings consist of three parts: the core, the wrap, and the ball. Flattop guitars designed for steel strings usually have *pin bridges*, which have a hole into which the ball-end is inserted and then held in place with a small peg made of plastic, wood, or in some guitars from the 19th and early 20th centuries, bone or ivory. The tailpieces of archtop and resophonic guitars are designed to accept ball-end steel strings as well. Steel strings can terminate in a loop, but this type of string is used primarily on banjos and mandolins, and very rarely on guitars. The only guitars that commonly use loop strings are those built in the Selmer/Maccaferri tradition. The tailpieces of these instruments are unique in that they can use strings with ball-ends or loop-ends.

D'Addario's production line.

The core of the wound string is made of a round or a hexagonal steel wire. A round core allows the maker to wrap the string more tightly, which some people claim gives the string more sustain. Round-core wire was standard a few decades ago, but it is relatively rare today. DR is one of the very few companies still making sets of acoustic guitar strings with a round-core wire. Their Sunbeams are popular with owners of vintage guitars who want a set of strings that closely resemble those that would have been used when their guitars were new. Because the wrap can slip or unravel from a round core if it's not carefully wound, most string manufacturers have switched to a hexagonally shaped core wire. The corners of the core wire help grip the wrap and keep the windings from slipping. All of the major companies, whether they are American, such as D'Addario, GHS, or Dean Markley, or European, such as Pyramid and Galli, use hex-core wire; and it is safe to assume that, unless labeled otherwise, that is the material used to make the wound string in question.

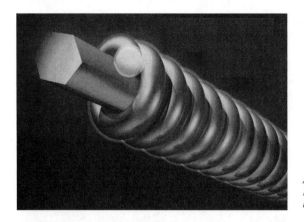

A D'Addario EXP string with hexagonal core.

The Austrian company Thomastik-Infeld makes a string that has a braided steel core, which is similar to the core found in some violin strings. These strings combine the flexibility of the floss core found in wound nylon strings with the bright ringing tone of steel strings.

The windings can be made from a number of different types of metal, but by far the most popular material for acoustic guitar strings is bronze, which comes in a variety of formulas. Other winding materials include nickel, silver-plated copper, gold, and steel, which it has to be said, is rarely used on flattop acoustic guitars.

Bronze Steel Strings

The windings on 80/20 bronze strings are 80% copper and 20% tin. These strings have a bright, golden color and a clear, ringing tone. The windings on 85/15 bronze strings are 85% copper and 15% tin, and sound slightly warmer than 80/20 bronze strings and, because of the extra copper, have a slightly darker color. The 80/20s are the default strings for many guitar makers, and most new instruments are shipped with them.

Brass Steel Strings

The alloy used in the windings of brass strings can vary from 80% copper and 20% zinc to 60% copper and 40% zinc, depending on the manufacturer. Brass strings are very bright and jangly sounding and last a bit longer than 80/20 bronze strings before losing their tone. The word "brass" can have bad connotations when it comes to tone, so many makers label them as bronze, or occasionally something like "bell bronze" or "bright bronze."

Phosphor Bronze Steel Strings

Phosphor bronze strings are usually an alloy of 90% copper and 10% tin that have had phosphorus added to the molten metal during the refining process. The phosphorus makes the strings slightly harder and more resistant to corrosion. Phosphor bronze strings sound slightly mellower than 80/20 bronze or brass and last a bit longer. They also have a slightly darker color than 80/20 bronze strings. Although they cost a little more than brass or 80/20 bronze strings, phosphor bronze are perhaps the most popular style of steel-string sold in music stores.

Nickel Steel Strings

Most of the strings marketed under the nickel label are actually made of a steel alloy that has been nickel plated. Because steel is a ferrous metal, it works well with magnetic pickups, which makes nickel-plated strings a good choice for flattop guitars with soundhole-mounted pickups and archtop guitars with pickups. Nickel-plated strings have a very mellow, almost dull tone, and are not commonly used on flattops without magnetic pickups. But some players with very bright-sounding guitars such as archtops find that nickel-plated strings can help their guitars sound a little warmer.

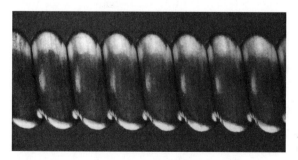

A close-up of a round-wound string.

Strings with pure nickel windings are made in very light electric guitar gauges, but they are rarely found in heavier acoustic guitar gauges. Heavier pure nickel and nickel-plated strings are sometimes labeled as jazz strings. DR makes an unusual set of strings called Zebras, which are wound with alternating strands of nickel-plated steel and phosphor bronze. Zebras work well with magnetic pickups, but still have a ringing acoustic tone.

Flatwounds

Flatwounds are steel strings that are wrapped in a ribbon-like metal tape instead of a round wire. Flatwounds have almost no finger noise but they also have a very dull sound. Flattop acoustic guitar players almost never use flatwounds, although some archtop players, particularly those who play jazz and use magnetic pickups, like the mellow tone.

Half-Rounds

Half-rounds, which are sometimes called *ground wounds*, are the steel-string equivalent of classical guitar polished basses. On half-rounds, a standard round-wound set of strings is carefully sanded and polished. Although the result resembles a flatwound string, half-rounds have more of the clarity and bass response of a standard round-wound set of strings. Half-rounds are popular with guitarists who spend a lot of time in the studio and want to avoid finger squeaks.

Coated Strings

Dirt, grime, and finger oils cause wound strings to sound dull much earlier than they should. In the early 1980s, Kaman, the parent company of Ovation, experimented with strings coated in Teflon, but with the technology of the time, they were unable to get the Teflon to adhere properly to the strings and withdrew them from sale.

A few years later, W. L. Gore and Associates, the company that makes the waterproof fabric Goretex, came up with a way of coating the strings with a polymer they called Polyweb. They called their new strings "Elixirs," and they became popular quite quickly; particularly when companies like Taylor began putting them on their new guitars. The Polyweb coating is applied to the strings after the core is wrapped, sort of like a stocking covering a leg, which keeps grit and oil from working between the windings. Coating the strings also reduces finger noise.

This close-up shows the coating of an Elixir string.

Some players felt that the Polyweb coating deadened the sound a little so, W.L. Gore developed Nanoweb strings, which were made using the same process as the Polywebs, but with much less material.

D'Addario uses a similar process for their EXP series of strings, but they coat the bronze wire before it's wrapped on the core. EXPs sound brighter than Elixirs, but because the coating doesn't fill in the "gaps" between the windings, they have more finger squeak. Coated strings have become so popular that most major string manufactures offer their own versions. A few companies have begun offering coated nylon basses, for classical players.

Silk-and-Steel Strings

Silk-and-steel strings are a cross between nylon strings and steel strings. The name comes from the fact that the core of the wound strings is a combination of a very small-diameter core wire and silk or nylon floss. As on a wound nylon string, the wrap is silver-plated copper (although GHS does make a set called Silk and Bronze with a phosphor bronze wrap). The two treble strings are plain steel.

Silk-and-steel strings have a lower tension than regular steel strings but higher than that of a normal set of nylons strings. They have a sweet tone that is well-suited to fingerpicking. Because of their lighter tension, they work well on lightly built parlor guitars from the early part of the 20th century, such as those built by Martin or Washburn, but they are still too heavy to use on a standard classical guitar.

Many people think that Savarez Argentine strings, a set of strings commonly used on Selmer/Maccaferri guitars, are silk-and-steel, but that is a misconception. Argentines, and strings made in similar fashion, are a very light set of steel strings with a silver-plated copper wrap. There is no silk in the core.

Cryogenically Frozen Strings

Cryogenics is a process where the strings are cooled in a computer-controlled refrigerator with liquid nitrogen down to a temperature of 320 degrees below zero, Fahrenheit. The strings are kept there for about fifteen hours and then are slowly brought back to room temperature. Many players feel this process somehow alters the molecular structure of the metal and increases the string's life. They also claim the cryogenically treated strings have more sustain and clearer trebles. Dean Markley popularized the process with their Blue Steel strings, although many other string manufacturers now offer cryogenically treated strings. The process only works on metal and can't be used on nylon strings.

Gut Strings

The first strings for acoustic guitars were made of gut. Although the material is sometimes called "catgut," it is really made from the intestines of sheep. Nylon strings basically superseded gut strings in the 1940s, but there are a few players, particular those involved in early music, who still use them. Gut strings are susceptible to changes in the weather—they absorb moisture and sound dull when the humidity rises and they can dry out and break when the humidity falls—but when the climate is right, they have a very clear sound with lots of sustain that many players still feel is the ideal tone. Thanks to the rise in popularity of the lute in early music circles, and the desire to recreate ancient sounds as accurately as possible, gut strings are once again available. La Bella is one of the few major string makers that offers gut classical guitar strings as part of their standard line.

Plain Nylon Strings

In the mid-1940s, Albert Augustine, at the urging of Andrés Segovia, introduced the first nylon classical guitar string. Segovia was looking for a string that had the tone of gut, but none of gut's problems with climate or durability. Nylon is now the most popular choice of material for the unwound strings of classical guitars, and over the years, string manufactures have been experimenting with ways to improve them. Plain, untreated nylon strings have a bright, clear tone, but because of minute variations in the diameter, they may not have good intonation along their complete length. Some makers have developed a process for drawing the string through a progressively smaller set of metal dies to give the string a uniform diameter. This process, which is known as *rectifying*, improves the intonation, but it also gives the string a slightly mellower tone and a rougher texture.

Some players, particularly flamenco guitarists, prefer black nylon trebles to clear ones. The black dye that's added during the process of making these strings does make them slightly stiffer, which makes some of the higher overtones sound a little more clearly.

Many string manufacturers have also been experimenting with other polymers besides nylon for the treble strings. Since many of these polymers don't have easily remembered trade names like nylon, Delrin, or Kevlar, but are instead referred to by their chemical names, string makers tend to describe them with vague phrases like "fourth-generation polymer." This is not very helpful, but it is better than trying to figure out what an adipic acid-hexamethylenediamine resin is. (That's the chemical name for nylon, by the way.)

The differences between the new polymers and nylon can be quite subtle, but Zyex, one of the few polymers with an easy name to remember, does offer a clear advantage in one respect. D'Addario uses a Zyex third string in their LP Composite series of strings. The Zyex string has a smaller diameter than a standard nylon third string, which gives it a bright tone that helps alleviate the tonal differences between the plain and wound strings. Savarez makes a third string with a nylon core wrapped in plastic that many players feel helps balance the tonal transition from the wound to the unwound strings.

Wound Nylon Strings

The three wrapped strings usually have a core of very fine nylon filaments, also known as *floss*, which replaced the silk filaments used in earlier years. The nylon floss is usually wrapped in silver-plated copper wire. Sometimes gold-plated wire is used, which gives the guitar a warmer tone. Because gold is more resistant to tarnishing than silver, gold-plated strings last a good deal longer than silver-plated strings, which helps offset the higher cost. By varying the diameter of the wrap with the thickness of the core, string makers can come up with a wide range of tensions and tones. Because classical guitars are more lightly built than steel-string guitars, subtle changes in tension and winding material can have a surprisingly major effect on tone. It's not unusual for players to use one brand of string for the trebles and another for the basses in an effort to come up with the best tone for their particular guitar. This is why it's possible to buy nylon basses and trebles separately. This is handy because the wound strings do go dead much faster then the plain strings do, so it's a simple matter for a player to just replace the basses and leave the trebles alone.

Both the basses and trebles of nylon strings are generally tied to the bridge, but some guitars from the 19th century were fitted with pin bridges similar to those found on modern steel-string guitars. In this case, a knot should be tied in the end of the string, which is then inserted into the hole in the bridge and held in place with a small peg made of wood, bone, or ivory. Some string manufacturers make nylon strings with ball ends. These are sometimes labeled as "folk strings," and they are almost never used on guitars used for classical music.

Carbon Trebles

The newest innovation in classical strings is the introduction of the so-called *carbon trebles*. The material is not actually carbon (don't confuse these strings with high-carbon steel strings), but is instead a fluorocarbon polymer known as polyvinylidene fluoride (PVDF), which string manufacturers wisely decided to simplify to just "carbon." Carbon trebles, which have a slight yellowish cast, have a sound that is more similar to gut than nylon. In fact, the feel, tension, and tone is so similar that many lute players have been using them instead of gut or nylon.

Polished Basses

Finger squeaks on wound bass strings are the bane of the classical guitar player's existence, particularly in the recording studio where every noise is amplified and then preserved for posterity. Some string makers offer a set of basses that have been lightly sanded and polished, which removes the top arc of the round wrap. This process greatly reduces finger squeaks, while not appreciably affecting the tone. D'Addario combines their polished basses with a core of Zyex floss.

Sets with polished basses cost quite a bit more than sets with round-wound basses, but because they last longer, many players consider them a better value in the long run. GHS makes a set of strings they call Vanguard Classic, where the pure nickel round windings of the bass strings are put through a roller, which flattens the top of the wrap, giving them the basic properties of polished basses. Vanguard Classics are also one of the very few sets of classical strings that offer a metal-wound third string.

Gauges and Tensions

Steel strings are sold in extra-light, light, medium, and heavy gauges. Strings are usually measured in thousandths of an inch, even in countries that use the metric system. The gauges are written in decimal form, such as .012 or .056. While there is no commonly agreed upon standard, the following chart will give you an idea of the general gauges used in most sets of strings. Most sets will be within a thousandth or two of these gauges. On all of these sets, the first two strings are plain steel and the rest are wound.

Extra-Light:	.010	.014	.022	.030	.038	.048
Light:	.012	.016	.024	.032	.042	.053
Medium:	.013	.017	.026	.034	.045	.056
Heavy:	.014	.018	.027	.039	.049	.059
Bluegrass:	.012	.016	.024	.034	.045	.056

Some string makers offer a set called "bluegrass gauge," which is a combination of light trebles that are easy to bend for solos, and medium basses, which have the power and volume for G-runs. Although a few manufacturers offer heavy-gauge strings, they are almost never used in standard tuning on flattop guitars. Heavy-gauge strings were common in the days before pickups, when the only way to get more volume from a flattop guitar was to hit it harder. But in the last twenty years or so, mediums have become the heaviest strings that most people use. In fact, many luthiers who build lightly braced flattop guitars will void the warranty if you use heavy-gauge strings. Players who use open tunings will sometime use heavy-gauge strings, but if you do, make sure you tune the strings below standard tuning.

In general, the lighter the string, the easier it will be to play, but the more likely it will be to buzz or rattle against the frets. Fingerpickers who play with a light touch tend to use lighter gauges. But players who play harder, such as swing guitarists or bluegrass pickers, need to use heavier strings to help keep the buzzes to a minimum. There is no hard and fast rule about which strings will work best on which size guitar, but generally, larger guitars such as jumbos and dreadnoughts work best with heavier strings, and smaller guitars like OMs and 000s sound better with lighter strings.

Wound strings that are made with identical metals and have the same diameter may still have a very different sound and feel. This is because one string may have a thin core and a heavier wrap, while the other will have a heavier core and a thinner wrap. A string with a thinner core will be more flexible and will sound brighter and be easier to bend. A heavier core will be stiffer and will have a warmer tone and will last a little longer.

Nylon strings are usually sold by tension rather than gauge. This is because different formulations of nylon can be tighter or stiffer and still have the same diameter. Nylon string sets are labeled light, medium, hard, or extra-hard tension. Some manufacturers label their medium set as normal tension. As with steel strings, the lighter the tension, the easier they are to play, but the more likely they are to buzz. Also, heavier strings drive the top more efficiently and tend to have more bass response.

Strings for Specialty Instruments

Most specialty guitars—such as tenor guitars, baritone guitars, 12-string guitars, Hawaiian guitars, and resophonic guitars—use steel strings that are identical to those used on standard 6-string guitars. The only difference is that the choice of gauges will be adjusted to suit the instrument's particular tuning.

The strings for acoustic bass guitars are made of the same materials as wound steel strings; that is, a hex core with 80/20 bronze or phosphor bronze windings. They are also available in all the various steel-string varieties, including half-rounds, cryogenics, and coated.

Like regular 6-string sets, 12-string sets are labeled light and medium, but the 12-string light set is actually based on the 6-string extra-light set and the 12-string medium set is based on the 6-string light set. This is important to remember if you ever have to make up a 12-string set out of single strings. If you make a medium 12-string set based on a medium 6-string set, the strings will be too heavy for the guitar and may damage it.

Harp guitars that are made in America, such as the Gibson or the Dyer, are usually built for steel strings. European harp guitars, which are also know as *contraguitars*, reflect their classical heritage and are generally built for nylon strings.

String Care

Strings wear out over time, but there are a couple of tricks you can use to extend string life. The easiest thing you can do is to wipe them down after you are done playing, which will remove oil and perspiration. Make sure you use a clean, dry, lint-free cloth and that you get the cloth between the strings and the fretboard.

You can also snap the wound strings by pulling a string a little distance from the fretboard and letting it smack against the frets. This can help dislodge bits of grit and grime that have become lodged in the windings.

But it's probably best to change your strings at regular intervals, because old strings become stretched out, lose their elasticity, and start to play out of tune. This is why the old picker's trick of removing old steel strings and boiling them to clean them isn't worth the effort.

Some unlucky players have particularly acidic body chemistry and will need to replace their strings more frequently. If your strings tend to get tarnished quickly where you touch them, you may be one of these people.

Body Styles

Although there are very few guitars that could be mistaken for another musical instrument entirely, it can be bewildering how many shapes and sizes are available. The basic hourglass shape of the instrument can be traced back to instruments built during the Middle Ages; but as the guitar has evolved, its shapes and sizes have been adapted to provide a better fit for each era's musical styles. While other elements of guitar design—such as the neck or headstock—may be of equal importance, it is usually the body style that we are drawn to when identifying an instrument. Not only does this largest part of the guitar seduce the eye, it is also the single most important element in creating a guitar's sound. As a balancing act between the necessity of being held by the player and creating optimum sound, the shape and size of an acoustic guitar's body is met with some limitations, but this hasn't kept luthiers and designers from creating a myriad of options.

When looking at an acoustic guitar, it is important to remember that the body shape is only one of many factors that define its sound. Different internal bracing, woods, and individual details can make one guitar of a certain shape sound drastically different from the next, quickly teaching the player or listener to keep an open mind to a shape associated with certain sounds or styles.

Flattop Shapes and Sizes

Dreadnought body shape shown on a Huss & Dalton guitar.

Dreadnought

Walking into a guitar store today, it is impossible not to notice that the *dreadnought* shape is the most popular available. Named after the largest battleship the world had seen at the time of its introduction, the style is also among the largest commonly made acoustic guitars. As such, it can offer incredible volume, bass, and dynamic range.

The first dreadnought was built by C.F. Martin under the Ditson brand (Oliver Ditson was a Boston-based distributor who had a line of instruments built under his own name) in 1917. At a time when most guitars featured comparatively small bodies, Ditson was seeking a guitar that could keep up with louder instruments, and the design he commissioned Martin to build delivered the goods. Featuring a width of 15⅝ inches at the lower bout, the new body maximized the possible internal airspace by using a much less pronounced waist and greater depth than previous designs. Martin adapted the long 25.4-inch scale from the era's 000 model (the company's largest guitar up to this point), giving the instrument's strings the tension to drive such a behemoth. These early dreadnoughts also featured a neck that joined the body at the twelfth fret, the same as the smaller parlor guitars Martin was making at the time. Due to the dreadnought's dramatic capability to rumble in the lower frequencies, it was even referred to as a bass guitar when it was introduced.

Although Martin approached the new design with a typical dose of conservative skepticism, the company couldn't deny that Ditson's idea worked. Accordingly,

Martin began offering the dreadnought design under its own name in 1931, creating the now legendary D-18 (with mahogany back and sides) and D-28 (with rosewood back and sides) models. Having refined the design through several years of building Ditsons, Martin's own dreadnoughts were successful from the start. Although the guitars have been subject to some changes over the years (most notably, a switch to a 14-fret neck in 1934 and non-scalloped top braces in the mid-1940s), the basic concept has turned into the root of the company's success.

Martin's D-28 is the most important dreadnought of all time.

Realizing the ongoing desirability of dreadnoughts built with the original specifications, Martin began offering "vintage" style models as early as 1976. Starting with the HD-28, which features herringbone purfling and scalloped braces, and currently ending with the company's "Golden Era" recreations of first generation dreadnoughts, players can choose from almost any design offered over the course of the years.

Not one to be upstaged by its main competitor, it didn't take long for Gibson to offer a dreadnought-sized guitar. Introduced in 1934 and aptly named "Jumbo," the guitar eventually became known as the J-45, which continues to be one of Gibson's most popular acoustic guitars. (It is important to realize that Gibson's Jumbo designation has to be seen in the context of the time, as it shouldn't be confused with the later J-200-style jumbo guitars that now define the term. See section entitled "Jumbo.") One interesting aspect of Gibson's design is that while the company essentially copied Martin's early elongated dreadnought shape, it matched it with a 14-fret neck by moving the bridge forward instead of shortening the body's upper bouts. Referred to as a "slope-shouldered" dreadnought, the shape has been used by various Gibson models, and it's also frequently copied by other manufacturers.

Gibson's "Round Shoulder" dreadnought J-45

Years later, in 1960, Gibson introduced the square-shouldered dreadnought with its Hummingbird model, in effect mimicking Martin's post-1934 shape. Still in production today, the fancy Hummingbird was joined shortly after by the equally gaudy Dove, and models such as the J-30, J-40, and Gospel eventually brought Gibson's square-shouldered dreadnought body to models with simple appointments and lower prices.

While it's not easy to make blanket statements about the tonal differences between square-shouldered and slope-shouldered dreadnoughts, there are traits that come to mind, particularly when discussing Martin and Gibson's original designs. While a Martin-style dreadnought will generally have excellent clarity, a punchy response, and long sustain, many Gibson-style instruments stand out by having a clear mid-range, a thumpy bass, and a certain "dryness" to their sound that's difficult to describe without having a guitar at hand to demonstrate.

Although both styles of guitars show up in virtually every style of music that requires a steel-string guitar, it can also be said that Martin-style dreadnoughts are the de facto flatpicking instrument. Owning a rosewood D-28 style dreadnought is almost a requirement for playing bluegrass, but they're also favorites for strumming acoustic rock, with players such as Stephen Stills having led the way early on (in 1998, Martin even issued a limited-edition Stephen Stills signature model). They're a common sight among folkies, and even fingerstyle players such as Harvey Reid and the late Michael Hedges have made dreadnoughts their guitar of choice. Gibson dreadnoughts tend to lack the admiration in the die-hard bluegrass crowd, but their balanced tone makes them popular with representatives of just about every other style, having particularly left their mark with blues fingerpickers.

A Gibson Hummingbird (left), and a newer Gibson Dove Artist show the "Square Shoulder" body shape.

Due to its large size and especially its wide waist, the dreadnought shape is not the most comfortable guitar to play, but the design's potential ergonomic shortcomings are made up for by its big sound. Strung with medium-gauge strings and played with a flat pick, dreadnoughts are easily the most powerful acoustic guitars available.

As should be expected from a design as omnipresent as the dreadnought, guitars featuring this design can now be found in all price ranges. Even many entry-level guitars made in Asia look like a Martin dreadnought from a distance, and high-end companies such as Bourgeois, Collings, and Santa Cruz continue to raise the bar of what these guitars are capable of.

A very Martin-like Collings D-2H (left), and the Gibson-inspired Bourgeois Slope-D.

0, 00, 000 (Concert, Grand Concert, Auditorium)

As was the case with the dreadnought (and really, most things related to steel-string flattop guitars), the 0, 00, and 000 (usually pronounced "oh," "double-oh," and "triple-oh") sizes were originally used by Martin, and have been adopted by other manufacturers as the years have gone by. Alternatively, these numerical designations also loosely correspond to models called *Concert, Grand Concert,* and *Auditorium.*

Contemporary guitarists used to today's larger instruments may be surprised to learn that when Martin introduced the 0-size in the early 1850s, it was the largest guitar in the company's catalog. The "0" designation continued the company's already existing method for identifying their instruments. Earlier models carried numbers from "1" to "5," with "1" being the largest, and "5" the smallest. With Martin's logic, it made sense that "0" would have even bigger proportions. Designed to meet player's demands for louder and more powerful instruments, the "0" featured dimensions of 13.5 inches at the lower bout, and a body-length of 19¹/₈ inches.

Although few contemporary builders make 0-size guitars, the style was popular with many brands up to about the 1930s. Many vintage guitars by companies such as Washburn, Lyon & Healey, and Vega feature measurements that would give them the 0-size designation. Comparatively delicate-sounding by today's standards, these instruments continue to have fans. Ranging from living-room pickers who appreciate the 0-size body's comfort to studio players who find that the guitar's "smaller" tone and lack of "boomy" low-end can be just what's needed when recording certain kinds of music. Jethro Tull's Ian Anderson is an example of a player who is successfully using 0-size steel-strings in an acoustic rock context (he plays an old Martin 0-16NY and a custom guitar built by British luthier A.B. Mansen).

Continuing the quest for more volume, the 00 was added to Martin's line in the early 1870s. As one would guess, the extra "0" signifies a further increase in size. Measuring about 14¹/₈ inches at the lower bout and 20¹⁵/₁₆ inches in length, the 00 body brings us into the territory of the modern small-bodied guitar. As an interesting bit of trivia, it's worth noting that Martin's original 12-fret 00-21 model had the longest run of being included in the

A vintage 14-fret Martin 0-15, and a modern, but vintage-inspired 12-fret 00-15S.

company's catalog in a fundamentally unchanged design from the late 1800s until 1993 (with later limited editions being offered). Rocker Steve Howe is perhaps the most visible player of the later 14-fret Martin 00 guitar, and he accordingly received a special signature model 00-18 in 1999.

Besides making what are essentially copies of older instruments, many companies use the 00-size as a basis for more contemporary models. Taylor's Grand Concert series is perhaps one of the most popular modern designs to feature these dimensions; and while it's particularly well-suited to fingerstyle playing, the line also impresses with it's versatility. The size and outline is also a frequent point of departure for acoustic-electric models, often matched with a cutaway and a shallower depth than what's found on the original design.

A Taylor 512ce, and a Gibson L-00 Blues King.

The 0 and 00-sized guitars also figure prominently into the history of Gibson flat-tops. However, identifying these instruments is quite a bit more confusing than it is with Martin's relatively straight-ahead method of naming its models. Gibsons that fall into this category include L, LG, B, and Nick Lucas body styles. Even within these designations, one needs to know that, for example, the L-1 started out as an archtop in 1902 before the name was used for the small flattop that most people think of when they hear the name. Similarly, the 0s and 00s in the L-0 and L-00 models refer to the amount of ornamentation, rather than body size.

First introduced in 1926, the L-0 and L-1 were Gibson's first regular production flattop guitars. With a width of 13^1/2 inches, the guitar featured a very distinctively rounded lower bout and a 12-fret neck. Forever associated with bluesman Robert Johnson (who is holding an L-1 in one of his two existing photographs), the guitar has been reissued numerous times, both by Gibson itself and other companies (including Samick, who offered an "official" Robert Johnson commemorative model in the early 1990s). Despite the legendary image bestowed on it today, the original L-style was short-lived in its day, as it was replaced by a slightly larger (14^3/4 inches wide) and less rounded body in 1929. Built in numerous versions featuring both 12- and 14-fret necks, this second-generation L-body-style lasted into the 1940s.

A very historically significant variation of Gibson's L models is found in the company's Nick Lucas model. Introduced as the first-ever official artist-endorsed signature guitar in 1928, the guitar was designed in collaboration with the early jazz star. Desiring greater volume and bass in a small-bodied instrument, Lucas suggested deepening the sides of an L-sized guitar (to 4^7/8 inches at the tailblock) as well as adding stylish, yet restrained, appointments. Initially featuring the same outline as the first-generation L-0 and L-1, the guitar was changed to the newer shape along with the rest of the L line in 1929. Early Nick Lucas models had an unusual 13-fret neck, and while some were made with 12-fret necks, the standard version of the instrument was eventually made with 14-frets to the body. Prized for its surprising volume and balanced sound that's suited to both flatpicking and fingerstyle, the guitar has been used by players such as Bob Dylan (who used it extensively in the mid-1960s), Norman Blake, and Roy Book Binder. Although still relatively obscure, the Gibson Nick Lucas style has inspired quite a few contemporary instruments. Santa Cruz's H model (named after its designer, Paul Hostetter) is based on the concept of a deep 00-size body. Taylor produced a number of dreadnought-depth Grand Concerts in the 1980s, and the trained eye will easily spot Tacoma's Parlor heritage. In addition, Gibson itself has frequently made limited production runs of the design in its Montana division.

A Santa Cruz H-Model.

Gibson introduced a new style for its small-bodied series in 1942. Although it was slightly narrower than the L model at the lower bout ($14^1/8$ inches); the new LG style featured a much wider upper bout, giving it an appearance that's not unlike that of a Torres–style classical guitar. Although the guitars coexisted in Gibson's catalog for a couple of years, the LG eventually replaced the older style in 1945. LGs were made at various price points, usually featuring mahogany or maple back and sides. Although appointments varied, these instruments were never offered in ultra-fancy version. Affordability and quality of tone were always primary concerns with these models, making them best sellers well into the 1960s. Eventually, the LG line was replaced by the B-15 and B-25, which feature the same-sized body, but different appointments, and, in some cases, narrower necks. These instruments lasted until the mid-1970s; and while abundant on the used market, Gibson has never reissued guitars featuring the LG- or B-style body.

Until Martin came out with a 0000-size body (a shallow-bodied jumbo, previously designated with an "M") in 1997, the 000 was the largest (15 inches wide) guitar carrying a string of 0s in its name. Particularly, the first-generation 12-fret design is highly coveted by fingerstyle players, who appreciate the instrument's balance, volume, and rich sound. In many aspects, 12-fret 000s are as close to a classical guitar as a steel-string gets; and after many years of neglect, the design has found a new group of friends in recent years.

A Martin 000-15S (left), and a Lakewood Auditorium.

Enjoying continued success since its introduction in 1934, the later 000 design with a 14-fret neck is a true workhorse. With a thinner neck and shorter scale, these guitars tend to be easy to play, and for many people, the design results in the quintessential "folk" guitar. However, before relegating 000s as incapable of playing anything beyond "Blowing in the Wind" or "Where Have All the Flowers Gone," consider that the guitars are also found in the hands of pop stars such as Elvis Costello, rockers like Eric Clapton, and skiffle pioneer Lonnie Donegan—the latter two of which have been graced with Martin signature models. This versatility has made the 000 the virtual blueprint for the many contemporary small-bodied steel-strings. Due to their near-perfect compromise between volume, tone, and playing comfort, this guitar type is also an excellent choice for players of physically smaller proportions.

OM (Orchestra Model)

OMs finish up this set of guitar styles that originated at Martin. Featuring the same exact body as a 14-fret 000, these guitars would seem virtually identical, if it wasn't for a long 25.4-inch scale and a wider nut of 1³/₄ inches, rather than the 1¹¹/₁₆-inch scale of the 000s . Visually, the most significant difference is a smaller pickguard. What may seem like extremely minor differences give the OM a significant boost in volume and power, and the wider string spacing gives the guitar better playability for fingerstyle techniques.

Martin OM-18V

The OM is of great significance in Martin's history, as it was the company's first guitar with a 14-fret neck, and its success caused the redesign of virtually the entire line to the new style in the early to mid-1930s. Once the switch was complete, Martin decided that it would rather use the same necks it was already making for the new 0 and 00-size guitars, and by late 1934, the original OM had been replaced by the 14-fret 000. As a result, the few hundred original OMs made between 1929 and 1933 became highly sought after, and remain in their position among the highest-priced vintage instruments today.

With the emergence of new American guitar makers in the 1970s, the glory of the OM would be revived. With vintage examples becoming scarce and prices getting out of reach for most musicians, luthiers began building copies or using the concept of a 14-fret 000-sized guitar with a wide neck and a long scale as an inspiration for original designs. Among the first of these builders were the Santa Cruz Guitar Company and Franklin Guitars, the latter of which received great recognition through their association with

A Santa Cruz OM with 42-style appointments.

fingerpicking stars John Renbourn and Stefan Grossman. While Franklin ceased to build guitars for many years, and only recently begun taking orders again, Santa Cruz remains one of the leading manufacturers of OM-style guitars, and the company's OM/PW has recently set new standards for affordable value in a high-end guitar.

The fact that Martin itself didn't offer an OM in its standard catalog (although it offered occasional runs of limited editions) until 1990 only increased the demand on the smaller manufacturers. Coincidentally, it was a direct collaboration with one of these tiny companies that would eventually get Martin back into the business of building this style of guitar. Long an advocate of the OM design, guitarist/designer Eric Schoenberg had started collaborating with a number of luthiers in recreating his favorite instruments. Ultimately, Schoenberg arrived at collaborating directly with Martin in building his own line of vintage-style OMs, which sometimes featured modern additions such as cutaways. The resulting instruments found enthusiastic approval among fingerstyle connoisseurs, and Martin eventually realized that it would be more profitable to sell similar instruments with its own name on the headstock. Testing the waters with a few limited runs of celebrity models, the company introduced the OM-28, and later the OM-28 Vintage Reissue, the latter of which has become a cornerstone of its offerings.

Today, OMs are made by many manufacturers. Not everyone uses the same name designation, but the specs are found over and over, and to many guitarists, the original OM remains to be the Holy Grail.

Martin's Switch from 12 to 14 Frets

Just when the 0, 00, and 000 sizes begin to make sense, along comes Martin's decision to switch the majority of their designs from a 12-fret neck/body joint to a 14-fret joint in 1934. With the decline of the banjo's popularity in the music of the time, many musicians switched to the guitar as their primary instrument; but being used to the banjo's easy access to higher notes, the 12-fret guitar design of the day seemed limiting to many players.

The change from 12 to 14-frets to the body: On the left a 12-fret Martin 000-28VS in the style of 1920's, on the right, a 000-28 featuring the later 14-fret design.

Gibson had begun offering 14-fret flattops in 1932, and even though it had introduced the design on the OM in 1929, Martin showed some initial hesitation. When the company did decide to make the switch, it charged ahead with full steam, revamping almost all their models to accommodate the new neck. Wanting to keep the placement of the bridge and bracing intact, Martin shortened and squared off the guitars' upper bouts, making room for the two additional frets. While they were at it, the company's luthiers also switched to a narrower neck (measuring $1^{11}/_{16}$ inches at the nut, rather than the $1^3/_4$ or $1^7/_8$ inches of the older design), replaced the classical-style slotted headstock with a solid one, and in the case of the 000, shortened the scale-length from 25.4 inches to 24.9 inches (0s and 00s already had the shorter scale with the old design). Dreadnoughts experienced similar changes, but as the largest guitar in the catalog, the instrument was the only model to keep the long scale length.

While all these changes effectively define what we have come to accept as the modern steel-string flattop guitar, they also changed the sound and feel of the instruments to the point where a Martin 000 made in 1929 didn't have much in common with the same model guitar manufactured in 1934 (the same confusion can be the case with Martin's vintage reissues, which feature similar specs depending on which year's model they're recreating).

Today, the majority of 0, 00, 000, and dreadnought-sized guitars feature the 14-fret design, although companies such as Collings, Santa Cruz, and Huss and Dalton are building instruments inspired by the older style. Some manufacturers offer their models with a choice of 12- or 14-fret necks, with Lakewood's Auditorium being an example of this approach.

In a final attempt to completely confuse even long-time experts, Martin began building 14-fret 000s with a long scale in the early 1990s. Indeed, 000s which are part of the 16 Series or below feature these dimensions, essentially making them OMs with narrow ($1^{11}/_{16}$ inches at the nut) necks. Standard Series (currently only the 000-28, 000-45, and various limited editions, such as the Eric Clapton model) are still made with the short scale.

Jumbo

More than with other body shapes and sizes, the jumbo is much less defined in the tonal qualities it offers. Although Gibson called their first dreadnought-shaped guitar a "Jumbo" (and later, "Advanced Jumbo"), it is generally the voluptuous shape of the company's later J-200 (also called "Super Jumbo") that is associated with the term. Featuring rounded upper and lower bouts (the latter measuring $16^7/_8$ inches across) and a tight waist, the guitar offered a completely new look and sound

Gibson's J-200 is the classic jumbo.

This F212XL is Guild's 12-string version of its popular jumbo shape.

when it was first introduced in 1937. With its gaudy appointments, outrageous mustache bridge, and generally bold aesthetic (including flamed maple back and sides; although rosewood versions have also been made), the guitar was an instant success with flashy country players such as Ray Whitley and Gene Autry.

Designed with strumming rhythm players in mind, most Gibson jumbos are relatively heavily built instruments. Although it became the guitar of choice for the late blues fingerpicker Rev. Gary Davis (who played with a deft technique and metal fingerpicks), most people find that the instrument is better suited for backup strumming—a quality that's appreciated by players such as Emmylou Harris, Pete Townshend, and Albert Lee.

Although smaller companies, such as Chicago's Larson Brothers, had also built jumbo-style guitars as early as the 1930s, it was Guild that would gain a reputation for the versatile tones of its F-50 model. Introduced in 1954, the guitar was the first serious competition for Gibson's pioneering Jumbo. Like many other Guild models, the guitar features a signature laminated arched back—a trait more often found on archtop guitars. While the version with maple back and sides is perhaps the most famous, Guild made the guitar in a variety of woods, including a rosewood model known as the F-50R, which was introduced in 1965, and remains popular with players of various styles. The late Dave Van Ronk was perhaps the most famous player of a Guild jumbo, using the instrument for his ragtime-inspired fingerpicking throughout his career. Guild had particular success with the 12-string version of its jumbo design. Used by artists as varied as Slash and Ralph Towner, this double-strung variation is a true classic; and for many years, it was practically without serious competition.

While Gibson and Guild continue to be popular with fans of jumbo guitars, several other brands have re-voiced the oversized body shape for a palette of tonal options. Goodall's Jumbo and Lowden's O Series are among the examples of models that combine a large airspace with lighter bracing and a carefully balanced voice. With a great response to a soft attack and excellent volume, these instruments are ideal candidates for fingerstyle playing. Taylor began offering jumbos early on in its history, and the company has always maintained that the guitars are tonally very similar to its dreadnought instruments. While the radically different shape might make this statement seem odd at first, it makes sense when it is considered that the internal construction and bracing of the two models are virtually identical.

On the left, a Lowden O25, on the right, a custom Steve Klein jumbo.

California luthier Steve Klein has long used a very large jumbo design (up to 18 inches at the lower bout) for his individually crafted high-end acoustics. Utilizing radical Kasha-inspired inside bracing (see page 156) and often elaborate inlay work, his guitars are among the most distinctive instruments being built today. Another unique Jumbo guitar is offered by the small Ryan Guitar company. Called the Cathedral, the guitar is designed to offer ultimate acoustic volume and presence for fingerstyle playing. An asymmetric design with a beveled armrest ensures ergonomic comfort that belies the instrument's gargantuan size.

Mini-Jumbo

What seems at first like a certain contradiction of terms is indeed one of the most popular contemporary body styles. Consisting of the curvaceous jumbo shape at a reduced size, these guitars can show similar variations as found in their larger

Gibson's J-185 was the first "small jumbo."

cousins, beginning with how they're called by the various manufacturers. In a continuation of the company's glory, Gibson practically invented the Mini-Jumbo when it introduced the J-185 model in 1951. Conceived as an affordable alternative to the pricey J-200, the instrument featured similar body proportions, but scaled down to a width of 16 inches at the lower bout. The guitar also lost the mustache bridge, and its appointments were toned down in order to save costs.

Although this size was new for a flattop, it actually shared an outline with the company's ES-125, ES-150, L-48, and L-50 archtops, but with a greater depth of 4^7/$_8$ inches. Although it had created an excellent instrument with great power and a friendlier, less "boomy" voice than that of the J-200, Gibson's marketing never gave the model its proper place in the company's line, and its original edition was discontinued in 1959.

Gibson did revive the shape soon after with the introduction of the special Everly Brothers signature model in 1962. However, while these guitars offered stunning looks and a celebrity endorsement, they were built with a shallower depth, and the sound was muffled by their distinctive, but oversized double pickguards. Custom orders aside, it wasn't until Gibson's acoustic division moved to Bozeman, Montana in the 1980s, where under the leadership of master luthier Ren Ferguson, a new version of the original J-185 Mini-Jumbo was reintroduced.

Santa Cruz Guitar Company founders Bruce Ross and Richard Hoover paid tribute to the J-185 body style early on in their careers when they introduced the F Model as part of their original line of guitars in 1977. Departing from Gibson's flashy appointments, the guitar had an understated appearance, and with his own signature voicing, the resulting guitar became an ultra-versatile instrument that's at home in many playing styles. In addition to the F Model, Santa Cruz used this

body shape as a point of departure when it created the FS model, a guitar specifically built with fingerstyle playing in mind. With its responsive cedar top and light bracing, ultra-plain appointments, and deep cutaway, the guitar's tone has little to do with the instrument that inspired its shape, but it set a trend that several of today's top luthiers followed. Among these are James Olson and Kevin Ryan, whose SJ and Mission Grand Concert models, respectively, feature similar dimensions, and which are considered to be among the finest instruments available by many fingerstyle guitar enthusiasts. This sentiment is shared by superstar James Taylor, who uses three Olson SJs as his main performance and recording guitars. In 2002, Olson began taking orders for a limited edition James Taylor Signature model, bearing a price tag of $25,000 each.

A Collings SJ

On the more affordable front, Takamine has had great success with its similarly shaped NEX body. Using the style on a whole range of instruments, starting in the affordable G-Series and continuing into the company's annual limited editions, Takamine has found a way of using the concept for instruments that impress with great all-around qualities for a variety of playing styles. Additionally, Takamine offers most of these instruments with its own pickup and preamp system, making them popular with frequent performers.

Takamine's mini-jumbo NEX design is one of the company's most popular shapes. On the left, an EAC48C, on the right, an ENV460SC.

Parlor Guitars

Parlor guitars have the smallest bodies of all flattops. Originally designed around the same time that steel-strings gained popularity (but many vintage parlor guitars are still best strung with nylon or silk and steel strings) in the late 1800s, these instruments represent some of the earliest examples of what we consider to be the modern American guitar.

In order to understand the parlor guitar, it helps to take a look at how the instrument's development differed in Europe and the U.S. Up to the 1840s, European and American guitars were essentially identical, with guitars made on both continents being quite small by today's standards. Following the lead of the Spanish luthier Antonio de Torres, most European builders began producing larger, fan-braced classical guitars. American companies, on the other hand, largely ignored the revolution in Spanish guitar design, and continued to build their instruments in the earlier pre-Torres style. As a result, while European builders such as Ramírez and Hauser had pushed the classical guitar to a highly advanced level by the beginning of the 20th century, American guitars were quite archaic by comparison. However, once American companies such as Martin and Washburn began experimenting with building stronger instruments for steel-strings, they adapted the now-familiar shape, thereby creating a classic instrument type.

On the left, an unidentified parlor guitar from the 19th Century. On the right, a Washburn parlor from the 1920s.

Larrivée's modern Parlour model.

Parlor guitars get their name from their intended use for entertaining guests in the parlors of the era's elegant Victorian homes, and as such, they were often played by women. In addition to their small bodies with narrow bouts, parlor guitars usually also feature a short scale length (between 22 and 25 inches) and 12-fret necks, giving them very compact dimensions all around. Great-sounding vintage examples can be found with names such as Washburn, Lyon & Healey, and Maurer on the headstock, and while these guitars don't tend to be "cannons," their sweet voices can make them outstanding choices in the recording studio. Players such as the Tin Hat Trio's Mark Orton have found ways to utilize Parlor guitars for their individual styles, and the folk revival during the 1960s created demand for the instrument style among folk singers.

As larger and more powerful guitars gained popularity, most manufacturers stopped building parlor-sized guitars in the early part of the 20th century. With sheer volume becoming less of an issue with modern amplification and recording techniques, many players have recently rediscovered the parlor guitar's charm; and today, several manufacturers are offering the style again. Perhaps the biggest success story is found in Larrivee's Parlor model, which was initially introduced as an inexpensive travel guitar, but has since been offered built with exotic woods to satisfy more refined tastes. Yamaha has recently introduced the parlor-sized CSF35 and CSF 60; and on the high-end, companies such as Santa Cruz, and luthiers such as Lance McCollum, are offering highly refined custom parlor guitars.

It is also worth mentioning that some manufacturers refer to certain models as "parlors" simply because they feature small-bodies with 12-fret necks. Many of these instruments would be more accurately described as being anywhere between an 0 and a 000 size, so it's a good idea to not go by name alone if you're looking for a parlor instrument.

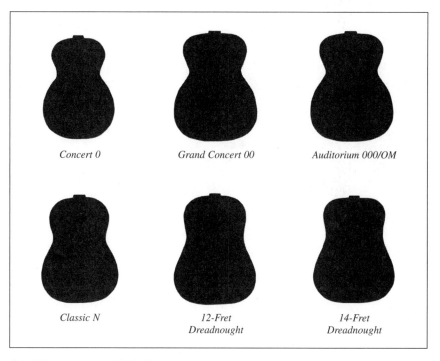

Six of Martin's most popular body sizes.

Other Flattop Shapes

In contrast to electric guitars, where solid-body construction enables just about any conceivable shape, acoustic guitar luthiers tend to be somewhat more conservative in just how far they will take the design. Ergonomics are often at the helm of experimenting with new shapes, and several luthiers have indeed come up with ways to build guitars that are more comfortable to play. Linda Manzer and William R. Cumpiano are using a "wedge-shaped" body on many of their flattops (with Manzer having trademarked the name), where the upper side (facing the player) is thinner than the lower side, therefore creating the comfort of a thin-bodied instrument without losing the tone of a deeper body. Michael Baranik and Harry Fleishman are among the builders advocating asymmetrical bodies, which some players also find more comfortable to hold. For something completely off the wall, Fred Carlson has designed a guitar he calls the "dreadnautilus," which resembles a spiral with a neck sticking out.

Fred Carlson's wacky-but-functional Dreadnautilus model.

It's not surprising that electric guitars have also served as inspiration for unusually shaped acoustics. Takamine's EA-360, which the company offered in the early 1980s, resembled Gibson's ultimate heavy metal axe: the Flying V. German luthier Boris Dommenget has recently built a similar pair of instruments (one a 6-string, the other a 12-string) for rocker Rudolf Schenker of the Scorpions. As their names suggest, Fender's Telecoustic and Stratocoustic are acoustic guitars styled after the company's classic Telecaster and Stratocaster models.

Guitars specifically made for traveling are a relatively new category—and with size being a major consideration, some interesting shapes have been invented. Martin's Backpacker is probably the most memorable, with a body that essentially flares out as an extension of the neck (its sides are actually the same piece of wood as the neck), with an overall width that's hardly greater than that of a typical guitar's bridge. Available in steel and nylon-string versions (and as ukulele and mandolins), the guitar is perfect for strapping onto a backpack, and a custom version has even been taken into outer space on board the Space Shuttle. Taylor has had immense success with its Baby model. With a dreadnought-shaped body that's about half the size of a standard guitar and a short 22-inch scale, the guitar is popular with frequent flyers and also makes an excellent choice for children.

On the left: Nylon and steel-string versions of Martin's Backpacker.
On the right: Tacoma's high-tuned Papoose.

For a guitar that's even smaller, look no further than Tacoma's Papoose. Although this diminutive 6-string may appear like a toy at first, it's actually a serious instrument. Tuned a fourth higher than a standard guitar (the equivalent of placing a capo at the fifth fret), the little fellow has a sound somewhere between a guitar and a mandolin.

Nylon-String Shapes and Sizes

Perhaps due to the narrower conception of classical guitarists' tonal ideals, the nylon-string guitar doesn't show nearly as much variation in shape and size as its steel-strung relative. The vast majority of nylon-string guitars feature a shape closely resembling the design conceived by Antonio de Torres in the mid-1800s. Surprisingly, this is even the case with instruments that offer radical departures from Torres's ideas elsewhere in their construction.

Widely regarded as the father of the modern classical guitar, Torres increased the size of the previously much more petite instrument (which was closer to the dimension of the parlor guitar described above), a move which, combined with his innovative fan-bracing system, gave the guitar a boost in volume, dynamic range, and greater control over tonal subtleties. Not only did Torres create an instrument that met the emerging generation of virtuoso classical guitarist's desire for a more powerful instrument, to many players, his general design remains the ultimate to this day.

In a quest to further extend the instrument's volume and tonal capabilities, the body's outline has often been experimented with, but none of the resulting instruments have had a lasting impact. Among the most noteworthy efforts is found in Manuel Contreras's Carlevaro (named after the Uruguayan guitarist Abel Carlevaro) model from 1983. In an attempt to maximize the active area of the top, the guitar featured an asymmetrical shape that eliminated the waist in the bass side of the instrument. In a further radical departure from standard guitar construction, the guitar has no traditional soundhole and features a second set of sides, which isolate the active part of the instrument from the player's body. Contreras continued to develop the design throughout the 1980s; and while many considered the idea a fundamental success, it never caught on among the often conservative classical crowd.

Although Torres came up with the definitive outline for the body of the modern nylon-string guitar, small variations in size have become the trademarks of certain schools of design. Torres's guitars had a body width (at the lower bout) of about $13^{15}/_{16}$ inches, which was followed by many other instruments. Early Hauser guitars are generally known for having relatively small bodies as well. Examples of larger-bodies nylon strings include certain models by Ignacio Fleta, Jerónimo Peña Fernández, and Thomas Humphrey's Millennium, all of which are around 15 inches in width.

The size differences between various classical guitars are demonstrated by this Contreras guitar on the left, and the small Torres–style Kenny Hill instrument on the right.

Classical vs. Flamenco

There is virtually no difference in the outline and size of classical and flamenco guitars. Sharing the same origins, little distinction was made between the instruments used for the two styles until the emergence of modern virtuosos such as Ramón Montoya and Andrés Segovia. Some flamenco guitars have evolved to feature slightly thinner bodies, and their use of cypress back and sides and lighter construction—combined with ultra-low action—gives them the typical percussive sound.

Flamenco guitars from Cervantes (left), and Yamaha (a model CG171SF).

Hybrid Instruments

As their name suggests, hybrid instruments are guitars that fuse features from different designs. Most often, the focus is on a guitar that is strung with nylon strings and sounds a lot like a classical, but feels more like a steel string. With narrower necks often joining the body at the 14th fret, radiused fretboards, and bodies that are closer to a steel-string 00 or 000 than the Torres design, these guitars depart from tradition.

Although "real" classical players will generally object to these instruments, players who are otherwise used to playing steel-strings often find them to be much more comfortable than standard nylon strings. Hybrid guitars are particularly popular with jazz players; and because they're often equipped with pickups, they're also found in pop and rock contexts. Some examples of these instruments include Takamine's NP-65C, which uses the company's NEX body as a point of departure, Taylor's Nylon-Series, which uses a deeper version of its Grand Concert shape, and Martin's 000C-16NGT, which relies on the company's proven 12-fret 000 body.

Popular nylon-string hybrids: Takamine's NP65C, and Taylor's NS-72.

Archtop Sizes and Shapes

Archtop guitars also don't tend to vary a great amount in shape, but there are several common sizes, usually measured at the lower bout. Even though Orville Gibson was building an early form of the archtop guitar by the end of the 19th century, the modern history of the instrument type really begins with the Gibson

L-5 designed by Lloyd Loar in 1924. Even though it appears small today—the guitar's width is 16 inches—the guitar was spectacularly large at the time. Designed to fit into the mandolin orchestras popular during the 1920s, the guitar's excellent volume and projection quickly allowed it to rise among players creating a new kind of American music—jazz.

Two eras of Gibson's L-5 archtop: On the left, the original 16-inch version, on the right, the later 17-inch version.

In a typical manner of bigger-is-better, Gibson replaced the original 16-inch L-5 with a new 17-inch design (which it called "advanced") in 1934. The same year, Gibson introduced its 18-inch Super 400 model, the largest archtop the company would offer. Initially remaining true acoustic guitars, both the L-5 and Super 400 eventually evolved into what are essentially hollow-body electric instruments with pickups mounted into their tops in the1950s. While these latest incarnations of the models—which also feature a cutaway—embodies what the L-5 and Super 400 designations stand for to many archtop fans, these are really instruments that have little in common with the original designs.

As swing bands got louder, archtops got bigger. Trying to squeeze as much volume out of an unamplified guitar as possible, luthiers began outdoing even Gibson's Super 400. Epiphone's Emperor featured a width of 18^1/$_2$ inches, and Stromberg's Master 400 even increased the size to 19 inches.

Two Epiphone archtops: On the left, a vintage US-made Emperor,
on the right, a recent Korean-made Emperor Regent.

With the electric archtop becoming the dominant type of guitar used in jazz, true acoustic archtops virtually disappeared by the 1960s. A few small makers, such as New York's John D'Angelico and his apprentice Jimmy D'Aquisto, continued to build this type of instrument; but none of the major manufacturers continued to offer them. With few exceptions, most of the archtops made today closely resemble the designs created in the instrument's heyday. Builders such as John Monteleone, Linda Manzer, Bob Benedetto, but also Europeans such as France's Maurice Dupont and Germany's Stefan Sonntag, continue to raise the bar in the various styles of acoustic archtops available.

Big difference in price: Guild's top of the line Artist Award on the left, and a S.S Stewart archtop sold in department stores in the 1940s.

Thin-Body Acoustic-Electrics

The better a guitar sounds as a true acoustic instrument, the more problems it tends to have when amplified at high volumes. The reason for this is that the qualities that create a full and rich acoustic sound with lots of volume and bass response— primarily a top that's flexible enough to move a considerable amount of air—are exactly the culprits for feedback when plugging in. As a result, many guitars that are designed specifically for playing loudly feature thinner bodies and stiffer tops. In an effort to appeal to players who are otherwise used to playing electric guitars, these instruments generally also feature deep cutaways and necks that are thinner than on many true acoustic guitars.

Appearing in the early 1980s, Guild's F-45CE and Washburn's Festival series were among the first widely available instruments in this category. Approximately the size of a 00 (but with a depth of around three inches), these guitars were equipped with under-saddle pickups and controls mounted in their sides, leading the way for many other manufacturers to follow.

Guild's F65CE thin-body, and Godin's radical Multiac.

Exactly how thin these guitars are varies among the available models. Some, such as Epiphone's PR-5, are only marginally thinner than standard models of otherwise similar dimensions. Other examples, such as the Godin Multiac or Rick Turner Renaissance are as thin as a solid-body electric, and these guitars really should be seen as electric instruments that happen to sound like an amplified acoustic.

Comparing the depth of a dreadnought (left) and a thin-body acoustic-electric (right). Far right: A Yamaha's APX9.

Ovations

Using a synthetic "bowl" in place of traditional wooden back and sides, Ovation guitars occupy a category of their own. Conceived and built by a branch of Kaman Aerospace (a famous manufacturer of helicopters), the guitars take advantage of their parent company's high-tech resources. Using similar fiberglass technology that he had successfully used in the construction of helicopter blades, company founder Charles Kaman started building Ovation Guitars in 1966. Also known as "roundbacks," Ovations looked like no other guitar from the start, even though the basic shape of the body is similar to that of a slightly enlarged classical outline. Early Ovations all featured what's now known as a "deep bowl," which has a similar depth as a traditional dreadnought guitar; and today, players can choose from medium-depth, shallow, and ultra-shallow bodies in addition to the original design.

An Ovation 1860 Custom Legend cutaway six-string and a 1751 12-string Balladeer by the same manufacturer.

Cutaways became an option on many Ovation models as early as 1982, and today, the majority of the company's guitars come standard with this feature. In 1998, Ovation came out with a limited edition parlor-sized model, but the model never attained enough popularity to be added to the standard line.

Over the years, both steel- and nylon-string Ovations have been popular with an impressive list of professionals. Because it was the first—and for most of the 1970s, practically the only—modern acoustic-electric guitar, it has been a frequent choice for performers who play acoustic guitar in a loud performance situation. Although today there are many alternatives for plugged-in acoustic playing available, many rock players in particular continue to appreciate an Ovation's hassle-free plug-in-and-go ability. This sort of popularity is reflected in an impressive roster of signature artists, who have included players as diverse as Glen Campbell, Josh White, Al Di Meola, and Melissa Etheridge.

Ovation's Al di Meola signature model, and the company's Celebrity Deluxe double-neck with both six and 12-string necks.

Cutaways

Enabling easy access to the instrument's highest notes, cutaways have become increasingly popular on all kinds of acoustic guitars. Modifying the guitar's otherwise symmetrical body by adding a curve at the treble side of the upper bout, a cutaway allows the player's fretting hand to move all the way to the highest position of the fretboard without being interrupted at the neck/body joint.

Although some examples of cutaways can be seen on guitars made in the early 1900s, their widespread popularity began as a feature on Gibson archtop guitars. First introduced with the L-5 Premier in 1939, the cutaway was quickly imitated by other manufacturers. Another example of first-generation cutaway guitars is found in Mario Maccaferri's guitar designs of the early 1920s, eventually evolving into the Selmer instrument forever immortalized by French Gypsy star

Django Reinhardt. American flattops were relatively slow to feature cutaway designs. With most players using this guitar type to strum first-position chords in folk and country music, notes past the third fret hadn't been a major concern, but evolving playing styles soon changed the conception of what flattops would be used for. 1951's Gibson CF-100 was one of the first cutaway-equipped flattops, but a lack of demand caused the company to discontinue the model by 1959.

As with many areas in the history of the guitar, rock 'n' roll would soon have a significant impact on flattop design. With more and more players coming from an electric guitar background, companies began answering the calls for increased playability by designing acoustics with cutaways. Guild was among the first to offer a guitar designed for rock rather than bluegrass, and its 1975 D-40C still stands as the blueprint for many contemporary instruments. By 1977, Martin had designed its first new body shape since the introduction of the dreadnought almost 50 years earlier. Initially introduced as the M-38, the style would become the first to receive a stock cutaway in 1981, with the resulting MC-28 becoming an instant success.

Although most concert-level classical and flamenco guitarist still prefer non-cutaway guitars (using their technical finesse to reach upper notes instead), the element has even found its way onto these instruments. Especially popular with jazz players, cutaways are now found on classical guitars in virtually all price ranges, including high-end examples by luthiers such as Robert Ruck, Linda Manzer, and Jim Redgate.

Whether or not a cutaway distracts from a guitar's tone is a frequent topic of debate. While obviously leading to a slight reduction of airspace inside the body, it is also a fact that, due to their stiffness, the upper bouts of most guitars have little affect on tone and volume. Because of this, most experts agree that with a properly designed guitar, there will be little or no difference between identical models with or without a cutaway.

A more personal decision is involved in deciding whether or not you need a cutaway in the first place. Classical players are a perfect example that virtuosity alone doesn't necessitate the design, and steel-string players such as bluegrass ace Tony Rice or fingerpicking legend John Renbourn also seem to get along fine without it. However, upper-register jazz voicings, lead-guitar playing, and even just the use of a capo can result in a cutaway easing a guitarist's existence.

Venetian, Florentine, or Maccaferri Style

The three types of cutaways found most often are called Venetian, Florentine, and Maccaferri styles. With a rounded point, the Venetian cutaway is bent from the same piece of wood making up the lower side of the instrument. Because of the sharp curve necessitated by the design, a Venetian cutaway can be hard to accomplish with particularly stiff or brittle woods, such as bird's-eye maple or padauk, which are difficult to bend without breaking.

A Florentine cutaway uses a separate piece of wood to create its distinctive shape, making it more labor-intensive to build. With its sharp point, the design allows a variety of actual shapes, making it the first choice for luthiers seeking as deep a cutaway as possible. An interesting variation on the Florentine cutaway is sometimes used by luthiers Judy Threet and Dana Bourgeois (the latter of which uses the design on his Martin Simpson signature model). After bending the lower side of the guitar as if it was to be built without a cutaway, a section of the upper bout is cut off and reversed, giving it a unique appearance, and making it

A Venetian cutaway on a Guild F-65CE.

unnecessary to bend a separate piece of wood.

A Maccaferri-style cutaway is made in a similar way to the Venetian variety, but it uses a distinctively different shape. Instead of curving toward the center of the guitar's body, this kind of cutaway is virtually flat on its way to meeting the neck. As its name implies, this type of cutaway is most often found in Selmer/Maccaferri–style guitars, but it's also used on Taylor's Leo Kottke signature model and a variety of other instruments.

On the left, a Gibson L-4C with a pronounced Florentine cutaway.
On the right, a Taylor LKSM6 with a cutaway in the Selmer Maccaferri-style.

A Dean Frana with double cutaways.

Double Cutaways

While common among electric guitars, double cutaways are a rare exception for acoustics. Although they re-establish the symmetry of a non-cutaway instrument, double cutaways have no added practical benefit, and many guitars that have used this feature have tonally suffered from the design.

Early examples of double cutaway guitars can be found in the Weissgerber instruments of German luthier Richard Jacob, and both Martin and Guild have unsuccessfully experimented with such guitars. Most recently, Dean introduced its acoustic-electric Frana with double cutaways, and luthier Abe Wechter has made them an integral feature on his Pathmaker design.

Variations

12-strings

Although multi-course metal-strung instruments like the cittern date back to the 16th century, they seem to have had little or no influence on the development of the modern 12-string guitar, which most likely was invented in Mexico in the latter part of 19th century. It was initially used in various Mexican folk styles, but sometime around 1920, blues musicians in America including Leadbelly, Barbecue Bob, and Blind Willie McTell began to play the large bodied, long, 26-inch scale instrument made by Stella. This version of the 12-string had a 12-fret neck and a slotted headstock. Some variations came with a pin bridge, while others were fitted with a tailpiece. These early guitars were designed to be tuned down to D or even C.

A Dell'Arte copy of a 1920s Stella 12-string.

After Leadbelly died in 1949, the popularity of the 12-string declined until the early 1960s, when it was revived by folk musicians like Erik Darling, Fred Neil, and Roger McGuinn, who played acoustic 12-strings on numerous recordings as a session musician before he founded the Byrds.

In the 1960s, Gibson's B12-45, which was a 12-string version of a J-45, and Guild's F-412, based on the 17-inch Jumbo F-50, were two of the most sought after models. Both companies also made smaller bodied 12-strings, but musicians overwhelmingly preferred the models based on dreadnoughts and jumbos. Players found that by stringing the guitars with extra-light strings, the instruments could be tuned up to E, rather than D or C. Since then, most new 12-string guitars have been designed to be played with the lighter strings and higher tuning, but the Taylor's Leo Kottke model was built to be strung with heavier strings and tuned down to C#.

A 12-string's first two pairs of strings are usually tuned in unison, while the remaining bass pairs are tuned an octave apart. The pairs are fingered in the same manner as a standard 6-string guitar. Twelve-strings have wider fretboards than regular 6-string guitars, usually measuring around $1^7/8 - 2$ inches at the nut. The bracing on most modern 12-strings is the same X-pattern that is used on six strings, but it is generally made slightly heavier to withstand the extra tension. Twelve-strings never have lightweight scalloped bracing. The older Stellas were built with simple ladder bracing. Old Stellas are scarce and highly prized by blues players, but there are a few modern luthiers making good reproductions, including the Dell'Arte company in California and Peter Howlett in Wales.

Selmer/Maccaferri–Style Guitars

In 1932, luthier Mario Maccaferri and the Selmer woodwind factory in Paris, France joined forces to build the Modèle Orchestre—a guitar designed by Maccaferri. Maccaferri's original design was for a gut-strung classical guitar—he was a virtuoso classical guitarist before he became a luthier—but he was persuaded to work up a steel-string version, which soon became the standard model.

On the left, the original, Mario Maccaferri–designed Selmer guitar with a large soundhole and 12-fret neck. On the right, the later model with smaller soundhole and 14-fret neck.

115

The Modèle Orchestre had many unique features, such as a large D-shaped soundhole and interior resonator that was designed to project the sound towards the audience. The guitar also had a cutaway, which was rare at the time, a 12-fret neck, and sealed, permanently lubricated gears, a now standard feature, invented by Maccaferri.

The guitars had a slightly arched spruce top, laminated rosewood back and sides, and were set up with a floating bridge and tailpiece, much like the archtops being built in America by Gibson and Epiphone. The guitar measured about sixteen inches across the lower bout, making it about the same size as a small-bodied Gibson L-5. Maccaferri's radical design was only partially successful—the interior resonator proved to be difficult to build, and guitarists weren't convinced of its benefits—and after a year or so, Maccaferri left Selmer to pursue other interests.

After he left, an unknown workman redesigned the guitar by eliminating the resonator, elongating the 12-fret neck to a 14-fret neck, and scaling down the large D-shaped soundhole to a smaller oval one. This model, which was renamed the Modèle Jazz was enthusiastically embraced by the Gypsy guitarist Django Reinhardt, and by the musicians who played the Gypsy swing he pioneered in Paris in the 1930s. Luthiers like Busato and DiMauro began copying the Selmer design almost immediately; and after the company stopped producing guitars in 1953, luthiers like Favino stepped up to fill the void. These days, Gypsy swing is more popular than ever, and there are builders all through Europe and America building fine replicas in the Selmer tradition.

Baritones

A baritone guitar, which is between the standard 6-string and bass guitar in pitch, has a long scale, up to 27 inches, and is designed to be tuned down three or four steps. Baritone guitars have become more popular in recent years, and are made mostly by independent luthiers like James Goodall, Michael Greenfield, and Ralph Bown. Guitarist Bob Brozman has been instrumental in pushing baritone guitars, and has inspired the

Alvarez-Yairi's JB1 baritone guitar.

Santa Cruz Bob Brozman model—a 12-fret mahogany dreadnought—and the National Reso-Phonic Style "1" baritone.

Baritones are generally tuned to B (B E A D F♯ B, low to high) or A (A D G C E A). There are a few larger companies building baritones, like Alvarez Yairi, who built the YB-1, and Ovation, who call their long-scale guitar the Long Neck. Both of these companies suggest that you tune their guitars down only one step to D (D G C F A D).

Acoustic Basses

Luthiers have been trying to come up with a workable acoustic bass guitar since at least the late 19th century, but it wasn't until Ernie Ball came up with the Earthwood bass in the early 1970s that someone came up with a usable design. Rather than try to make a guitar version of a stand-up bass, like earlier luthiers tried to do, Ball worked on coming up with an acoustic version of the popular Fender Precision bass. The Earthwood bass was slightly larger that a jumbo guitar, but it was built lightly enough to be resonant enough to still have a good low end. In 1976, Guild introduced the B-50, which was six inches deep and eighteen inches across the lower bout. The Guild was popular enough to stay in the line, but it didn't inspire any other builders to make their own versions.

Then in the late 1980s Martin introduced the B-40, which was based on their 16-inch jumbo body. The B-40 was smaller than the Guild, and consequently quieter without as much low end; but players began using it with transducer pickups to make up the difference. In the wake of Martin, other companies began to offer acoustic basses of their own, many with built-in pickups. Some of the more interesting acoustic guitars basses include the Steve Klein–designed Taylor Bass which features a Kasha-style bracing pattern, and the Dobro Bass, which has an aluminum resonator. Acoustic guitar basses tend to have a scale length between 31 and 34 inches, and they are generally strung with brass or phosphor bronze strings.

On the left, an Ovation Celebrity bass, on the right, two acoustic basses by Guild: a B-4E, and a fretless B-30.

Another variation of the acoustic bass is the guitarron, a large Mexican guitar with a short, fretless neck, six wound nylon strings, and a distinctive, V-shaped back.

Resonator Guitars

Resonator guitars use an aluminum cone-shaped diaphragm to amplify the string vibration, rather than the wooden top of a conventional guitar. The first resonator guitar was invented in the early 1920s by Rudy Dopyera, who started the National Guitar Company. Dopyera came up with two versions of the resonator guitar, both of which had metal bodies. The first design had three small cones that were connected by a T-shaped bridge. The tricone, sometimes called a tri-plate, usually had a square neck for playing Hawaiian slide style. These instruments are sometimes called steel guitars, but the name refers to the playing technique, which

Left: A metal-bodied National Tricone. Right: A square-neck Dobro with a wooden body.

uses a metal bar known as a steel, instead of the body material, which was nickel-silver.

The other style of National guitar had a larger, single cone. The strings ran over a small wooden disc, called a "biscuit," that was attached to an aluminum cone that resembled an upside down pie-plate. The tricone had a smooth, mellow tone that was well-suited to Hawaiian music. The single-cone National had a louder, rougher tone that made it a favorite for blues players, particularly those who played with a bottleneck.

National's Estralita model with a wooden body, round neck, and single-cone resonator.

In the late 1920s, Dopyera left National to form the Dobro Company. Rather than take the National designs along with him, he invented a third style of resonator guitar. The Dobro, which had a wooden body, used a bowl-shaped resonator that was set up with an 8-armed aluminum spider that held the bridge. The Dobro guitars were almost always built with square necks, and they became quite popular with country musicians and later bluegrass musicians.

Today there are a number of companies making resonator guitars, including National Resophonic—who make excellent resonator guitars in the old styles even though they have no direct connection to the original National company—Beltona, who are based in New Zealand, and Dobro, who are now owned by Gibson. There are also a number of companies making inexpensive resonator guitars in Asia, such as Johnson and Regal.

Requintos and Terz Guitars

The requinto is a smaller-bodied guitar that is usually tuned a fourth or a fifth higher than a standard guitar. Requintos are played throughout Spain and Latin America, but they are especially popular in Mexico. The Mexican version of the requinto tends to have a deeper body than a standard guitar, while the Spanish version is about the same depth. The scale length tends to measure between 570 and 585 millimeters.

Left: A Pimentel requinto. Right: A Martin 5-18 compared with a dreadnought.

The terz guitar is small-bodied guitar that was popular in the 19th century. Terz guitars had a small body and were tuned up a third from a standard guitar. They had a bright, penetrating tone and were commonly used in duets with full-sized guitars. Terz guitars are basically extinct as nylon-string guitars, but the body sizes live on in the Martin 5-18, which although it has steel strings, is based on a 19th-century body mold.

Tenor Guitars

Tenor guitars were invented in the early 1920s to help 4-string tenor banjo players make the switch to guitar, which was fast replacing the clanky-sounding banjo in dance bands. Many guitar builders in the 1920s and 1930s made

A Martin 0-18T tenor guitar.

numerous models, ranging from inexpensive styles like Martin's 2-17, a tiny bodied all mahogany guitar, up to Gibson's TGL-5, a tenor version of the top of the line L-5 archtop.

Most players at the time tuned the tenor guitar in fifths to CGDA, the same tuning as the tenor banjo. But in the late 1950s, Nick Reynolds of the folk group the Kingston Trio tuned his tenor to DGBE—the same tuning and pitch as the top four strings of a standard 6-string. The tenor guitar was primarily an American phenomenon, but the French company Selmer made about 150 tenor guitars.

Seven-Strings

Seven-string classical guitars were popular in Russia in the 19th century, but the style died out in the early part of the 20th century. In the late 1930s, the jazz guitarist George Van Eps had Epiphone build him an archtop with seven strings, a style of guitar he played until the end of his life. Van Eps tuned his seventh string, which was in the bass position, to low A, although many of the guitarists who followed him tuned the seventh string to B.

Lenny Breau went the other direction and placed his seventh string above the high E string and tuned it to A. Flattop seven strings are very scarce, with the custom Gallagher made for bluegrass flatpicker Steve Kaufman being one of the very few. Ibanez is perhaps the only large builder making a flattop steel-string, the AJ-307CE, a cutaway with a pickup.

Solid-Bodies

Some players need more volume on stage than their amplified acoustics can give them before feeding back, and so the solid-body acoustic was born. One of the first solid-body acoustics, introduced in 1982, was the Gibson Chet Atkins CEC (for cutaway electric classic), which had the silhouette of a classical guitar from the front, but was only about an inch and a half thick. The Chet Atkins CEC had a bridge-mounted piezo pickup, and although the guitar looked like a solid-body electric, it had hollow chambers to both cut down on weight and to give the guitar a bit more acoustic tone. The success of the nylon string led Gibson to introduce a steel-string version and a 12-string version.

Other companies latched onto the solid-body acoustic idea. Guild launched the FS Series of guitars in 1983, but discontinued the series a few years later. The most successful challenger to the Chet Atkins guitars has been Rick Turner's Renaissance series, which is actually a very shallow hollow-body with a solid top and no soundhole. The Renaissance comes in a variety of styles, including 12-strings, baritones, and basses.

Perhaps the most unusual solid-body acoustics are the Parker Fly Concert, a solid spruce guitar with a transducer pickup in the bridge, and the Spanish Fly, which is the nylon string version of the same guitar.

Electric guitars with acoustic sounds: Turner Renaissance Nylon, Parker Fly Concert, Yamaha AEX500NS.

Harp Guitars

Harp guitars have a standard 6-string neck and anywhere from one to twelve extra bass strings, which are supported by an extra neck, elongated upper bout, or a post. The harp strings can be plucked with the right or left hand, but because they are usually floating without a fingerboard beneath them, they are never fretted.

A vintage Gibson harp guitar with ten bass strings.

There are two major types of harp guitars: European style and American style. The European style was developed in the 19th century by Austrian builders like Stauffer and Schertzer, Italian builders like Mozzani, and French builders like Lacôte. The European models were set up for gut strings and they were used primarily for playing classical music. In the latter part of the 19th century, a style known as Schrammel music, which used a harp guitar as a rhythm instrument became popular in Vienna. In America, builders like Knutsen, the Larson Brothers, and Gibson built numerous harp guitars that were heavily braced for steel strings.

The harp guitar had a brief vogue in the early part of the 20th century, but it faded from popularity by the 1930s. In the 1980s, Michael Hedges was often photographed with a Larson Brothers harp guitar. Even though he rarely played it in concert, and only recorded a handful of tracks on it, he sparked a mini-revival of the instrument—and there are probably more people playing harp guitars today than at anytime in the last 200 years.

Weissenborns

Sometime around 1910, a luthier based in Washington named Chris Knutsen started building guitars with hollow, square necks for playing slide guitar in the Hawaiian style. A number of builders on the West Coast began making guitars in the same style; and by the early 1920s, a luthier in Los Angeles named Hermann Weissenborn gained the reputation for making the best version—and his guitar eclipsed that of the man who invented it.

Guitars in the Knutsen/Weissenborn style were popular in the 1920s, but they faded into obscurity with the ascendance of the resonator Hawaiian guitars made by National and Dobro. In the 1970s, players like Bob Brozman and David Lindley began playing old Weissenborns, sparking a revival of interest. Perhaps the best-known contemporary player is Ben Harper, who plays an interesting blues style. Modern builders include Bill Hardin (who builds under the name Bear Creek), Michael Dunn, the French luthier Maurice Dupont, and the German company Manzanita. Marc Silber has Weissenborn-style guitars made in Mexico, which he sells under the K & S label.

On the left, a vintage Weissenborn Style 1, on the right, a Weissenborn copy by Manzanita.

5 The Top

It's the Most Important Part of the Guitar

The *soundboard*, or top, is the most important component of any guitar, for it is responsible for a majority of the instrument's sound. The back and sides certainly affect both tone and volume, as does the density and rigidity of the neck, but these influences are of little importance if the top doesn't produce a worthy sound right from the start. On the other hand, if you give a first-class luthier a cheap guitar of the lowest level, and instruct him to replace its soundboard with one of his best (if he's willing), the result will be an instrument that sounds far better than anyone would expect.

Solid or Laminated

For all of the guitar styles in question, soundboards are either of solid wood or laminated wood veneers. "Solid" means that the thickness of the top is all one piece, not that the top is one piece of wood across its width; for, as with violins, virtually all guitars with solid tops are made of two halves, joined at the center. Tradition, and the desire for symmetry, dictates the two halves of the top be *bookmatched*, meaning that a thicker piece is sawn to yield two thinner sections, which then have their edges glued together so that the right and left sides are mirror images of each other.

Laminated tops are made of thin veneers, usually with the uppermost layer, and the layer on the underside, having grain that runs longitudinally (perpendicular to the frets). There is usually one layer, and sometimes two or more, between these two veneers, with grain running at a 45-degree or 90-degree angle to the outer layers. On the most inexpensive instruments, such laminates are chosen only for convenience and economy, but some laminated soundboards made of thin spruce veneers can sound good enough to fool even educated listeners. To add to the confusion, the outer veneers on virtually all laminated tops are also bookmatched, making it difficult to distinguish from a genuine solid spruce top.

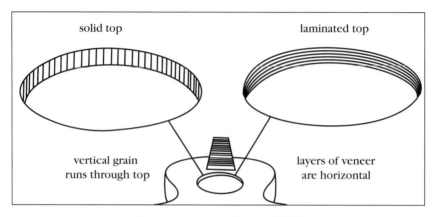

Inspecting a guitar's soundhole can reveal whether it has a solid (left image) or laminate (right image) top.

Usually one can detect a laminated soundboard by looking at the edge of the soundhole. If the grain lines seen on the outer surface can be traced through the thickness of the wood where it is exposed at the soundhole's edge, then it is a solid top. If a darker line can be detected around the edge, with lighter spruce both above and below it, then the top is probably laminated.

Spruce

For as far back as guitars can be traced, spruce has been the preferred wood for the soundboard, just as it has been the first choice for members of the violin family. As the type of guitar most directly connected to the violin family tradition, acoustic archtops featured spruce exclusively for their carved soundboards. Until about thirty years ago, most guitar builders only paid attention to the origin of the spruce used for soundboards, and European spruce was considered superior to spruce that grew in North America. Today, however, there is much more attention paid to the actual species of spruce, and at least three distinctly different types of spruce grow in Canada and the U.S.

The most common spruce is Sitka, which grows in the northwestern portion of the continent. This is the type of top wood found on virtually all American steel-string guitars made between the late 1940s and the 1990s, when manufacturers finally began to explore the tonal characteristics of other species of spruce for specific models (Sitka is still used for a vast majority of North American–made guitars, as well as most guitars made in Asia). Thanks to the large diameter of many Sitka logs, and the large forests from which they are harvested, Sitka spruce is still widely available. It is known for being remarkably strong; and though often quite light in color when first cut, Sitka darkens with exposure to light, turning honey-colored in just a few months. This wood is excellent for steel-string guitar tops, but too hard and stiff for most classical builders. It delivers a clear, bright tone and can be played very hard, but has fallen out of favor among builders of high-end guitars, mostly because it is common and comparatively inexpensive.

Englemann is another North American species, but is usually more expensive because the trees are smaller and the grain tends to spiral, making much of the wood unsuitable for guitarmakers. This tendency to spiral is one of the reasons that many Englemann tops tend to show considerable "run-out," giving the guitar soundboard a distinct color shift at the center seam. Englemann is softer than Sitka, and thus more easily damaged. It's also lighter in color and never develops the brownish color of well-exposed Sitka. Englemann is most ideally suited for fingerstyle players, as it yields a warm, open tone without being played hard.

The most desirable tonewood for guitar tops, at least among flattop steel-string players, is Adirondack spruce, sometimes called Appalachian, and as the name implies, it only grows in the Eastern U.S. This was the type of wood used by the Gibson and Martin companies prior to World War II, which is no doubt a large part of its appeal. Adirondack is stiff like Sitka, but is lighter in color. It's known for its ability to be played very hard without sounding forced or harsh, and is popular among flatpickers and fingerstylists alike. It is the wood of choice for builders making replicas of Martins and Gibsons from the 1930s—the "Golden Era" of American guitarmaking. Martin uses this top wood exclusively for its GE models, which occupy the highest rung in that company's vintage reissue series.

European spruce, still given top ranking among classical builders, looks much like Englemann, but is a bit harder and stiffer, though lighter in both weight and color than Sitka. European spruce, often dubbed "German spruce" regardless of where it grew, is a popular option listed on the price lists of most North American manufacturers both large and small. This top wood seems to combine the best qualities of all the North American spruces, and works well for any type of playing under every possible condition.

Spruce tops await further work at the Froggy Bottom shop.

Cedar tops, such as on this Goodall Concert Jumbo, can provide a quick response for fingerstyle playing.

Cedar

For flattop guitars, both classical and steel-string, western red cedar is also popular, and has been widely used by Spanish guitarmakers since the mid-20th century. Cedar reigned supreme in Madrid during the classical guitar's tremendous popularity during the 1960s and 1970s, for instance, and during that time the rich, dark tone of the cedar-topped Ramirez IA Segovia model essentially defined the sound that was expected from the best classical guitars. Since flamenco guitars need a brighter, snappier tone, however, spruce is still the preferred wood for those models, regardless of the maker. Cedar didn't really catch on with steel-string builders until the 1980s, when it was widely used for fingerstyle guitars, especially those made or sold in Europe.

Cedar has a warm, brown color, and is softer and less stiff than the spruces. It's known to respond quickly to even the lightest touch, and to need a very short "break-in" period. Among American builders, Taylor has used it the most extensively, but most all of the smaller companies offer it as an option, and James Goodall has had particular success with cedar. Other softwoods that have been used with some success are larch and redwood.

Martin has been very successful with its all-mahogany D-15 model.

Mahogany

Mahogany made its first significant appearance as a wood for guitar tops when Martin began using it in the early 1920s. Although technically a hardwood, mahogany is light in weight and soft enough to work well as the soundboard on steel-string guitars. It lacks the quickness and clarity of spruce, but the warmth and depth of the tone is appealing to many players. Mahogany tops are usually only found on guitars with mahogany backs and sides. The C. F. Martin company used this combination to great advantage on its Style 15 and 17 models, as it allowed them to eliminate binding on both the top and bottom edge of the guitar body, and thus market a guitar model at a much lower price. Sometimes called "chocolate Martins," these unassuming little 0-15 and 00-17 model guitars, discontinued in the early 1960s, became so desirable that Martin repeated their success by introducing them again in the late 1990s.

Koa

Koa soundboards are the result of the Hawaiian music craze of the late '10s and '20s, when such woods were used for making Hawaiian guitars, especially by the Martin company. When it was found that such instruments had an interesting tone for steel-strings played in the conventional (Spanish) style, the guitar's

Taylor has long offered koa tops on guitars such as this 12-string K-65.

traditional list of materials was expanded, and today some players prefer the tone of a koa soundboard.

As with mahogany tops, koa soundboards are only found on guitars with a koa back and sides. Because of its weight, koa tops yield a somewhat compressed sound with lower volume, but with excellent sustain. In the last decade, Taylor has sold far more all-koa guitars than has Martin. The greatest appeal of koa guitars is no doubt the rich coloring and dramatic figure—a far cry from the monotony of even-grained spruce soundboards.

Other Woods

Maple has been used for guitar tops, but usually only on acoustic-electric models where the dampening effect of such a hard and heavy wood helps to slow feedback when amplified at higher volumes. Some guitarmakers, especially Taylor and Adamas, have also used walnut for soundboards. As the acoustic guitar's role continues to expand, and builders search both for new sounds and alternatives to depleted supplies of the traditional guitar woods, many other species will no doubt be put to use, especially on acoustic-electric models.

Alternative Materials

Alternatives to spruce and similar soundboard woods made an appearance long before wood shortages were an issue. Since spruce is chosen primarily because of its high strength-to-weight ratio, logic suggests that a material with similar properties, but with an even higher strength-to-weight ratio, might be even better. This was the thinking behind Kaman Corporation's choice of ultra-thin carbon graphite fibers on either side of a thin birch plywood core for the tops of its Adamas models introduced in the mid-1970s.

On the left, RainSong's all-graphite DR1000. On the right, an Ovation Adamas 1597 with a graphite top.

Since that time, Martin has forged ahead with its own approach to alternative top materials. Martin uses a high-pressure laminate of wood fiber (similar to Formica), with a print—yes, a photographic image—of spruce as the outer layer for the soundboard of its low-cost X-Series guitars. Not to be accused of being wood-obsessed, Martin has also used aluminum for the tops of some thin body versions in this same X-Series. Chris Martin explains that he doesn't want to try to replace the traditional wooden guitar, but he does want to expand the guitar-buying public's idea of what guitars can be made of, and wants Martin to be ready for the day when wood is simply too expensive for lower-priced, American-made guitars.

Top Bracing

It's ironic that the most important part of the guitar, at least in terms of its sound, is the most difficult part of the instrument to observe, and is even harder to measure. While the bracing of the soundboard cannot be completely obscured, as can a varnish formula, it still eludes the casual observer, and forces other builders to peer inside through the soundholes with lights and mirrors. When guitar builders gather, soundboards and the bracing that supports them are probably the most heavily discussed topic, and for good reason.

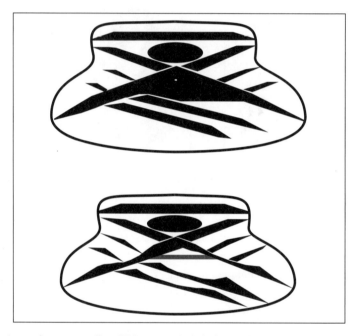

The top image shows non-scalloped X-bracing, which the bottom drawing illustrates the scalloped variety.

A beautiful piece of spruce or cedar, topping a perfect set of sides and back and linked to the ultimate neck, will still be only average, or worse, if the builder doesn't use the same care and knowledge when bracing the soundboard. For many instruments, such as Flamenco guitars, it's a delicate balance between bracing the guitar for longevity, or for a short but brilliant career. When everything comes together as it should, however, the guitar will sound its best and still survive for generations of players.

Function

The braces on the underside of a guitar's top serve two important functions. The primary one is to keep the soundboard from collapsing, bulging, or becoming distorted from string tension— and about this role there is little argument among luthiers. All guitar tops show some signs of deflection from their original smooth surface as a result of laboring under approximately 75 to 200 pounds of pull from the strings; but with adequate bracing—and reasonable care—most guitars can survive such tension for decades of use with little or no repairs needed.

The second function of the top bracing is to maximize the tone and volume of the guitar—and here is where the most heated controversy about guitarmaking has been focused, especially in modern times. But this argument has often surfaced in print during the last century and a half, and we have no reason to think discussions about the soundboard bracing of guitars only began in the mid-19th century. Rather than confuse matters by describing the various theories involved, we'll simply describe the various guitar soundboards and how they are usually braced for nylon-string and steel-string flattop guitars, and also for archtops.

Bracing Materials for Soundboards

Even on the earliest known guitars, soundboard braces were almost always made of spruce, even if the back braces and other internal structures on the instrument were made of other woods. Exceptions to this are usually in the classical guitar field, where cedar is sometimes used by individual builders. One exception to the spruce monopoly is the bridge plate, which is usually a hardwood such as maple or birch (Martin also used rosewood for several years). Bridge plates on classical guitars, or guitars with pinless bridges, are often spruce, simply because without the wear from string balls or knots to worry about, the weight penalty of a hard, durable material isn't needed. Many companies have also used plywood for bridge plates, but this is only on high-production instruments. Laminated braces have also been used on steel-string guitars, with the most unusual featuring a rosewood core, as patented by Chicago's Larson Bros. in the 1920s.

Alternatives

Since soundboard braces need to be strong but light, many alternative shapes have been used, but usually only on an experimental basis. Braces shaped like I-beams, or even braces drilled out for lightness, are not unusual among steel-string guitars

135

by independent makers. Some builders have used carbon fiber laminates for top braces on steel-string guitars. The radical classical guitars of Greg Smallman of Australia demonstrate just how far the lighter-stronger approach can be taken, with carbon fiber in minute amounts strengthening the top braces. Despite all the high-tech developments, most soundboard braces are still shaped like a dull blade, with the thick edge glued to the soundboard.

Soundboard Bracing on Flattop Guitars

Although there are countless different bracing patterns used on flattop guitars today, most all of them fall into about a half-dozen different broad categories. Since virtually all flattop guitars were originally strung with gut until about a century ago, when steel strings led to the American guitar revolution, we'll discuss both types together. Steel-string guitar bracing hasn't had much effect on modern classical guitars, but steel-string builders often borrow ideas from the field of classical luthierie.

Braces are glued to the top in the Santa Cruz shop using "go-bars."

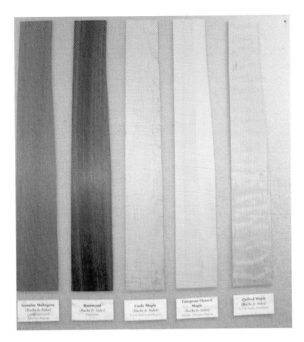

Five popular woods for a guitar's back and sides (from left to right): Mahogany, rosewood, curly maple, European flamed maple, and quilted maple.

Traditionally, a guitar's sides are bent by hand. The wood is moistened, and then shaped over a hot metal cylinder.

137

After the pre-shaped braces have been glued to the top, a worker at Martin fine tunes their fit.

A body is sanded prior to finishing.

Taylor uses a special press for installing the frets.

This picture shows how Taylor's bolt-on neck is attached to the body.

A traditional dovetail neck joint (in this case at Martin) takes a lot of skill and hand work for a proper fit.

Finishing a guitar takes several layers, which are usually applied by hand (in this case at Garrison).

Introduced in 1931, Martin's D-28 is probably the most important acoustic guitar of all time. Its large body can produce respectable volume, and the guitar has become the standard instrument for playing bluegrass.

Before the dreadnought was introduced, the 000—shown here as a 000-28 Vintage Reissue—was the largest guitar that Martin made. Even though its 12-fret neck-body joint and slotted headstock may be similar to a classical guitar, the instrument is designed for steel strings.

Martin's OM was first introduced in 1929. It has the same body as the later version of the 000, and it was the company's first guitar with a 14-fret neck. Due to its balanced sound and easy playability, the model has become a favorite with players of many styles.

Selmer guitars became famous through the Gypsy jazz of Django Reinhardt. Originally designed by Mario Maccaferri, they continue to be used for this style. Pictured here is the original 12-fret design with a large soundhole. Later versions have a 14-fret neck and a small soundhole.

Taylor has become the second largest manufacturer of acoustic guitars in the US (after Martin). Founded in 1973, the company has become known for the use of ultra-modern manufacturing techniques. The guitar on the left is a top-of-the-line PS-14c Grand Auditorium. Pictured on the right is the company's Leo Kottke signature model 12-string.

Guild has become famous for its 12-strings. This F212XL is a typical example of the company's jumbo-size model, and it features mahogany back and sides and a spruce top.

Since Guild was founded in 1952, it has placed an emphasis on archtops. The guitar pictured is an Artist Award (for a while the model was named after guitarist Johnny Smith).

Originally designed by Lloyd Loar and introduced in 1923, the Gibson L-5 was the first modern archtop.

Gibson's SJ-200 (also called Super Jumbo) is generally considered to be the first true jumbo flattop. With maple back and sides and fancy appointments, the guitar stands out in a crowd.

Three custom guitars (clockwise from top left): A Rose Jumbo featuring Kasha design elements by Steve Klein, a Goodall Grand Concert, and a special California Edition by Larrivée.

Two of the most important classical guitars of all time: On the left, a José Ramírez 1a, which has become a virtual standard to be measured by, and on the right, a 1888 Antonio de Torres, which introduced important design elements such as fan-bracing.

Top left: Ireland's Lowden guitars have become known for having their own individual style. With a jumbo body, mahogany back and sides, a cedar top, and minimal appointments, the O10 is luthier George Lowden's original design. Top right and bottom: Two guitars by Lakewood, Germany's biggest maker of flattop steel-strings.

Bob Benedetto is one of the most famous contemporary archtop makers. This La Venezia is now built under license by Guild, and it shows Benedetto's typical austere, yet ultra-precise aesthetic.

Germany's Stefan Hahl is one of the most important archtop builders in Europe. Shown here is his Jazz Supreme model.

A trio of modern acoustic-electric nylon-strings (clockwise from top left): Takamine's NP-65c with a Santa Fe theme, Rick Turner's Renaissance, and Godin's MIDI capable Multiac.

Ovation was the first manufacturer who successfully used synthetic material in the construction of acoustic guitars. Additionally, the company pioneered the development of the modern acoustic-electric guitar, which made the instruments popular with performers. Pictured on the left is an Ovation Adamas 1597 with an unusual soundhole configuration and a carbon-fiber top. On the right is the company's Adamas Q prototype, which may be a glimpse into what the future could hold.

Three guitar made for playing lap-style slide (clockwise from top left): A metal-bodied National Tricone with three resonators, a wooden Dobro Square-neck with a single resonator cone, and hollow-neck Weissenborn-style guitar made by Manzanita.

Ladder Bracing

The earliest and most simple style of top bracing is "ladder bracing," which gets its name from the fact that the braces look like the rungs of a ladder. This style almost mirrors the bracing used on the back of the instrument, so looking inside the soundhole at a typical guitar's back braces gives you a good idea of what ladder bracing is about. There is usually one brace above the soundhole, under the fretboard. A second brace is below the soundhole, in front of the bridge, with another brace below the bridge. With this pattern, the bridge plate often goes all the way across the top, acting as another brace.

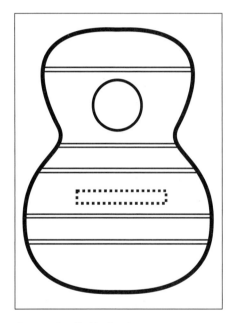

An example of ladder-bracing.

Most early European guitarmakers used some variation on this pattern, and it dates back to the time of Stradivarius or earlier. Since it is easy to manufacture guitar tops with this type of bracing, it is still found on many inexpensive, mass-produced instruments at the lowest price ranges, especially nylon-string guitars. In the first big guitarmaking factories in the U.S. around 1900, such as Washburn, the braces below the soundhole were often angled, resembling a shallow zigzag pattern. Gibson used ladder bracing on its least expensive steel-string models as late as the 1960s, and also on the acoustic/electric J-160E. Ladder bracing is still used on contemporary versions of the French Selmer guitars, such as played by Django Reinhardt, and on a few other historical reissues; but with those exceptions, it is rarely seen on guitars of high-quality today.

Although ladder bracing, which is also called "straight bracing," delivers a quick response with lots of brightness, it lacks the sustain and complex overtones of the more sophisticated patterns.

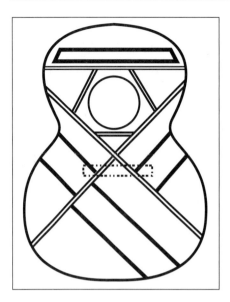

A typical example of X-bracing.

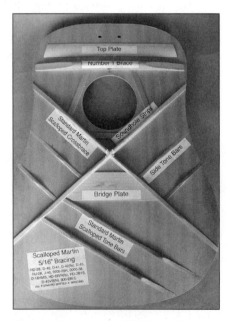

Martin's X-bracing is the most popular, and most often copied bracing pattern for flattop steel-strings.

Cross or X-Bracing

"X-bracing" is characterized by two main braces which intersect between the soundhole and the front edge of the bridge. The bridge plate is then wedged between the lower legs of the "X," with one or more braces below that. This pattern is ideal for the greater torque placed upon the soundboard by steel strings, as it strengthens the top at its weakest point near the soundhole, which is where ladder-braced guitars often fail. The area between the lower legs of the X and the side of the guitar is usually stiffened with "finger braces," which run parallel to the upper arm of the X on either side. The soundboard is also protected against deflection from string tension by the fact that the lower legs of the X run beneath the bridge tips. This is the most commonly seen top-bracing formula for flattop steel-string guitars today, and although the sizes and outward appearances of such guitars vary widely, the underside of their soundboards are remarkably similar.

Although other builders may have used it earlier, X-Bracing is commonly attributed to the C. F. Martin Co., which first used it in the 1840s. Martin was using X-bracing on most of its higher models by the 1850s, although it wasn't widely copied by other American guitarmakers until the use of steel strings became popular around 1900. Martin always used one, and later two, transverse braces below the bridge plate. This made the treble side of the top stiffer, accentuating the treble, while the bass side of the soundboard was left freer. Common variations include placing these lower braces horizontally, parallel to the brace above the soundhole, or using a modified fan pattern, where the braces radiate out from the bridge somewhat like on a classical guitar.

X-bracing comes in so many variations that it is difficult to generalize about its sound, but for steel-string guitars, most builders agree that it is the best way to get the necessary stiffness to support a thin top without adding a labyrinth of braces to do the job. The result is excellent sustain, and under the best conditions, a soundboard that responds to a light touch but still withstands a heavy attack without sounding forced.

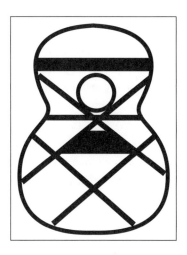

Double X

A variation of the X-pattern that has appeared more than once is the double-X, in which there are a second set of intersecting braces below the bridge plate. Yet another version repeats the X above the soundhole, beneath the end of the fretboard (Gibson has used both these variants). The second version doesn't have much effect on tone, as the primary bracing of the top where it matters most is not significantly altered.

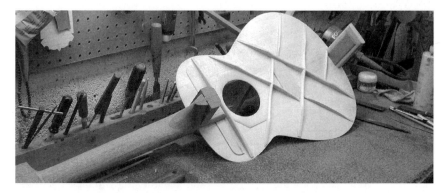

Some steel-strings, such as this Pimentel, use a double-X bracing pattern.

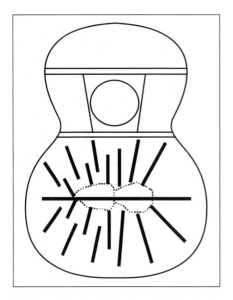

Kasha-style bracing is based on scientific theories about top movement.

Kasha

Although originally intended only for classical guitars, Michael Kasha's radical theories regarding soundboard bracing have also been adapted to the steel-string guitar. Although Steve Klein's Kasha-influenced instruments have found some success, the Gibson Mark Series, which exhibited a watered-down Kasha pattern, was deemed a failure. In theory, Kasha's bracing pattern, and the accompanying asymmetrical bridge, was intended to do a better job of transmitting the energy from the vibrating strings throughout the soundboard, making better use of a larger area. His theories also treat the bass and treble side of the soundboard more differently than do any of the more conventional bracing patterns. Without two nearly identical guitars—one Kasha-braced and the other X-braced—to compare, it's difficult to evaluate what the Kasha pattern actually achieves, since guitars made with that pattern also exhibit a host of other differences in both size and construction.

A-Frame

C.F. Martin designed a simpler bracing pattern for its new D-1 guitar, which was introduced in 1994. The "A-frame" is actually the bracing around the soundhole, with the upper portion of the "A" going up beneath the fretboard. This design strengthens the typically weak portion of the guitar's top, extending from above the soundhole to the intersection of the X-braces. Martin's variant of its own venerable X-bracing pattern has only one transverse brace below the bridge, and the braces are tapered but not scalloped. Other companies have been using A-frame bracing for many years, including Lowden and Ovation. In all cases, the pattern has long vertical "legs" which taper towards each other in the upper bout, with one or more braces running horizontally between them. The pattern that describes an "A" is seen when facing the underside of the soundboard, with the neck of the guitar pointing up.

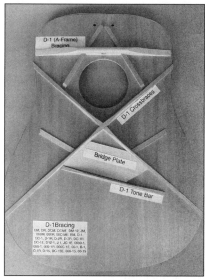

The A-frame pattern derives its name from the set of braces above the soundhole (otherwise it's similar to a standard X-pattern). On the right, Martin's A-frame pattern from the company's 1-series.

Scalloped Braces

From the beginning, Martin relieved, or scalloped, its top braces. The part of each lower leg of the X near the bridge tip was scooped out, leaving a small peak in the brace before it was again cut down as it neared the lining at the edge of the soundboard. The center of each transverse brace was scalloped in a similar fashion. Martin ceased scalloping its top braces in 1945, as the absurdly high tension from string gauges intended for archtop guitars caused too much "bellying" of the top around the bridge. As the use of heavy-gauge strings all but disappeared, and as the public outcry about the superior tone and volume of "prewar" Martins increased, the company returned to scalloping the top braces on many models. Today, most X-braced guitars, such as those by Taylor, Gibson, and other manufacturers, are also scalloped to some degree. Not all luthiers agree on the superiority of this feature, however, and builders like Jeff Traugott prefer steeply tapering the lower legs of the X rather than scalloping them.

Most players find that scalloped-brace guitars have more bass response—specifically, more sustain in the bass—than a similar guitar with non-scalloped braces. On large guitars, especially those with rosewood back and sides, the result can be a lack of clarity and a weakened treble register that cannot match the bass. These shortcomings can be overcome in a number of different ways, and the scalloped X-brace guitar top has vastly outnumbered all other bracing styles combined for over twenty years, especially in American-made guitars.

Tapered X-bracing is still widely used, however. Many Martin models still feature it—such as the standard (non-herringbone) D-28 and D-35, as well as all Martin's lower-priced models with A-frame bracing. Most Canadian and European builders also rely on tapered bracing.

Ovations

Although the first Ovation Balladeer used a modified X-bracing pattern with a kind of H-pattern above it surrounding the soundhole, that was as conventional as any Kaman (parent company of Ovation) guitar ever got. At least six different bracing patterns have been used at Ovation, many of them fan-like patterns with braces running almost the entire length of the top. Some of the patterns were only made possible by the multiple offset soundholes on either side of the upper bout. In general, Ovation bracing is lighter than what would be found in a more conventional steel-string guitar, partly because the hard finish, to which the bridge is glued, is an integral part of the soundboard's strength.

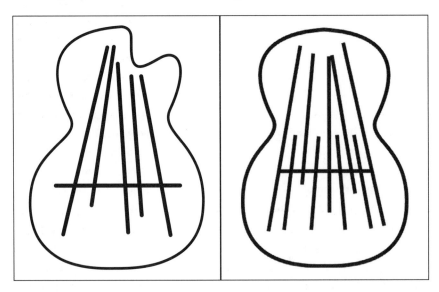

On the left, a bracing pattern used on certain Ovation Elite models. On the right, one of Ovation's Adamas bracing patterns.

The Bridge Plate

On flattop guitars, especially steel-string models, the string tension on the bridge, and the portion of the top directly beneath it, requires special reinforcement. This is achieved with a wide, flat brace, with the grain running perpendicular to the grain in the soundboard.

On nylon-string guitars this brace is optional; and when present, it is usually made of spruce. On steel-string guitars, specifically those using bridge pins, the bridge plate is an important part of the bracing, and is crucial to the top's survival against tremendous string tension. The bridge plate on steel-strings is usually maple, and is wedged tightly between the lower legs of the X-brace, just below where the braces intersect. The Martin company used large bridge plates of rosewood in the 1970s and early '80s, but it was felt these muted the response, and the company went back to using maple.

Nylon-String Bracing

The top bracing on nylon-stringed guitars poses a number of problems not shared by steel-string instruments. Perhaps the greatest obstacle is the very low tension of the typical classical guitar string set, making lightness a high priority. Other common difficulties include getting an adequate balance between the wound D string and the unwound G, a typical weak point in many lower grade classical guitars. As more steel-string players have moved to embrace nylon strings, many of the hybrid instruments they choose have cutaways and built-in pickups—features usually associated with the steel-string guitar. Most of these instruments lack the robust tone and volume of true acoustic classical guitars, and should be addressed as acoustic-electric instruments only.

Fan Bracing

In mid-19th century Spain, about the same time that C.F. Martin was experimenting with X-bracing, Antonio de Torres was perfecting an equally influential style of bracing the soundboard of the flattop guitar. Continuing the work of luthier José Pages, Torres left the heavy horizontal braces above and below the soundhole, but below those he placed a number of much smaller and lighter braces that radiated out into the lower bout beneath the guitar's bridge and beyond. Since these braces resemble the spines of a small hand-held fan, the pattern has come to be called "fan bracing."

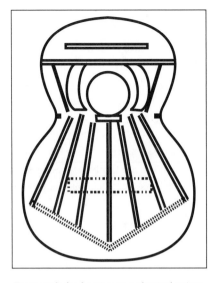

Torres-style fan bracing on a classical guitar.

Some early Spanish makers used as few as three fan braces, but Torres used as many as seven, while also increasing the size of the guitar and its scale length. This style of top bracing, combined with a larger, more robust body, became the model for the modern classical guitar.

Unlike the American guitar, which has gone through major evolutionary changes in size and stringing, the Spanish guitar has seen more steady refinement. Although other top-bracing patterns for classical guitars have been developed, most lost favor and disappeared; and today, Torres bracing is still the standard for a vast majority of nylon-string guitars built in Spain, Latin America, and throughout the world. It supports a thin soundboard with minimal weight, permitting excellent volume despite the low tension of nylon strings. The most common variant is with the brace below the soundhole, called a "harmonic bar," set at an angle to tighten up the treble side of the soundboard. Many guitarmakers also add two braces below the tips of the fan, one on each side of the tailblock. These braces run almost horizontally, forming a shallow "V" shape.

Lattice Bracing

One of the more popular bracing patterns recently developed for classical guitar soundboards is a grid-like structure of tiny interlocking braces, intersecting at right angles.

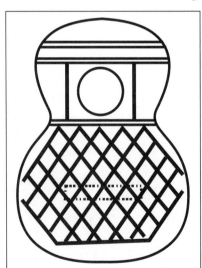

The lattice bracing pattern used by some contemporary classical builders.

Kasha Bracing

Acoustic engineer Michael Kasha developed a radically different top-bracing pattern for the classical guitar in the late 1960s. This pattern utilizes a large number of small braces radiating out from around an asymmetrical bridge. Although many luthiers experimented with Kasha's theories, Richard Schneider was the builder who championed the radical approach with tenacity. It was also adapted for use with steel-string guitars, most notably by luthier/designer Steve Klein.

Although popular among a limited number of builders as recently as a decade ago, Kasha bracing is no longer considered new or revolutionary, and is rarely seen on new classical guitars today.

Archtop Bracing

The reinforcement of an archtop guitar's soundboard is quite different from the bracing used on a flattop guitar. The carved top, due both to its arch and its greater thickness, is inherently far stronger than any flattop design. Even more importantly, with strings anchored to a tailpiece, the archtop's soundboard is subjected to downward pressure from the strings, rather than the tendency of string tension to pry up or even fold the soundboard, as frequently happens on flattop models.

Bracing for Round and Oval Soundhole Archtops

Although other earlier builders constructed guitars or guitar-like instruments using a soundboard carved in an arch, much like that of a violin, Orville Gibson is generally credited as the father of the archtop guitar as we know it today. Gibson's earliest guitars had tops carved with a low arch, an oval soundhole, and a single brace below the soundhole just in front of the bridge. By the 1910s, the bracing was more of a narrow H-pattern, with two long "tone bars" on either side of the soundhole and a horizontal brace spanning the gap between them—again, just ahead of the bridge. As the Gibson company began to use steeper neck angles to increase the guitar's volume, the bracing on its archtops was made stronger to withstand the increased string tension. In general, the early round soundhole archtops have a sweeter treble tone, sounding a bit more like a flattop guitar, but lack the percussive power and projection of an *f*-hole model.

Tone Bar Bracing

The first truly modern archtop guitar was Gibson's L-5, which first appeared in 1923. Violin-style *f*-holes on either side of the bridge eliminated the weakening effect of the large soundhole between the end of fretboard and the bridge. The L-5, like its companion, the F-5 mandolin, had a carved soundboard supported by twin tone bars, each one much like the single bass bar in a violin. (Note that these two braces are not symmetrical, and the treble side brace is closer to the guitar's center-line than is the brace on the bass side, which runs quite close to the *f*-hole.) This type of archtop bracing is still used today, although on many guitars with large pickups mounted in the top, there is also one or more horizontal braces running between the tone bars.

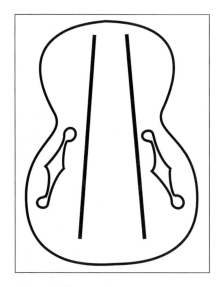

The parallel bracing found on many archtop guitars.

On archtop guitars, the biggest difficulty is fitting the braces to the internal parabola of the carved top. One shortcut employed by some manufacturers is to cut notches in the braces, much as linings are notched, but with the cuts spaced farther apart. This allows the brace to be bent to fit the curve. After the braces are glued to the curved surface, they are usually topped with a thin strip of wood to add the needed rigidity. This is considered a shortcut, however, and one that is probably detrimental to tone. With the advent of CNC (Computer Numerical Control) machining, the inside of the carved top and the underside of the top braces, whether tone bars or X-pattern, are both shaped from the same computer model, insuring a perfect fit.

X-Bracing on Archtops

Gibson's next version of the L-5 was an inch wider in the lower bout, and debuted in 1934. Called the "Advanced L-5," it featured an X-braced top, with the "X" intersecting approximately beneath the bridge. Though these X-braced L-5 models are not as highly valued today as Gibson's later L-5s, which were again given twin tone-bar top bracing, the X-brace is more commonly used by contemporary archtop builders than any other design.

The archtop guitar has moved beyond the heavy pounding such models often had to endure in the days before electric pickups, and as a result, contemporary builders are often making their tops much lighter than was commonly found on jazz-age giants of the 1940s. X-bracing seems more ideally suited to fingerstyle jazz, the playing style that now dominates the archtop market.

The tone and volume of archtop guitars depends heavily on the graduation (thicknessing) of both the top and back, but bracing still plays a key role. In general, it is felt that X-braced archtops have a warmer tone with more sustain than does a comparable tone-bar braced instrument. For those players seeking the classic rhythm chop and piercing projection often required of an archtop when playing acoustically in a jazz combo, however, tone-bar bracing is usually still the best choice.

The Soundhole

Throughout the long and varied history of the guitar, its soundhole(s) have been one of the strongest identifying features. For many builders, the headstock, soundhole, and bridge are where they leave their mark, even if many other parts of the instrument are nearly identical to other makers' examples of the same type of instrument. Today, with an ever-widening array of guitar types vying for attention, soundholes are often a badge of identity, indicating not only the maker, but also the type of music or specialized playing style for which the instrument is intended.

Although early guitar-like instruments, such as the vihuela, often had more than one soundhole, or a soundhole that wasn't round, by the time the guitar was becoming more thoroughly defined in the early 19th century, the single, round soundhole was the norm. But while the size and shape of the soundhole was virtually standardized, there was tremendous variation in the decoration around the soundhole, called the "rosette," after the intricate carved "rose" that graced the soundhole of earlier lutes and of many guitars dating back to the Renaissance.

Some soundholes, like the one on this Takamine Garth Brooks model, deviate from the norm.

Size

The size of the typical round soundhole found on flattop guitars has evolved along with the size of the guitar itself. Soundholes on early parlor guitars were usually about $3^1/2$ inches in diameter, but on most modern dreadnoughts and jumbos the size is about four inches.

Round

Round soundholes are still the norm today, for both steel-string and nylon-string guitars. In the past, this was not only a fashion preference, but was also the result of convenience for builders, as center-guided circle cutters were the easiest way to cut both the hole and the ring(s) around it. Now that laser cutters and computer-driven routers are used for more and more of these cutting applications, guitar-makers may break with tradition and use alternate shapes of approximately the same size. So far, however, this option has only been applied by a few independent builders.

Oval

One variant to the round soundhole design that keeps popping up over and over again is the use of an oval. Oval soundholes were common on the earliest Gibson archtop guitars, but have also appeared on numerous flattops over the years. Until recently, the C.F. Martin Company used an oval soundhole on its cutaway models, simply because the shorter but wider hole allowed more room for a primary top brace that had to be moved to accommodate the cutaway. Perhaps the most famous guitars with oval soundholes were the instruments made by Selmer in Paris in the late 1930s through the early 1950s.

Some guitars, like this Guild, have oval soundholes, which make it possible to extend the fingerboard by a couple of frets.

Rosette

Even when early guitars were still being made with carved work covering the soundhole, decorative rings around its perimeter were often employed as additional decoration; and when soundholes were left open, the inlaid lines and figures surrounding the hole were often the dominant decoration of the guitar's front view. Although concentric rings of inlaid wood were often all that was used, some builders added pearl and ivory inlays. These were often a repeating pattern of small pearl diamonds and dots, but leaves and vines, or simplified floral patterns, were also common. More ornate examples might have a soundhole surrounded by complex figures such as birds, animals, or even stylized faces. On many guitars, these inlays were simply pressed into a black, or sometimes white, background made of glue and lampblack, or glue and white filler, filling a routed channel around the soundhole.

By the mid-19th century, however, the most common decoration around the guitar's soundhole consisted of small strips of marquetry made from colored woods. As the Spanish classical guitar and the American guitar headed down their separate evolutionary paths, the soundhole decorations were also distinctly different. The American guitar, as typified by Martin, used two or three sets of inlaid rings with groupings of black and white lines, sometimes with a narrow band of marquetry in the center. This marquetry was made in strips and sometimes came in patterns such as the famous herringbone design that Martin often used. The Spanish guitar, however, most often had a single, wide band of decoration, composed of miniature wooden tiles arranged in a repeating pattern with concentric lines at the edges.

The wide rosette found on classical guitars was usually the most elaborate decoration on the entire instrument. Along with the decorative cuts at the top of the headstock, the strict style code of the classical guitar often left the rosette as the only other place in which a luthier could leave any artistic statement or signature.

Cutting the channel for the rosette at Albert & Müller.

After continuing with virtually no change from Martin's multi-ring style established in the mid-1800s, Gibson, as usual, added characteristic variety when that company began making flattop guitars as well as archtops in the late 1920s. Ever loathe to be too much like Martin, Gibson used single-ring rosettes on many of its flattop models, sometimes adding binding on the inner edge of the soundhole to match the body binding.

During the 1910s and early '20s, Lyon and Healy used a raised bead of ivoroid binding on the inner edge of the soundhole as its sole decoration. But these were about the only exceptions to the Martin style until the late 1960s and early '70s, when independent luthiers and small companies began to challenge icons such as Martin, Gibson, and Guild. For Michael Gurian, for instance, his years as a classical builder resulted in a steel-string guitar rosette more like what would be found on a nylon-string instrument.

As independent luthierie blossomed in the 1980s, so did the variety of soundhole decorations employed, as many builders strove to give their instruments a unique identity. Rather than multiple rings of plastic, most independent builders began using wood purfling, and pearl designs again flourished. Wide, single-band rosettes of solid wood, often matching the headstock overlay and the back and sides of the body, also became more common. The leaves, flowers, and tendril motifs often used on instruments from hundreds of years earlier, again began to adorn the guitar soundhole, but with new materials and techniques.

A simple rosette in the Torres style.

Lakewood uses "magic symbols" for the rosettes of its New Century models (top), while Takamine's Santa Fe series makes use of turquoise and other gemstones (bottom).

ƒ-Holes

On archtop guitars, the evolution of soundholes and soundhole decoration has been quite different. Early Gibson archtops from before the 1920s had oval or round soundholes, with a wide rosette similar to those used on flattop guitars. When Lloyd Loar introduced Gibson's L-5 around 1923, its soundboard had violin-like *ƒ*-holes with no binding or decoration whatsoever. In the mid-1930s, Gibson began adding three-ply binding to the *ƒ*-holes of its larger and more ornate archtop guitar models, and for the most part, this is still the only decoration commonly seen on archtop soundholes today.

During the archtop's heyday, there were a few variants in the *f*-hole design. Gibson used an aperture shaped more like an "S," with round holes at the top and bottom of the curved line and an enlarged diamond-shaped area in the middle. Some manufacturers made these upper and lower holes separate from the rest of the cutout. Martin chose more violin-like *f*-holes for its ill-fated archtops. On many guitars, the small notches near the center of the *f*-holes were intended to indicate the bridge position, although this isn't something one can count on as being exact. Gretsch, typically bolder when it came to design, used elongated teardrop shapes for the soundholes on some of its Synchomatic archtops. These are often called "cat's eye" soundholes.

Two examples of f-holes on archtops: On the left, an Epiphone Emperor Regent, on the right, a Guild Artist Award.

In Europe, archtop builders seemed less fettered to violin-like soundhole designs; and especially in the post WWII period, German builders like Hopf, Hofner, and others often displayed highly original soundhole variations, both in terms of shape and decoration. When the archtop guitar revival began in the 1970s, new builders stretched the design code for archtop soundholes. The most interesting and radical of these designs came from Jimmy D'Aquisto, John D'Angelico's former apprentice and the sole link between the Golden Age of American archtops and the new trend towards archtop guitars that served dual roles of musical instrument and fine art object. D'Aquisto first streamlined his mentors traditional *f*-holes, eliminating the notches in the center altogether. Later, he made soundholes shaped like elongated diamonds on some models, and towards the end of his career even included moveable "shutters" (made from the spruce removed when the hole was cut) within the soundholes themselves that could be used to alter tone. Now freed from the traditional restraints, archtop builders today use an ever-widening array of soundhole designs.

Unusual Placement

The structural "error" that results from placing a large, single soundhole, right where the soundboard needs maximum strength to withstand string tension, has not been ignored by all builders. Placing the soundhole, or an aperture of similar size but a different shape, in the upper bout(s) is not uncommon. The first of these designs to gain widespread acceptance was found on the Adamas guitars, but other offset soundholes have appeared as well. The Tacoma Guitar Company uses a single soundhole in the upper bass-side bout on everything from high-strung travel guitars to 17-inch-wide guitar basses. The flattop guitar variant used for Hawaiian slack-key playing is often seen with two smaller soundholes on either side of the end of the fretboard, each decorated much like a traditional soundhole in the usual position.

This Steve Klein guitar has the soundhole on the treble side of the upper bout.

The quest for a stronger, lighter, soundboard, with a greater effective vibrating surface, will no doubt continue, and with it will come more designs that take the soundhole out of the stress line beneath the stings.

Steve Klein guitars with traditional and offset soundholes (left). Tacoma has made a name for itself by offering models with offset soundholes, such as this Chief (right).

Enlarged Soundhole

One exception to the same-as-usual soundhole on traditional, Martin-style instruments is an enlarged version, patterned after the 1935 Martin D-28 formerly owned by the late flatpicking legend Clarence White. This instrument gained a majority of its fame as the principal guitar used by Tony Rice since White's death. Before White acquired the guitar, the soundhole had been damaged by pick wear, and in evening out the ragged edges to a smooth circle it wound up being about 4 1/2 inches in diameter (also prior to White's ownership). The Santa Cruz Guitar Company was the first to build a Tony Rice model with this soundhole size, and since that time numerous other companies, including Collings, and even Martin, have issued dreadnought models with an oversized soundhole. The largest of the enlarged soundholes is probably the D-shaped holes found on the first guitars Selmer built to Mario Maccaferri's designs in the early 1930s.

This John Monteleone archtop features extra soundholes in the side.

Side Soundholes

Soundholes in the sides of the guitar, as well as in the top, are another variation. Soundholes in the side of the guitar facing the player are often used as mini monitors, allowing the guitarist to more easily hear the sound of his own instrument. Classical builder Robert Ruck has added additional small soundholes on either side of the neck block.

The Bridge

The three acoustic guitar types discussed here each have radically different bridges. As with headstocks and soundholes, bridges are often the way individual luthiers and large guitar factories alike express their identity, though this is truer of flattop steel-string guitars than of classical guitars or archtops. With a few rare exceptions, the bridges on classical and steel-string guitars are glued to the face of the instrument; and though the two types of bridges have looked quite different for more than half a century, they both share a common ancestry.

History of Bridge Designs

Although similar early instruments, such as lutes, had bridges that served as a hitching post for tying the strings to the soundboard, many early guitars used pin bridges. By the mid-19th century, well before the common use of steel strings on guitars, two bridge types had become popular. In North America and much of

Europe, guitars were usually given bridges that used wood or ivory pins to hold the knotted end of each string in place at the bottom of one of six holes extending through the bridge to the underside of the soundboard. This type of bridge construction had already been in use on similar instruments for over a hundred years. Guitars descending from the Spanish tradition, however, used a bridge with a lute-like tieblock, instead of holes and pins, to fasten the strings. Today, of course, nylon-stringed guitars never have pin bridges, but even as recently as the 1920s, American guitars with gut strings often used the same bridge as their steel-string cousins.

Pin bridges on guitars were often quite ornate in the early-19th century, with elaborate shapes or filigree decorations borrowed from lutes and similar instruments. Martin, while still building in the Austro-German style, used ornate bridges on many of the guitars constructed in the company's earliest days in New York. By mid-century, however, American guitars, regardless of who made them, had quite simple rectangular bridges with six pins. Martin's design had carved peaks at each tip, now usually called a "pyramid" bridge.

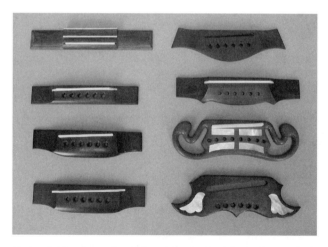

Various bridge shapes, from left to right: Standard classical guitar, Taylor, Martin from the end of the 19th Century, Guild, Martin "belly" bridge with closed saddle-slot, Gibson J-200 "mustache" bridge, Martin with open saddle-slot, and Gibson Dove.

Flattop Steel-String

For most all American makers, the narrow rectangular bridge would remain largely unchanged until the 1930s, when the need for more substantial footing to withstand the tension of steel strings resulted in bridges with a bulge, or "belly," behind the pins. As steel strings came into fashion, the bridges on flattop guitars became more vital to the structural integrity, and hence longevity, of the guitar. Bridges became both wider and longer as a result. Today, there are an infinite variety of such shapes in use on steel-string guitars of all sizes and shapes, regardless of origin. In some cases, such as the Gibson Super Jumbo introduced in the mid-1930s, the bridge became a fanciful showpiece that was uniquely tied to the rest of the guitar's decoration.

As guitar bodies became standardized into only a few shapes, bridges became an important part of any maker's identity. Martin's "belly" bridge, for instance, was so recognizable that although Gibson also needed a bridge that offered more substantial footing on the soundboard, Gibson put the bulged portion on the front edge of the bridge, rather than use a design that looked too much like Martin's. Both Guild and Taylor have bridge shapes that are easily recognizable, and companies such as Breedlove and Tacoma have continued this tradition. For over thirty years, however, Martin's bridge shape has been so widely copied that it is now by far the most popular bridge design for steel-string guitars, and most contemporary players probably have no idea of its origin.

An interesting variant in steel-string guitar design is when the builder separates the string saddle from where the strings anchor in the soundboard. This leaves the lower part of the bridge, where strings are anchored to the face with pins, to function much like the tailpiece on an archtop, while the separate saddle is almost like a floating bridge. Some Alvarez Yairi steel-strings use this design currently, but it was also used in the past by a few obscure builders in the U.S., and has historical roots in a number of early guitar-like instruments. While such designs often appear awkward, at least to those accustomed to standard bridge shapes, they do eliminate the problem of bridges coming unglued from the face of flattop guitars.

Pinless Bridges

Pinless bridges were widely used on inexpensive steel-string guitars such as Harmony in the 1950s and '60s, but the design reappeared on Ovations in the late 1960s, and has since become standard on certain high-end brands. Breedlove and Lowden are two companies that use pinless bridges exclusively on their guitars, but similar designs also appear on quite inexpensive instruments. One advantage, of course, is that the player never has to worry about losing a bridge pin! The downside of this design is that the string balls tend to dent or scratch the top when strings are changed quickly, prompting some builders to provide a thin, removable scratch guard to fit behind the pinless bridge when changing strings. Yet another disadvantage is that a shallow neck angle on the guitar will result in an inadequate "break angle" of the strings over the saddle on a pinless bridge, because the string is anchored above the guitar's top, not beneath it. The difference in how the string is anchored probably results in some changes in tone, but no thorough studies without prejudice on that issue have been conducted.

Pinless bridges on steel-string guitars such as this Breedlove, are based on the classical guitar nylon-string bridge design.

Nylon Strings

Thanks to its role as a classical instrument, with the same type of strings as used decades earlier, the Spanish guitar's bridge has not undergone dramatic changes, and for the most part luthiers have been content with subtle modifications. Many times the builder's "signature" on the bridge is little more than a different decoration of the tieblock itself. There have been significant changes, however, such

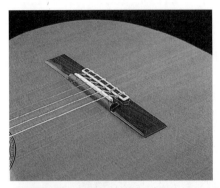

as strengthening the bridge across its width to limit flex. The current trend towards historical models, however, means that more and more high-end classical guitar bridges look like those made by great luthiers of the past.

For luthiers looking to improve the plight of the hapless guitarist tying strings over the tieblock and hoping

Top: A typical classical bridge on a Hopf guitar.

Bottom: This double-drilled string block allows simpler string changes and a steeper angle of the strings passing over the saddle.

they will hold, tieblocks with double holes for each string are increasingly popular. This not only reduces the chance that a string will unwrap from the tieblock and mar the top of the guitar, it also relieves the tendency of the wrapped string to pull up slightly on the string as it enters its hole in the tieblock, thus reducing the downward pressure on the saddle and possibly reducing the tone. This is especially true of guitars with a shallow neck angle and low saddle height.

Bridge Materials

The material used for bridges is another difference between steel-string and nylon-string guitars, especially today. On early instruments, the material used was directly related to the price: cheap guitars had birch or maple bridges stained to look like ebony, while higher quality guitars used rosewood, with ebony reserved for the finer examples. Martin even used solid ivory bridges for its highest models until 1916.

Most bridges are made out of wood, but some vintage guitars, such as this 19th-century Martin use ivory.

Now all but the very cheapest imported guitars use rosewood bridges, while Taylor currently uses ebony on every steel-string instrument they make, even down to the Baby models. Martin uses both ebony and rosewood, but is also using black Micarta for both the fretboards and bridges on many of its less expensive models.

With a few exceptions, such as Ovation and Lowden, who both use walnut on some models, rosewood or ebony have been the standard materials for bridges until quite recently, when cocobolo, Madagascar rosewood, and other exotic hardwoods began to appear more often on instruments by independent builders.

With a few exceptions, the fretboard and bridge on steel-string guitars are usually made of the same wood. This is not true of nylon-string classicals, however, where it has long been felt that rosewood produces a better sound than does ebony, most-ly due to the difference in weight. On archtop guitars, bridges are always rosewood or ebony, with a few rare exceptions. The adjusting mechanism is usually of brass or steel, with a threaded thumbwheel for raising or lowering the saddle.

Saddles

Both nylon- and steel-strung guitars use similar saddles as the lower string bearing. These are usually made of bone (ivory before the 1960s), though hard plastics have been widely used since the 1960s, especially on high-production guitars. Many early guitars, especially inexpensive ones, used a metal fret, like those found on the neck, as a saddle. This was standard even on fairly expensive guitars in the 19th century. Saddles of a hard, dense wood, such as ebony, were also common. In the 1970s and '80s, when the influence of electric guitars was strongest, metal saddles, especially brass, were also sometimes used, though never as standard equipment from a manufacturer.

Since the 1970s, Micarta, a phenolic, has been widely used by large manufacturers, though a much harder plastic, sold under the Tusq trademark, is now gaining in popularity. A current trend among custom builders is towards fossilized ivory for string saddles, sold as an after-market accessory, often with matching nut, bridge pins, and endpin.

"Drop-in" saddles may look like a part you should be able to buy off the shelf, but they usually need to be fitted to the guitar's bridge and the height adjusted for the individual's playing style and string choice. Proper fitting of the saddle is probably the most important concern, especially as poor-fitting ones can wedge against the sides of the saddle slot and crack the bridge.

Much as been said about the effect of different materials on a guitar's tone and volume, but little real research has been done. Hard materials like bone and Tusq definitely last longer than softer materials like Micarta, which tend to develop notches or grooves in the top of the saddle, especially from wound strings. Thanks to softer string materials, this is less an issue with nylon-stringed guitars. Many independent builders still feel that bone is the ideal material for saddles on acoustic guitars, as it is hard, shapes well, takes a nice polish, and is readily available.

For archtop guitars, the saddle is effectively the upper portion of the adjustable, floating bridge, and is compensated as needed. Ebony is still the preferred material, and harder synthetics are felt to make the tone too harsh.

Saddle Slot

Bridges usually have a slot to accept the saddle, and the slot is either a long kerf in the bridge, open at each end, or a routed slot in which all four sides are surrounded by the bridge material. Although the first type of slot, now usually called a "through-cut" saddle, was used by Martin, Gibson, Guild, and many other companies up until the mid-1960s, or even later, it has the disadvantage of requiring that the saddle be glued into the bridge. This need is dependent on string tension and the height of the saddle protruding above the bridge, however, so nylon-string guitars' saddles rarely need to be glued.

For a steel-string guitar with a steep neck angle and high-tension strings, however, the need to glue in the saddle (to protect against cracking the bridge at the saddle slot), may cost the owner considerably more in upkeep over the life of the guitar. Glued-in saddles make adjusting the string height at the bridge much more time-consuming and expensive, as well as making the installation of under-the-saddle pickups a nightmare.

With modern milling equipment, the closed, or "blind-end" slot (sometimes referred to as a drop-in saddle) is both stronger and more convenient, but the desire to emulate the building styles of the past has resulted in the return of the antiquated style on most all new guitars designed as vintage reissues. The closed saddle slot offers numerous advantages to players and luthiers alike, such as being able to change saddles quickly to accommodate different playing styles, string gauges, or climates.

Compensation

One of the most noticeable improvements on steel-string flattops during the last two decades has been for more accurate compensation of the saddle, to allow for accurate intonation, especially as the player moves up the neck. Although Gibsons had reasonably good intonation almost 40 years ago, thanks to the saddles being at a steeper angle, most other guitar manufacturers never bothered to ensure that the fretted octave note matched the pure octave harmonic sounded at the 12th fret. Because of the narrow saddle, and the shallow angle, the B string usually sounded slightly sharp, and the low E decidedly so, while the high E and the D were often the only strings that played in tune up the neck.

One of the most frequently requested repairs was for a compensated saddle, with notches in the top edge to position the B string further behind the high E, then the

G forward again, and the A and low E moved back. On an instrument with a comparatively shallow saddle angle, such as Martin, this required either routing an unusually wide slot, or filling in the saddle slot and re-routing it at a steeper angle in the bridge (often moving the slot back closer to the pins). Beginning in the 1970s and early '80s, manufacturers such as Ovation and Taylor began making such saddles standard equipment.

Another solution adopted by Lowden, Takamine, and others, was the use of a split saddle. This meant two separate saddles—a short one for the unwound E and B strings, and a second longer saddle for the wound G through low E. This saved the extra weight of a saddle wide enough to accommodate the different string bearing points necessary for adequate compensation, but it introduced a whole new set of problems for players who wanted to add under-the-saddle pickups.

Lowden's split saddle is an attempt to achieve better intonation.

Today, virtually all guitarmakers, large or small, ensure that their instruments have far more accurate intonation than was expected in the past, and virtually all new high-end guitars have saddles with the tops notched or angled to accommodate the intonation needed for different strings. Some builders go beyond working only at the saddle end to improve intonation, and also shorten the distance between the nut and first fret a minute amount. Yet intonation can only do so much, however, and knowing how to temper the tuning of a guitar is probably more important to the player than having each string play a perfect octave at the twelfth fret.

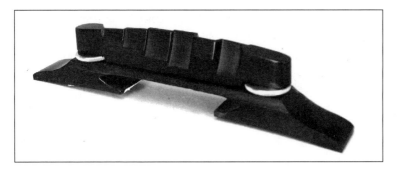

Most archtop bridges feature a compensated saddle for improved intonation.

Archtop Bridges

Unlike steel-string and nylon-string guitars, archtop guitars do not have bridges that are glued to the soundboard. Instead, bridges on archtops are "floating," and are held against the soundboard with the downward pressure of the strings as they pass over the bridge and then angle steeply downwards to where they're anchored at the tailpiece. Thanks to the floating bridge, archtops have had better intonation than flattops almost from their inception.

Archtop bridges are never glued or otherwise fixed into place. Instead, they're held in their position by the strings' tension.

Although early Gibson archtops—with round soundholes—had bridges that were not adjustable, they still had a compensated top portion—serving as a saddle—as early as 1910. Even if the standard compensation on such bridges did not quite do an adequate job, the entire bridge could be angled slightly to bring the guitar closer to playing in tune.

Another Gibson innovation, the adjustable archtop bridge, was patented in the early 1920s, around the same time the company began using truss rods in its necks.

The adjustable bridge, with compensated saddle, gave archtops a decided advantage for any player with a well-trained ear. Besides improved intonation, archtop players could make minute adjustments in string height without even removing the guitar's strings.

For the most part, archtop bridges do not show the wide range of shapes and styles as found on flattop models. During the golden age of the jazz guitar, however, some stylistic flourishes did surface, most notably the art deco "stair-step" bridges used by Gretsch, and the triangular inlays on both the top and bottom portion of the earliest Gibson Super 400 bridges, which echoed the inlays used on the fretboard and headstock.

Bringing such a convenient capacity for adjustment to the flattop guitar seemed like a good idea, and Gibson began using adjustable saddles in its flattops beginning in the late 1950s. By the 1970s, however, only inexpensive guitars still had adjustable saddles, simply because it was widely recognized that they robbed both tone and volume from the flattop design.

6 The Back and Sides

Woods and Their Sounds

The materials used for the back, sides, and top are sometimes referred to as "tonewoods." Luthiers choose the wood for the back and sides of the guitar for strength, stability, and beauty, but most of all, for tone. Everyone agrees that different species of wood produce different tones, but beyond that, all agreement ends. Players and builders can, and do, get into endless debates over the superiority of one species of rosewood versus another, the tonal variations of slab-cut and quarter-sawn wood, and even if the color of the wood makes a difference. All of these arguments can be boiled down to the generally accepted idea that the denser and darker the wood, the more bass response the guitar will have; the less dense and more lightly colored, the brighter the tone.

Luthiers and musicians have also been debating for centuries about whether good tone comes from the material used or the skill of the builder. In the 1850s, the famed Spanish luthier Antonio de Torres made a guitar with a papier-mâché back and sides to demonstrate that a skilled craftsman can make a good guitar out of anything. In 1998, Bob Taylor made the same point by building a fine sounding guitar using an oak shipping pallet he found on his loading dock for the back and sides, and a pine 2×4 leftover from a construction project for the top.

Even though Torres and Taylor have shown that just about any material can be used to make a guitar, rosewood is still the most popular wood for building flattop steel-strings and nylon-strings. Mahogany is used quite a bit by steel-string luthiers, while archtop builders overwhelmingly prefer maple.

Slab-Cut, Quartersawn, Veneers

Tonewoods are cut from a log in one of three different ways: quartersawn, slab-cut, and in ultra-thin slices called "veneers." On quartersawn wood, the log is cut along its length into four wedge-shaped pieces. The wood is then cut from the face of each wedge, which gives a piece that has the grain running more or less perpendicular to the growth rings. On slab-cut wood, the log is cut into planks along its length. This method yields more material from a log—and in the case of maple and Brazilian rosewood, harvests some pieces of wood with fancy figures. But on many of the pieces that come from wood that's been cut using the slab-cut method, the grain runs at an angle or even perpendicular along its width. When quartersawn wood shrinks as it dries out over time, it tends to shrink evenly in all dimensions, while slab-cut wood has a tendency to shrink more on one side than the other, which sometimes causes the wood to warp.

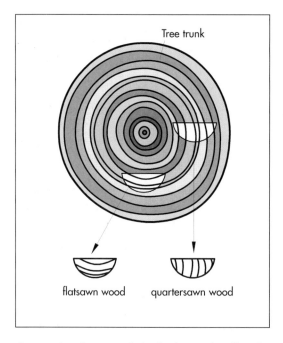

Cross-section of a tree trunk showing how cutting affects the grain pattern in the neck.

Builders prefer the stability of quartersawn for tops and necks, as well as for the sides, where it is easier to bend. But some builders are willing to use slab-cut wood in the back, where the structural stability of the material is not as much as issue. But generally, builders and players want quartersawn wood whenever possible.

The third method of getting wood from a log is to cut it into veneers. A veneer is cut from a log in a long continuous slice, much as one would peel an apple. Veneers are very thin and have to be glued to a core of some sort.

Solid or Laminate

The back and sides of guitars are made of either solid wood or laminates. In general, solid woods give a richer, fuller tone than laminates, which tend to be fairly bright-sounding without a lot of depth or resonance. Most of the inexpensive guitars made around the world, particularly those built in Asia, have laminated backs and sides. Cheap laminated guitars are made with a very thin veneer of rosewood or mahogany glued to a core of a relatively soft wood. Because the cost of materials is so low, this is an inexpensive way to build guitars. On guitars built in this style, the choice of veneer is purely a cosmetic choice and has almost no effect on tone.

But even though solid wood construction usually produces the finest guitars, not all laminate guitars are cheaply built instruments. In the 1800s, it was common for luthiers to make the back out of a wood like spruce or cedar and to laminate a veneer of maple or rosewood over it to add a bit of structural stability.

It was also common to make the side of laminated material, because it resisted splitting and cracking. In the 1930s, the Mario Maccaferri–designed Selmers featured mahogany backs veneered with Indian rosewood. Maccaferri did this to increase the treble response and to build a guitar where the back and sides wouldn't crack or split under heavy use.

In more recent years the classical builder Greg Smallman has built classical guitars with very heavy, laminated rosewood backs and sides. His feeling is that this design, when coupled with his ultra-thin tops, help project the sound forward.

Mahogany

Mahogany has a light, golden-brown color with a fine, even grain. The best mahogany comes from Central America; and even though it can come from any number of countries, it is generally sold as Honduran. Guitars made of mahogany tend to have a bright, clear tone, excellent treble response, and a quick attack. It works particularly well on larger-bodied guitars where the inherent bright tonal qualities of the wood balance out the potentially boomy quality of the bigger soundbox.

The back and sides of this Martin D-18 are made out of mahogany.

Mahogany is rarely used for building archtops or higher-end classical guitars (many student-grade classicals are made of mahogany), but it is prized by steel-string guitarmakers. Mahogany is cheaper than rosewood as a raw material, so it has always been used by builders for their plainer instruments, such as Martin's D-18 and Gibson's J-45. But many players prefer the crisp tone of mahogany, particularly when recording.

Honduran mahogany usually has a straight grain pattern, but occasionally a tree will have a striped figure that is sometimes referred to as a "ribbon pattern." There is also a highly figured mahogany that has a quilted pattern. So far, all of the quilted mahogany in the world appears to have come from a single, huge tree, which may have produced the pattern as some sort of genetic mutation. Quilted and ribbon mahogany are both more brittle than the straight-grained variety, and a few luthiers feel guitars made of it sound too harsh. Mahogany also grows in the Philippine Islands, but most luthiers consider the island variety too soft to use. Even so, a few large-scale factories use it on very cheap instruments. There is also a wood from Sierra Leone called *khaya invorensis* that is sometimes sold as African mahogany. It has similar tonal properties to true mahogany and more and more builders have been working with it in the last few years.

Indian Rosewood

The color of East Indian rosewood (scientific name *dalbergia latifolia*) ranges from dark chocolate brown to reddish brown and even dark purple. The grain tends to be straight and even with a fair amount of color variation between the dark and light shades.

On the left, a Taylor 810 with back and sides out of Indian rosewood. On the right, the back of a Collings D-2H made out of the same wood.

Indian rosewood has been used on guitars for decades, but it wasn't until the ban on exporting Brazilian rosewood in the mid-1960s that it became the standard rosewood in the guitar world. Indian rosewood is quite dense and has a full, rich bass response with clear trebles, which has made it popular with builders of both steel-string and nylon-string guitars. Archtop guitars are almost never made from Indian rosewood.

Indian rosewood is sorted by quality at Martin.

Brazilian Rosewood

Brazilian rosewood (scientific name *dalbergia nigra*) ranges in color from almost black to dark brown to light chocolate brown. It can also have streaks of red, orange, and even bright green. When quartersawn, the grain is straight and even, while slab-cut wood can have extremely wild curves and extreme color variations. Because of the flamboyant grain patterns, Brazilian rosewood is one of the few tonewoods that is routinely sold in slab-cut form.

Brazilian rosewood has a great bass response—deep without being muddy—and bright, clear trebles. In 1965, the government of Brazil put an embargo on log-form wood leaving the country in an attempt to boost the local milling industry. Guitarmakers such as Martin weren't happy with the quality of the milled timber coming from Brazil, so in 1969, they switched to Indian rosewood. The change caused the value of guitars to go up immediately, and as early as 1970, used Martins made of Brazilian rosewood sold for more than new guitars made of Indian rosewood. Brazilian rosewood was available throughout the 1970s and 1980s, but it was so expensive that guitarmakers rarely used it except for limited runs. During this period, companies such as Guild and Taylor gradually switched to Indian rosewood, as did most of the classical builders in Europe and America.

Then in 1992, Brazilian rosewood was added to the list of banned materials kept by the Convention on International Trade in Endangered Species (CITES). Since then, the only Brazilian rosewood that could be legally imported needed a CITES document stating that the timber was cut prior to July 11, 1992.

Rough-cut Brazilian rosewood at Lakewood. On the right, a Santa Cruz OM with Brazilian rosewood back and sides.

This cut the supply of newly logged wood to zero, which drove the already high price up even further. Paradoxically, as the price rose, more Brazilian rosewood came on the market as luthiers and wood brokers who had been hoarding wood began to cash in on their stashes. The need for CITES documentation has also led to people harvesting old Brazilian rosewood stumps—a process that was previously too expensive to be profitable.

Luthiers and players have been debating about the superiority of Brazilian rosewood over Indian for decades, with strong positions being taken on both sides. The common consensus that dark, straight-grained, quarter-sawn Brazilian is the best-sounding wood, but that Indian rosewood with the same attributes is nearly as good. (Again, the general feeling is that darker wood is denser and has a better bass response.)

Many fine luthiers refuse to build with Brazilian rosewood, feeling that its supposed superiority is primarily hype. But even though it may sound a little bit better, the best Brazilian rosewood can cost 15 to 20 times more than the best Indian rosewood, pricing it out of reach for all but the wealthiest guitarists.

Maple

Maple is a pale, yellowish wood that becomes darker and more golden with exposure to light. Maple sometimes exhibits a variety of figured grain patterns—the most common of which is a series of stripes, which when widely spaced is known as "tiger striped," "flame," or "curly maple." When the stripes are more narrowly spaced the wood is sometimes called "fiddleback maple," because it resembles the figure found on better-quality violins. Curly maple is usually found on quarter-sawn wood, but when it is slab-cut it can exhibit a pattern known as "quilted," or a pattern made up of tiny knots known as "bird's-eye."

When used in flattop guitars, maple has a smooth, mellow bass with a clear, but not too bright, treble. It's most commonly used on flattop jumbo models like the Gibson SJ-200, the Taylor 615, and the Guild J-50. Although maple was commonly used on classical guitars made in France, Italy, and Austria between 1820 and 1860, the practice faded out when the rosewood guitars of Spanish makers like Torres became popular. Today nearly all classical guitars made in Spain are built of rosewood or mahogany, but maple is still used by builders in other European countries.

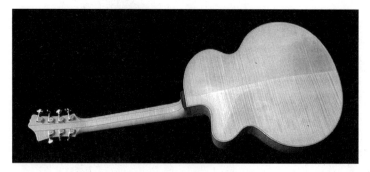

A seven-string Henneken archtop with maple back and sides.

Many of the first carved guitars and mandolins made by Orville Gibson at the end of the 19th century had the sides and back made from walnut or birch. After he was bought out by a group of Kalamazoo businessmen in 1902, the new company slowly began switching to maple, and by the early 1920s, all of their high-end instruments had maple backs and sides. Maple had been used on bowed instruments such as violins and cellos for centuries, and the Gibson catalogs of the 1920s went to great lengths to compare their guitars and mandolins to the violins of the great Italian builders. Gibson even went so far as to name their new sunburst finish "Cremona Brown" after the birthplace of Amati and Stradivarius.

Maple turned out to work so well for archtops that builders have rarely even considered using another kind of tonewood. Three varieties of maple are commonly used in building guitars. In the past, the most sought after variety was European maple (scientific name *acer pseudoplatinus*) which was used on many of the greatest violins. In recent years, the scarcity of European maple has led archtop builders to start using two North American varieties: eastern rock maple (scientific name *acer nigrum*), which is a very dense, pale wood with a tight, smooth grain that builders like because it is relatively easy to get a good finish with it; and western bigleaf maple (scientific name *acer macrophyllum*), which has a slightly coarser grain and is less dense than either rock or European maple. It's also a little darker in color, with more of a golden hue. Taylor's use of bigleaf maple since they started the company in 1974 has led to more builders using it in their own guitars.

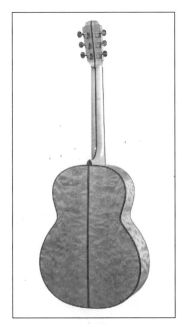 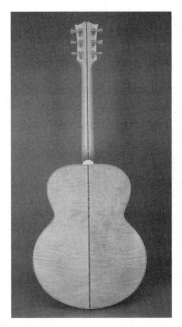

Although maple is mostly used on archtops, it is also frequently used on flattops. On the left, a Lowden F35 whose maple back and sides has a "quilted" pattern. On the right, Gibson's J-200 was one of the first flattops with maple back and sides.

191

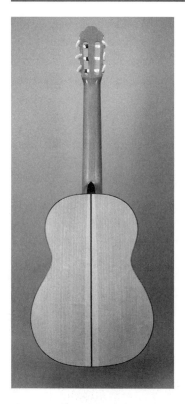

Cypress is the traditional choice for the back and sides of a flamenco guitar.

Some spectacular "flame" in the koa back and sides of an Albert & Müller guitar.

Cypress

Cypress has a pale yellow color, sometimes with a hint of orange or red. It's a very light wood in terms of density, which gives it a very bright, percussive tone that has made it the wood of choice for flamenco guitars. The most highly sought after species of cypress grows in Spain, but Monterey cypress, which grows on the West Coast of North America is also popular with builders.

Occasionally, you might see a wood called "Canadian cypress," which is actually a misnomer, as the tree is really a variety of cedar. Cypress usually has a straight, even grain; but some builders actually seek out wood with knots, which they feel gives the guitar a slightly rough appearance in keeping with the wildness of flamenco music.

Koa

Koa grows in Hawaii and has a brownish orange color. It can exhibit a striking figured pattern similar to flamed maple, which makes it highly prized by both luthiers and players. Koa has a bright, clear tone with a strong mid-range. Koa was first used on ukuleles in the late 1800s, and guitars very soon after. In the 1920s, Hawaiian music was extremely popular in the U.S., and consequently, many builders used koa for their guitars—particularly Martin, and Weissenborn, who built a guitar with a hollow-neck designed for playing slide. When Hawaiian music faded in popularity during the 1930s, the use of koa in guitars declined.

In the 1970s, there was a revival of the use of koa led by smaller builders like James Goodall and the Santa Cruz Guitar Company, who felt the wood offered an interesting addition to the usual choice of rosewood, mahogany, or maple. Although koa is relatively scarce, it is currently used by a large number of builders.

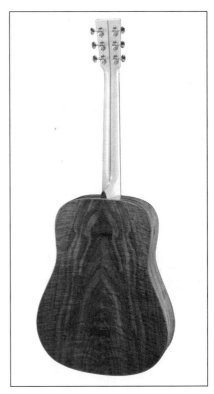

Martin has long used koa for its guitars, and even offers the wood in its relatively inexpensive models, such as this SPD16K2. On the right, the walnut back and sides of a special issue Martin NWD.

Walnut

Walnut has a medium dark brown color, which can sometimes have a reddish or grayish cast to it. Guitars made of walnut tend to have a tone somewhere between the bassy tones of rosewood and the brighter mahogany tones. Although walnut has been used in furniture for centuries, luthiers have only started using it over the last few decades. Larger companies such as Martin and Taylor have both made instruments out of walnut, as have numerous smaller builders. The most common varieties used by builders are California walnut (scientific name *juglans California*) and claro walnut (scientific name *juglans hindsii*). Walnut both sounds and looks good; and since it's not endangered, more and more builders are likely to start using it in the future.

Cherry

Cherry is a pale blond wood with sonic qualities similar to maple. It is relatively inexpensive as a raw material, and has become a popular choice for larger companies seeking a good-looking, fine-sounding wood to use on their cheaper guitars. The Canadian company Godin has been using cherry on its Seagull line with great success. Because cherry grows so quickly and it's not endangered, it has also been used occasionally by Martin and Gibson.

Other Woods

There are many other types of wood that can be used for the back and sides. In the 1920s and 1930s, birch and oak were widely used, particularly on less-expensive instruments; but these days, they are scarcely used at all. In the last few years, luthiers have been experimenting with a wide variety of different tonewoods. Most of these woods come from the tropical forests of South America, Africa, and Southeast Asia, and are generally too expensive or too scarce for the larger companies to use for large numbers of guitars. Many of these woods are members of the rosewood family.

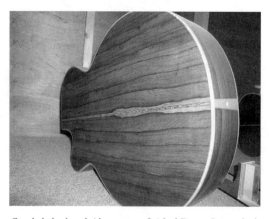

One of the most common alternative woods is cocobolo (scientific name *dalbergia retusa*), a rosewood that grows in Mexico and Central America. Cocobolo ranges in color from golden yellow to reddish orange, and has a tone that many builders feel resembles Brazilian rosewood.

Cocobolo back and sides on an unfinished Froggy Bottom body.

A Taylor 414 with ovangkol back and sides.

A rarer rosewood is African blackwood (scientific name *dalbergia melanoxylon*). This tree grows in Africa and is almost as dense and as dark as ebony. African blackwood is very difficult to bend for the sides, but guitars made from it have a deep, rich bass response and sparkling trebles.

Zircote (scientific name *cordia dodecandra*), is not a member of the rosewood family, but its grain and color look very much like Brazilian rosewood.

Macassar ebony (scientific name *diospyrus celebica*), grows in Indonesia and is deep black with golden-brown streaks. Breedlove has built some good-sounding guitars out of this wood.

Wenge (scientific name *millettia laurentii*), grows in Central Africa. It's heavier than most rosewoods but is also softer. It has a chocolate brown color, and when built into guitars, has a strong mid-range and smooth bass response.

Sapele (scientific name *entandrophragma cylindricum*), is a mahogany-like wood that has been used by Spanish luthiers for decades. Taylor in California was one of the first steel-string guitarmakers to use it.

Ovangkol (scientific name *guibourita ehie*), is a rosewood-like wood that has been used by European builders for decades, and is just now being taken up by American builders.

Palo Escrito is a wood that grows in Mexico and is favored by the builders of Paracho, a town where nearly every inhabitant is a luthier, or works for a luthier.

Backs made out of various woods await further processing.

Synthetic Materials

With the availability of high-quality tonewoods becoming increasingly questionable, synthetic materials are frequently considered as alternatives. It probably comes as no surprise that the first attempts to make guitars out of synthetics came in the plastic-happy 1950s. Fascinated with the possibilities of injection molding, luthier Mario Maccaferri designed a line of plastic stringed instruments after his immigration to the U.S. during World War II. Initially spurred by the desire to make an inexpensive ukulele to be sold on a popular TV show, the line eventually included several models of guitars, as well as a violin that was once the centerpiece of a special performance by the New York Philharmonic. While the ukuleles turned into a huge success with millions being sold, the guitars never caught on.

Although the guitars were innovative in ways beyond the fact that they were made out of plastic (including tuning machines whose planetary gears were integrated into a hollow headstock, and an easily adjustable neck angle), they simply couldn't compete with the sound of wooden guitars. Disappointed by the lack of interest, Maccaferri put several thousand of the instruments into storage, where they were practically forgotten until they were found in a New Jersey warehouse in the late 1980s. For a period of a couple of years, these "brand-new" guitars made in the 1950s were suddenly available, delighting collectors and Maccaferri buffs. Today, the guitars are still a relatively frequent sight on the vintage market of Internet auction sites. Usually costing a fraction of other collectable guitars, they are an affordable—and fun—option if you want a really cool guitar designed by one the most colorful luthiers in the history of the instrument.

Another early attempt at using synthetic materials for acoustic guitars is found in National's line of Res-o-Glass instruments from the 1960s. Featuring a body made out of fiberglass, these single-cone resonator guitars were designed with student players in mind. Limited commercial success and a sound that didn't really compare with the company's famous wooden- or metal-body instruments lead to their discontinuation after only a few years in production.

Ovation Guitars

Founded in 1966, Ovation Guitars was the first company to have widespread success with largely non-wooden guitars. As a subsidiary of Kaman Aerospace (a company primarily known for their helicopters), Ovation had the resources to experiment with a variety of new materials and designs, eventually leading to a unique design featuring a synthetic bowl ("round-back") as the main element of the instrument's body. Dissatisfied with wooden guitars' susceptibility to crack with changes in temperature and humidity, company founder Charles Kaman looked to fiberglass as the solution. By choosing a rounded shape, Ovation's designers were able to manufacture the guitar's back and sides as a single unit, eliminate the need for internal braces, and create a distinctive feature that would make it easy to immediately identify the instruments. Additionally, Kaman believed that the resulting parabolic shape of the back would result in a superior sound, as it was less likely to trap sound waves than a traditional design.

Realizing that he was more likely to find market acceptance if he used a wooden top with his fiberglass back, Kaman initially relied on relatively traditional guitar construction for the top, neck, and other parts of his Ovation guitars. Having already found success in the fact that famous guitarists, such as Josh White, Glen Campbell, and Charlie Byrd, began using Ovations shortly after their introduction (it was Byrd who suggested the name "Ovation"), the company achieved its real triumph by introducing one of the first modern pickup systems on an acoustic guitar in the early 1970s. A perfect match for the instruments' already unusual appearance and image, the proprietary pickup system allowed the guitars to be played at high stage volumes without feedback, but retain the sound of a true acoustic guitar. For over a decade, Ovation made virtually the only mass-produced, professional, acoustic-electric guitar, giving the company a huge boost in popularity.

Not one to be easily satisfied with his company's ascent as an industry leader, Kaman continued to experiment with composite technology, eventually leading to the Adamas line of guitars. Featuring a top that sandwiches an ultra-thin birchwood core between two layers of carbon fiber, the instrument took high-tech guitarmaking to a new level by making almost the entire body out of composite materials.

Today, Ovation offers a large selection of models in many price ranges. Having switched the material for its back from fiberglass to a material called "lyracord," the instruments are based on four different depths for their bowls, each with its own tonal character. Generally, a player concerned with good acoustic tone will choose a model with a deeper bowl, while someone faced with loud stage volumes will benefit from the less feedback-prone shallow bowl.

Ovation's catalog starts out with the inexpensive Celebrity line. These instruments feature the same backs as the more expensive U.S.–made models, but are generally paired with laminated tops, less elaborate electronics, and basic appointments. These guitars offer the classic Ovation look and feel, as well as representing many qualities of the basic Ovation sound. As their low price suggests, the quality of these guitars is no match for the company's higher-end models, but for many players on a budget, these are a good option for getting a real Ovation at an affordable price.

At the time of the writing of this book, Ovation's U.S.–made line starts out with the evergreen Balladeer model. This is basically the classic Ovation, with a deep bowl, spruce top, round soundhole, and onboard electronics. An increasingly popular choice is found in the unusual-looking Elite series. Featuring multiple soundholes in the top's upper bouts, the model fuses a feature that was first introduced in the carbon-topped Adamas with more traditional wooden-top construction. This design has frequently been the basis for many of Ovation's annual limited editions, featuring tops made out of redwood, bubinga, flamed maple, and other exotic choices. The wood-topped line of guitars reaches its climax with instruments such as the Custom Legend and the Al Di Meola Signature model.

While first-generation Adamas guitars gave many guitarists a case of sticker shock, recent additions to the line have become more affordable. First introduced in 1998, the line of SMT guitars is available with single or multiple soundholes and different depth bowls, creating a multitude of choices for guitarists who wish to own a carbon-top guitar.

The latest development in Ovation's R&D efforts is found in the radical Adamas Q. Constructed almost entirely from graphite (including the neck), the instrument features a radical new look that shows the graphite's woven fibers. Currently, the instrument remains in the prototype stage (although it has appeared at trade shows), but it nevertheless offers a fascinating glimpse into the company's future.

Graphite Guitars

Perhaps the most radical acoustic guitars are those made out of carbon fiber graphite. The largest inroads into this market have been made by a company called RainSong. Founded in Hawaii, where extreme climates and high humidity tend to challenge wooden instruments, RainSong is now located in Washington state. While early RainSongs simply substituted graphite for wood in an otherwise traditionally built guitar, the company eventually came to the conclusion that a different approach was necessary in order to maximize the benefits available in the new material.

Using layers of carbon fiber (a process the company calls "projection tuned layering"), current RainSongs take advantage of the material's incredible strength and use no braces in their internal construction. Designed to be completely wood-free, the instruments use carbon fiber in the construction of the neck, fingerboard, bridge, and other parts in addition to the body. Sounding remarkably similar to wooden guitars, they are currently available in the way of various steel-string and nylon-string models, based on OM, Grand Auditorium, dreadnought, and jumbo shapes.

On the left, RainSong's WS9000 guitar made out of graphite.
On the right, Martin's Cowboy X, made out of a high-pressure laminate.

Currently the only other manufacturer making graphite guitars is a relatively new outfit called Composite Acoustics. Using the know-how of NASA engineers, the company began offering guitars in 2000. Featuring an appearance that's very similar to that of a RainSong, at first (displaying graphite's silverish gray color and showing the material's woven pattern), the guitars actually differ in their construction. While RainSongs use a regular-looking neck-body joint with a heel and an internal neckblock, Composite Acoustics uses a neck with no heel—making upper-fret access easy—and no internal reinforcement, claiming that their material doesn't require such traditional features to get the necessary strength. On the other hand, Composite Acoustics utilizes a standard X-bracing pattern for its tops, using braces made out of composite material. Besides a dreadnought model, the company also offers the radically shaped small-body "X" model, a long-scale baritone, and an acoustic bass guitar.

Martin's acoustic-electric DCXME made out of high-pressure laminate.

Martin X-Series

Introduced in 1998, Martin's X-Series of guitars took the industry by surprise. With a body made out of high-pressure laminate (HPL) the guitars represent Martin's attempt to use alternative materials, which is an inexpensive way to build an entry-level instrument. A wood-fiber derivative that's laminated under extremely high pressure, the material is similar to what is used on many kitchen counters and other furniture. With an ultra-hard surface, HPL is very strong, can easily be brought into the desired shape, and is resistant to warping under the influence of heat or extreme humidity. Coated with a photo finish, HPL can be made to look like anything. While the standard DXM looks like it has a mahogany back and sides and a spruce top, Martin has also used Brazilian rosewood finishes, solid colors, and—in the case of the Cowboy X—scenes of cowboys sitting around a campfire playing Martins.

Few players would argue that X-Series Martins sound as good as their wooden cousins, but it's undeniable that they have enabled the manufacturer to make an instrument that looks and feels like a real Martin at an unprecedented price. Since their introduction, the line has been expanded to include guitars that feature HPL backs and sides with a real, solid spruce top (which offers a more mature acoustic sound), thin-body acoustic-electric versions (such as the 00CXAE), and most recently, models with aluminum (!) and carbon fiber tops.

Construction

In contrast to the endless debate about which species of wood is best, most players and builders basically agree on how the back and sides should be assembled. Together with the top, the back and sides are essentially a box; and given that the box needs to be strong, light, and resonant, builders of flattop steel-strings, nylon-strings, and archtop guitars have all come up with similar solutions to the same problems.

Arched vs. Flat Back

In general, steel-string guitars with flat tops have flat backs, and those with arched tops have arched backs. But like everything having to do with guitars, there are exceptions to the rule. As early as 1930, Epiphone was making flattop guitars with an arched back that was pressed into shape and made of maple laminates. A laminated arched back doesn't vibrate as freely as a solid flat back, but it does seem to help project the sound forward. Epiphone continued to experiment with the laminated-maple arched design, and in 1947, they offered the unique design, which they dubbed the "Tone Back," on their top-of-the-line flattop, the FT-110.

In 1952, Epiphone moved part of their manufacturing facility from New York to Philadelphia. Some of the workers left behind in the move formed the Guild guitar company, and within a few months, they were building flattop guitars with arched maple backs like the Aragon F-30 and the Navarre F-50. Over the years, Guild also made guitars like the D-25 that had arched backs made of laminated mahogany.

The arched-back, flattop style has become something of a Guild trademark, but Gibson did try their hand at the technique when they built the J-55 and the Gospel in the early 1970s, and the reissued Gospel in the 1990s. In the early 1980s, the Santa Cruz Guitar Company offered a model called the FTC that had a solid, carved back. Using its experience with violins and archtop guitars, Eastman Strings introduced a line of flattops with arched backs in 2003. In the 1930s and 1940s, Martin experimented with putting carved, arched tops on bodies with flat backs. The design proved to be a failure, and other builders didn't take up the style.

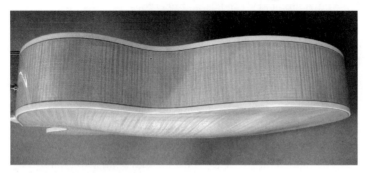

The arched back on a Guild Artist Award.

Carved or Pressed (for Arched Backs)

Arched backs can be carved from a solid piece of wood and pressed into shape using thin pieces of solid wood, or pressed into shape using laminates. Just about everyone agrees that to get the best acoustic tone, a carved, solid back is the best way to go. The feeling is that the solid wood helps give tonal depth, particularly in the bass, while the arched shape helps project the sound forward. Backs that are too thick tend to sound rather thin and produce little bass response, while backs that are too thinly carved can sound tubby with an ill-defined treble.

During the archtop guitar's most popular period in the 1930s and 1940s, builders of cheaper guitars would sometimes take a thin piece of wood and bend it into an arched shape over a mold. While this practice was mostly used for the tops, some backs were formed in this way as well. Guitars made in this way had a thin, trebly tone. This technique was not very sound, structurally, and over time, many of the guitars made in this way have slowly succumbed to string tension and have collapsed. Almost nobody makes arched backs in this way today.

The third way of making an arch-back is to press it out of laminates. Laminate backs are usually found on inexpensive guitars like many of the new archtops from

Asia, and most of the archtops made by the now-defunct American companies Kay and Harmony. Laminated backs are also found on many expensive archtops designed to be plugged in, like Gibson's ES-5, ES-175, and ES-150, and Epiphone's Zephyr series. On these models, the laminates aren't used as a cost-cutting measure, but to take advantage of the inherent stiffness and to help cut down on feedback caused by a too-resonant guitar.

Two-Piece vs. Three-Piece

The vast majority of guitars are made with a two-piece back. The usual technique is to take a piece of wood, split it in half along the edge, and open the two new pieces like a book. This technique, which is called "bookmatching," means that the two pieces will be closely matched in grain pattern and color. This process is particularly important with slab-cut pieces of wood, which can exhibit wildly varying figure and color shifts.

Occasionally, a guitar will be made with a three-piece back. In this case the third piece is set in the center in a triangular shape with the point at the heel. The third piece can be made of the same wood, usually in a contrasting color, or it can be of a different wood altogether. The most famous three-piece guitar is Martin's

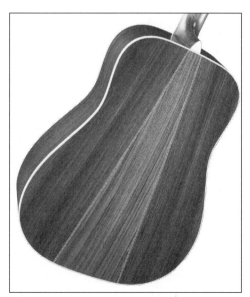

D-35, which was introduced in 1967. Martin came up with the idea of using three pieces for the back when their supplies of Brazilian rosewood started to dwindle after the 1965 ban, and they discovered they had lots of pieces that were too small to use in a two-piece back, but could be used in a three-piece back.

Taylor and Goodall will occasionally use a three piece back on their maple and koa guitars. Very rarely you will find a guitar with a one-piece back, but those that exist are almost always smaller-bodied guitars. Luthiers also

Martin's D-35 is probably the most famous example of a guitar with a three-piece back.

occasionally make backs out of more than two or three pieces of wood, but again, this is very rare.

Taper

When viewed from the side, the bodies of steel-string flattops are generally deeper at the endblock than they are at the neckblock. This taper is more pronounced on larger-bodied instruments, such as dreadnoughts and jumbos, than it is on smaller guitars like OMs. Some Gibson flattop guitars, like the Nick Lucas and L-00, have almost no taper at all. The taper makes it a little easier to play large guitars. Classical guitars also exhibit a small amount of taper, but it's not as extreme as that seen on steel-strings. Like classical guitars, the bodies of archtop guitars have very little taper.

Bracing and Back Strip

Back braces are used primarily for structural support, but they do have a definite, if subtle effect on tone. The most common back-bracing style is a simple ladder pattern. The braces can have a variety of shapes, including wide and flat, tall and blade-like, and short with a square, or sometimes a rounded, top. Like the top braces, back braces are usually made of spruce, although a few makers use mahogany or cedar. The famous classical guitarmaker Ignacio Fleta even combined spruce and mahogany braces for the backs of many of his instruments.

Most luthiers believe that lighter bracing, which makes the back more flexible, has a bassier tone, while stiffer bracing, which makes the back less flexible, makes the guitars sound a bit brighter. It's common for luthiers to use wider, flatter braces in the lower bout, and thinner, taller braces in the upper bout—but this is not a universal rule. Some builders use a cross-brace pattern on the back, similar to the one used on the top. Many guitars also have a back strip—a length of spruce, or sometimes mahogany, that is glued along the center seam to help keep the two pieces that make up the back from separating. Because the arch shape is so strong and stable, guitars with arched backs never have back braces. A few builders like Boaz Elkayam use back braces that arch like a bridge, and only touch the back at the edges and one or two places in the middle. These builders feel that this system offers structural support while allowing the back to vibrate more freely.

Lining

The lining is the thin strip of triangular-shaped wood that provides a gluing surface, and runs along the seams where the top and back join the sides. The lining can be made of spruce, cedar, mahogany, or basswood. Linings can be made from a single piece of smooth wood and bent into shape, which is fairly common on classical guitars, or it can be made from a piece of wood with a series of saw cuts that make it more flexible. This style of lining is sometimes called "kerfing." Many guitars made in Spain and Latin America use linings made from many separate blocks of triangular wood.

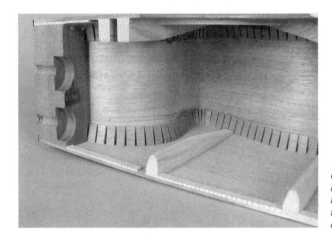

Cut in half, this Taylor body allows a view of its kerfing, which connects the sides with the back and top.

Side Reinforcements

On guitars with solid sides, the luthier will sometimes reinforce each side with small strips of cloth, or perhaps small wooden braces. These don't affect the sound at all, but they do stop cracks and splits from spreading. Because plywood doesn't split, guitars with laminated sides don't need reinforcement.

Endblock

The endblock, sometimes called the tailblock, is a piece of wood set inside the lower bout of the guitar where the sides join together. The endblock is usually made of mahogany. On many steel-string guitars, a strap button is attached to the neckblock. On older guitars, and modern guitars without pickups, the strap button fits into a tapered hole drilled into the endblock and is held in place by friction.

On acoustic guitars with pickups, the jack and strap button is an integral piece. On these instruments, a hole is drilled completely through the endblock so the wiring can be fed into the interior of the guitar. Very few guitars have the strap button held in place by a screw. Because classical- and flamenco-guitar technique require the player to be seated, nylon-string guitars almost never have strap buttons. A few modern builders will make the endblock out of laminated wood for extra strength.

Neckblock

The neckblock, sometimes called the headblock, is the large piece of wood that the neck fits into. The neckblock is almost always made of mahogany. On classical guitars built in the Spanish tradition, the neckblock is an integral part of the neck—and the sides, back, and top are actually built around the neckblock. The neckblock has two extensions: one that runs under the fretboard, and the other that extends two or three inches onto the back. The shape of this extension has led luthiers to call this neckblock style the "Spanish boot" or "Spanish foot." On most steel-strings, and on many classical guitars built in Austria, Germany, France, and Italy, the neckblock is built into the body separately from the neck. In this case, the neckblock will be carved with a slot to accept the dovetail joint or the tenon of a mortise-and-tenon. On bolt-on necks, the neckblock will have two holes drilled through it.

Martin's HD-28CW (Clarence White model) features herringbone binding.

Binding

The strips of plastic or wood inlaid around the outside of the top and back of the guitar are called "binding." The small strips of wood, marquetry, or pearl inlaid between the binding and the wood on the top or back are called "purfling." (For example, on a Martin HD-28, the white plastic trim is the binding and the herringbone strip is the purfling.) Binding is more than decorative, in that it helps protect the corners of the guitar from cracking when they are accidentally bumped. Binding also keeps the endgrain of the top and back near the neckblock and tailblock from absorbing moisture. Some Martins with mahogany tops have no binding at all. Some inexpensive guitars made in the 1930s by Gibson were only bound on the top and not the back. On some very cheap guitars, the binding is just painted on. In the 19th century, some expensive guitars were bound in ivory, which, because it was brittle, didn't offer much protection. In the 1920s, luthiers began using celluloid that had the same color and grain as ivory. This material is called "ivoroid" or "French ivory."

Binding is glued to the body, and held in place with tape and rope (at the Martin factory).

Center Strip

The center strip is the length of purfling that separates the two pieces of wood that make up the back of the guitar. The center strip is purely decorative, and generally matches the purfling that runs around the back. Steel-strings almost always have a center strip of some sort, as do many classical guitars. Archtops never have a center strip running up the back.

Glues and Finishes

Glue

Whether in a large, modern factory, or in an individual luthier's shop, the process of joining wood parts is always performed by hand. Today's most efficient factories use computer controlled machinery to make precision parts and may also have specialized fixtures for assembly, but it is the job of individual handcrafters to apply the adhesive and put the parts together for gluing. With the bewildering array of adhesives available, there are many potential choices for each operation of the guitarmaking process, from the oldest known glue to the most modern catalyzed polymer. A luthier or factory will make these choices based on workability, reliability, application, worker skill, cost, and safety of use.

Hide Glue

Hide glue is exactly what the name implies: an extraction of proteins from animal skins. While there are many specialized glues made from rabbit skin, sturgeon swim bladders, and other exotic animal sources, the primary hides utilized for glue production are from cattle and pigs. Using a combination of steam and acid or alkaline treatment, the collagen protein is extracted from the skins in a form of gelatin (in fact, there is essentially no difference between the "technical gelatin" that is commonly called "hide glue" and the gelatin we eat as food).

The use of hide glue dates from ancient times; and until the 20th century, hide glue was the best adhesive for assembling wood products. Even today, traditional hide glue remains one of the least-expensive glues to manufacture, and is used extensively for making paper products such as corrugated cardboard boxes, envelopes, and sandpaper (when you lick a stamp or the flap of an envelope, you eat a bit of hide glue). When properly used as a wood adhesive, hide glue can develop a tensile strength up to about ten thousand pounds per square inch, which is about the same strength as the strongest modern wood adhesive.

In centuries past, instrument makers used hide glue for the simple reason that it was the best adhesive available among a very short list of choices that included starch pastes and casein (milk) glues. As a matter of training in general woodwork, the techniques of using hide glue were taken for granted. Hide glue must be mixed with cold water and then heated to achieve a smooth consistency. Care must be taken not to allow the glue to become overheated for too long, or it will deteriorate and lose much of its strength. The glue must be applied while it is hot (140 degrees Fahrenheit), and parts must be clamped before it starts to set to a gel state. In order to keep the glue liquid as parts are assembled, it is customary to work in an uncomfortably hot room, and to warm the parts as well. Hide glue is particularly sensitive to contamination and/or oxidation of the gluing surfaces, so it is desirable to sand or scrape the surface of the parts prior to gluing. Hide glue has essentially no cohesive strength (the ability to fill gaps in the woodwork) so parts must fit perfectly to obtain the best joint strength. Hide glue carries with it a high water content, which can cause wood parts to swell, requiring a long drying time and calculation to avoid deformation.

Today, hide glue is considered one of the most difficult adhesives to master for woodworking because we have such an impressive array of synthetic products with many desirable qualities and ease of application. So why do some modern makers still use the stuff? Hide glue does have a couple of very important characteristics that make it an ideal instrument glue. First, it dries completely hard and rigid. Unlike aliphatic resin or PVA glue, hide glue will never stretch, even microscopically, which may allow parts to slide, particularly in the high heat of a parked car. Even the slightest amount of glue "flow" can allow a guitar neck to bend forward under string tension and create a permanent warp. Hide glue is extremely heat resistant. Again, in heat stress, a bridge, neck, or other joint is far less likely to deform as a result of glue failure. Epoxy and regular wood glues all tend to fail catastrophically above 160 degrees Fahrenheit, where hide glue will remain rigid far beyond that range. Unlike other wood adhesives, hide glue dries and sets entirely by evaporation, so an old hide-glue joint may be revitalized by the addition of a hot, diluted glue solution, which will dissolve the original glue.

Loose neck joints, for example, may be reglued successfully by injecting new hide glue. Some instrument makers feel that the hardness of the dried glue contributes to tone propagation between the various parts of a guitar.

Today, none of the three largest American manufacturers—Martin, Taylor, or Gibson—uses hide glue for any part of assembling their instruments. Even most of the smaller factories, such as Collings and Santa Cruz, use aliphatic resin exclusively. Individual luthiers who build high-end classical guitars or vintage steel-string replicas are the most among the modern builders who have continued the use of hide glue. Hide glue is still used extensively in Latin America, but that is most likely a matter of cost and availability.

White Glue

Most of today's guitars are produced in quantity by factories, both large and small. The difficulty in working with hide glue eventually caused most of the factories to switch to modern wood adhesives. C.F. Martin, America's most conservative guitar factory, finally made the switch around 1965, when the factory moved to a new, large building, eliminating the heated glue-up room. Production of guitars increased, and it was impractical to continue the tradition of using hide glue. At that time, the choice was made to use aliphatic resin glue, a modern woodworking glue often referred to as "yellow woodworking glue," to differentiate it from the polyvinyl acetate glue (PVA) commonly known as "white glue."

(A bit of confusion arises because the aliphatic resin glue sold to consumers in small quantities is packaged in the same plastic bottles as the PVA glues. To avoid confusion on store shelves, the aliphatic resin glue usually has a yellow tint added. In fact, the aliphatic resin glue used in the guitar factories is white in color, just as is the PVA consumer glue. It's not all that significant, but when a guitar factory says, "We use white glue," it may mean either type. In the following discussion, I'll use "white glue" in the same way, to mean either PVA or aliphatic resin, because they have so many similarities.)

White glue is the ideal instrument glue from a factory standpoint. It is strong and very easy to use. It cleans up with water and is relatively non-toxic. Workers need no special training to use it, and working temperature is not critical. White glue has the same low-cohesive strength as hide glue, so it is still necessary for parts to fit well and to be clamped properly so as to squeeze out any excess glue from the joint. Drying time is shorter than with hide glue, and parts may be unclamped sooner, which can speed production. The wood parts absorb less water from the glue, making certain operations a bit more predictable. And white glue is relatively inexpensive, so cost is not a factor in making the choice.

It is often necessary to take apart glue joints for various repair operations such as neck resetting, bridge regluing, and structural restoration. Curiously, white glue has the reputation of making a joint that is much more difficult to disassemble than a hide glue joint. In fact, while the two types of glues present different problems, neither is appreciably less desirable from the standpoint of disassembly for repair. For example, a dovetail neck joint made with white glue is just as easily disassembled by steam injection as one made with hide glue. Hide glue is less water resistant, and white glue is more easily disassembled with heat.

All in all, white glue is the dominant adhesive used in the acoustic guitar industry for factories of all sizes and individual builders as well. That makes sense both from the logical consideration of its working characteristics, and the fact that it has been two generations since the use of hide glue has been taught as a part of school woodworking courses.

Solvent Glue

Many acoustic guitars have celluloid and plastic parts, such as pickguards and bindings, which are glued to the necks or bodies. The customary glue used for this purpose is a kind of plastic dissolved in a solvent that is common to the plastic part as well. Thus, celluloid dissolved in acetone makes a fine glue to adhere celluloid to wood. This kind of glue has been used for the last hundred years to glue celluloid bindings on the edges of guitar bodies and necks.

In general, it is necessary to use a solvent-type of glue to get good adhesion between plastic and wood parts. Plastic is very unlikely to be held by hide or white glue alone. Care must be used when working with these adhesives because of the toxic and volatile solvents. Additionally, the solvents can cause the plastic parts to swell considerably. If too much glue is used, the plastic binding will swell before it is sanded to be level during the finishing process. Then, as solvents evaporate over the following weeks, the binding will shrink back to an unattractive level. Too little glue, and the solvent action won't be enough to allow good adhesion between the parts. Solvent alone can also act as a good adhesive, particularly for plastic bindings that must be "welded" together to form decorative layers or to hide the joints where ends meet.

Epoxy

Since its invention around 1939, epoxy resin has been an increasingly important adhesive in many industries, and it eventually made its way into acoustic guitar production. It was the first of a class of modern adhesives that cures by chemical reaction rather than evaporation. Epoxy is a two-part liquid which, when mixed, forms a very strong, solid polymer mass. Unlike hide and white glues, there is no solvent to evaporate or to be absorbed by the wood. The resin hardens without shrinking, so it is the ideal gap-filling adhesive. In fact, the polymer is so strong that it isn't strictly necessary to clamp the parts being joined. The parts need not actually touch, because the cured resin has at least as much strength as the wood surrounding it. Epoxy is ideal for use with dissimilar materials, such as the steel carbon filament reinforcement used as stiffening rods in guitar necks. It makes a good filler material for inlay work, and is sometimes used as an open-pore, woodgrain-filling material in the finishing process. Some makers like epoxy because it contains no water, so parts don't deform from water absorption as they are glued.

Epoxy is expensive and messy to use, and cleanup requires the use of solvents that are at least mildly toxic. The cured resin is resistant to any commonly used solvents, so disassembly of some epoxy joints is considered impossible for practical purposes. Regluing damaged epoxy joints can be problematic because of poor adhesion between the new and old glue.

Super Glue

Cyanoacrylate, commonly called "super glue," has been around almost as long as epoxy, but it wasn't on the market officially until 1958, and not commonly available until much later than that. Like epoxy, it cures by a chemical reaction, solidifying into a solid with high-cohesive strength. It is available as a liquid with a very low viscosity, so it can be used to seal microscopic cracks in exotic hardwoods, such as Brazilian rosewood and ebony. This feature alone makes cyanoacrylate an important part of the guitar industry, saving innumerable pieces of rare woods that might otherwise have been discarded for cosmetic reasons.

Cyanoacrylate is legendary in its ability to cure quickly. We've all heard the stories of users getting stuck in their own glue! The speed of use makes cyanoacrylate an irresistible choice where speed of production is a major consideration. It sticks to all kinds of materials, including a variety of plastics, making it a good choice for gluing binding and purfling. It sets hard and rigid, so it also makes a good glue for frets (while no glue really sticks to metal, the cyanoacrylate runs into the fret slots and bonds to the wood of the fingerboard, filling gaps and helping to hold the frets in place mechanically). Some high-production factories even glue acoustic guitar bridges right on top of the finished surface of the guitar using a thicker-viscosity cyanoacrylate.

Acetone is a common solvent for cleanup, and it is also a solvent for the cured cyanoacrylate.

Conclusion

One large Asian guitar factory uses white glue for the entire guitar construction because of its workability and convenience, with three exceptions. Plastic bindings are glued with plastic solvent glue. The dovetail neck joint is set with epoxy because it is not necessary to make the joint perfectly, or to shim it until it fits tightly—the epoxy simply fills up all the gaps and holds well. Hide glue is the choice for the fingerboard, to help keep the neck rigid and straight even if the guitar is exposed to excessive heat while tuned to pitch. These are good examples of making logical choices for each application.

A manufacturer of fine, higher-priced guitars would probably not choose an epoxy for the neck joint because of the eventual need for removal and resetting of the neck. A more costly, well-fitted dovetail or bolted neck joint would be more appropriate.

Finishes

Almost any guitarmaker will tell you that the most difficult and frustrating part of the guitar-building process is the finish. The finish is the first thing a player or potential buyer experiences, and it can have a profound effect on the desirability of a guitar. It's a bit ironic, because most players believe that the finish is not as important as either tone or playability.

Historically, guitars have been finished with materials and techniques that were common to other woodworking industries, such as furniture making. In Stradivari's day, it was common for violinmakers to formulate and make their own varnishes, and that practice was common among cabinetmakers as well. As modern finishes have become a part of standard woodworking, they have been adopted by large guitar factories first, and later by individual luthiers.

French Polish

In the 19th century, guitars were customarily finished with shellac, using a process called "French polishing." Shellac is the oldest known clear finish for wood, dating back to the time of the Egyptian pharaohs. It is a resin secreted by *laccifera lacca*, a small insect also known as the "lac" bug. In India and Thailand, these insects infest certain indigenous trees, eventually forming huge masses of secretion that covers entire limbs. The resin is harvested by hand by scraping the resin from the limbs. After it is refined and bleached, the shellac resin is packaged and sold as flakes ranging in color from a dark orange-brown to nearly colorless. The shellac resin is mildly soluble only in alcohol. Dissolved in alcohol, shellac is sometimes known as "spirit varnish" or "shellac varnish." Other, softer and more elastic natural gums and resins, such as copal or sandarac, may be added to give the shellac a bit more elasticity or toughness.

Shellac is the oldest type of wood finish, and it starts out as flakes.

Shellac resin has an interesting feature in common with hide glue: It is another guitarmaking product we have all eaten. Shellac is the shiny coating on many medication tablets, candies, and other food items.

French polishing is an ancient technique of applying shellac by hand-rubbing. This technique takes advantage of the fact that shellac is only mildly soluble in alcohol. The finisher uses a thick cloth pad and rubs on a coat of a dilute shellac solution. Immediately, the alcohol starts to evaporate, leaving a microscopic layer of shellac on the surface. Within seconds, the finisher wipes again, and again, slowly building up a sticky film. As the film gets sticky, a drop or two of lubricating oil, such as linseed oil, provides a barrier between the wet shellac pad and the drying surface on the wood. After hundreds of passes with the shellac pad, a significant layer of finish is left on the surface.

Sessions of French polishing proceed with days of drying, until the desired finish is achieved. It is brought to its final gloss by a process called "spiriting off," in which the polisher uses only alcohol on the rubbing pad, lubricated with a bit of oil on the surface. As the pad moves across the surface, it removes tiny streaks and high spots, leaving a level finish with a fine reflective shine. This is another classic woodworking technique that takes a lot of instruction and practice in order to master. Today, French polishing is sometimes thought of as a lost art by many modern woodworking enthusiasts, even though it is still a primary style of guitar finishing in parts of the world where solvents, lacquer, and spray equipment are in short supply.

Before the 20th century, French polishing was known as the finest of all finishes. It is important to put that comment in a historical context. It was, indeed, the most level and shiny wood finish, because the other techniques included less sophisticated rubbing and brushing, both of which left characteristic marks behind. With today's spray equipment, synthetic finishes, and buffing equipment, it is commonplace to produce a finish of higher gloss and clarity than a French-polished shellac finish. Many guitarmakers believe that the thinner the finish, the less likely it is to have a detrimental effect on tone. French polishing allows the finisher to produce a high-gloss finish that is only a fraction of the thickness of a modern lacquer finish. Shellac finishes are more resistant to cold and less resistant to heat than nitrocellulose lacquers or polyester finishes. The player's body heat may be enough to soften the finish on the back of a French-polished guitar, and the finish may blister in the high heat of a parked car.

Nonetheless, French polish has the right romantic ring about it. It tugs at our nostalgic longings, and it has a soft glow all its own. Perhaps because it is applied in such a thin layer, some makers and players feel it is important to the tone of a guitar, particularly for the tops of classical guitars. Clearly, something that has this kind of skill attached with its application is special in today's world!

French-polished shellac finishes can be repaired by the same technique by which they are applied. It is not unreasonable to add a bit more finish from time to time as it wears away or is injured. Unfortunately it is by far the most easily injured and worn of any finish, and the repairs can be expensive. While it is theoretically possible to apply shellac by spraying, it is not practical. Shellac simply does not flow out evenly as does paint and lacquer, but instead tends to "gather" and run, causing more difficulty than the French polish application. The shellac resin has an extremely long life as a wood finish because it does not deteriorate appreciably with age.

Nitrocellulose Lacquer

The first entirely synthetic finish, nitrocellulose lacquer consists of a clear, plastic resin dissolved in various petroleum distillates. It was first developed by DuPont as an automobile finish, and was quickly adopted by the woodworking industry. By about 1930, nitrocellulose lacquer had replaced most French polishing in American steel-string guitar factories. Like shellac, nitrocellulose lacquer dries entirely by evaporation, leaving a film behind. Because it is usually applied by spraying, the lacquer film tends to be level and uniform, and builds up easily on the surface. Once it has dried, the lacquer can be sanded and polished with abrasives and buffed with power equipment to produce a perfectly level, high shine.

Chemical additives result in finishes appearing anywhere from a dull satin to super high gloss.

Compared to French polishing, lacquer requires far less training and skill, and it saves a terrific amount of time, particularly in the factory setting. Lacquer accepts a wide variety of transparent dyes, opaque pigments, and even metallic flakes to produce the widest variety of finish colors and styles of any type of wood finish. Chemical additives can be used to make the lacquer dry with a high-gloss or "dead-flat" finish, or any degree of "satin" between the two. In most situations, the low-gloss finish is used to save time and money on modestly priced instruments because it saves the labor-intensive steps of leveling and polishing. A low-gloss finish is often preferred as a matter of personal taste, or to avoid reflections when an instrument is played under the intense lighting on stage.

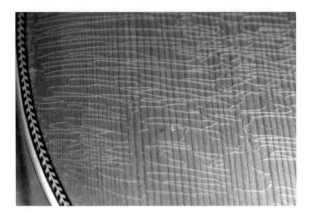

Cracks in the finish can be the result of poor application, or be caused by extreme temperatures.

If the lacquer is applied too thickly, or if the formulation is not correct, it will develop long cracks, or "checks," very quickly as the coating begins to shrink with age. Sudden exposure to cold can also cause finish checking, as will prolonged exposure to sunlight. The thinner the finish, the less likely it is to crack with temperature changes. Old lacquer finishes become less resistant to water and abrasion. As the lacquer ages, it loses volatile components and becomes more brittle, presumably decomposing altogether, eventually. As with adhesives and the plastic components that may replace wood, ivory, or bone parts, the synthetic finishes have a shorter lifespan than their natural predecessors such as shellac.

Because nitrocellulose lacquer is an evaporative finish, it can always be redissolved in its original solvent. At any time, a new layer of lacquer can be applied, and it will melt right into the original finish, amalgamating with it and becoming a seamless part of the original. With care, a luthier can do nearly perfect touchups and finish-blending on a high-gloss nitrocellulose finish. It is much more difficult to touch up a satin or low-gloss finish because it is nearly impossible to recreate the uniformly dulled surface. In most cases, it is necessary to cover the surface with a new coating of low-gloss lacquer to avoid having an uneven or blotchy appearance.

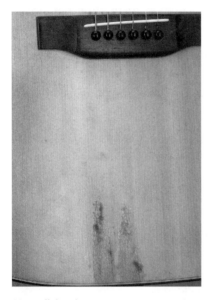

Nitrocellulose lacquer can react to certain materials such as vinyl. This Martin's finish was damaged by prolonged contact with a guitar strap.

Nitrocellulose lacquer is more resistant to body heat and scratches, and is generally more wear-resistant than shellac. It does, however, react to a wide variety of chemical influences, including human perspiration, which, depending on the individual, may soften the lacquer film to the point of becoming sticky (on an acoustic guitar, this usually means the neck and the area where the playing arm crosses the face of the guitar). The only real cure for this problem is to refinish the neck or other area with a different type of finish—usually a more modern, inert surface coating. Other agents, such as the rubber or vinyl pads on guitar stands, or vinyl guitar straps, can have the same effect, causing spots of softness, or even blisters to appear in the lacquer.

Vinyl damage usually does not require refinishing whole surfaces because, unlike the player, the vinyl can be removed from contact with the guitar. It is usually sufficient to remove the affected lacquer by careful application of solvent, and to touch up the area by applying new lacquer, and leveling and blending it with the surrounding surface.

Catalyzed Polymer Finishes

Today most factory-made guitars are finished with a variety of catalyzed polymer materials. Some of these finishes work like epoxy, with a two-part mixture that reacts to form a relatively inert polymer coating on the wood. While this type of finish is very effective, it presents special problems in handling. Care must be exercised to keep it from clogging spray equipment, for example. Newer, more convenient finishes have been developed that consist of a liquid that is catalyzed once it has been sprayed on the surface of the wood. Some are, like the cyanoacrylate glues, catalyzed by atmospheric moisture. Once they are sprayed, the reaction begins, and in a relatively short time, the finish is fully hardened. Because atmospheric moisture is pretty much everywhere, it is difficult to keep these finishes fresh and usable once the container has been opened.

Currently, the most popular, convenient, and effective catalyzed finish uses very specific, high-intensity ultraviolet light as a curing agent. The finish remains in a liquid state indefinitely unless exposed to this specific light radiation, so it is easily kept fresh and ready to use. Exposed to the light, it cures completely in less than a minute, so it lends itself perfectly to high-volume factory production. It is, however, among the more toxic finishes so extra ventilation and care are required for its use. Additionally, the high-intensity light is dangerous, so the worker must be protected from the radiation. It is common for finishers to wear complete isolation suits and masks when working with this kind of finish.

Most guitar factories still spray finish by hand.

The catalyzed finishes have very desirable characteristics as coatings for acoustic guitars. They are perfectly clear and can be polished to a very high gloss, or they can have flatting agents added to achieve any degree of satin or dull surface when they harden. Catalyzed finishes will accept a full range of pigments and dyes to achieve almost any level of transparency or color desired. Properly handled, the finish can be applied in the same thickness as conventional nitrocellulose lacquer, and can look just the same. There is no hard evidence suggesting that the finish is detrimental to tone when properly applied.

A body is sprayed at Larrivée.

It is common for inexpensive guitars to have very thick catalyzed finishes that cover flaws in the woodworking, and that are easily handled with power-sanding and buffing equipment. For this reason, the catalyzed finishes have developed an association with cheaper, poorly made instruments. Some musicians mistakenly assume that it is the finish that causes these instruments to be inferior to those made with nitrocellulose lacquer, so it has taken the high-quality acoustic guitar industry a while to overcome a prejudice against polymer finishes. Finally, though, even the most conservative producers are starting to accept and use this type of finish.

Catalyzed polymer coatings have all the desirable characteristics needed in an acoustic guitar finish. They are extremely scratch resistant, and have no susceptibility to chemical agents such as perspiration, vinyl, or rubber. They can be applied quickly and economically, and have much less tendency to check with exposure to undesirable temperature changes. While their ultimate longevity is not known, it is presumed that catalyzed polymer finishes will far outlast nitrocellulose lacquer.

The only undesirable quality is a matter of repairability. Touching up a catalyzed finish is problematic because there are no solvents to melt the surface so that the new material may be blended with the original finish. The most common material used in repairing these finishes is cyanoacrylate glue, which cures to a clear solid that nearly matches the polyester finish in hardness. It adheres well to the surface, but since it does not actually blend with it, there is always a telltale line between the original finish and the repair. In order to get a "seamless" look and avoid a detectible line between new and old finish, it is necessary to add a full coating to an entire surface, such as a back or side of a guitar. But, compared to lacquer and shellac, there is less often a need for such touch-up finish work. As with many other technological advances, the cost of catalyzed finishes and the specialized ultraviolet light equipment has become low enough to be affordable for individual luthiers. Year by year, we see more use of these modern finishes.

Colored Finishes

It is impossible to think of colored guitar finishes without associating them with the instruments made by Gibson. Starting with black-faced guitars at the company's inception in 1902, Gibson has led the way with brightly colored instruments. Before Gibson's influence, the coloring used on guitars followed the violin-making tradition of using natural transparent colors to tint the finish. And, the guitar factories used the colors and finishing techniques common to furniture-making at the time, such as using a reddish-brown stain on mahogany, or "faux grain" painting to cover inexpensive, plain woods.

Before the Great War, Gibson had made instruments with black or white painted tops, and had developed the first colored finish that would become their trademark and a standard of the acoustic guitar industry. It was a shaded coloration that blended from a bright yellow stain in the center of the instrument to very dark red at the edges. The instrument's sides were similarly colored, with yellow highlights at the upper and lower bouts, shading to dark red at the waist, neck area, and endblock.

It seems likely that the inspiration for this coloring might have come from observing the pattern of wear on old violins, where years of handling causes the finish to become thin in various areas, producing a characteristic light and dark shaded finish. For centuries, it had been a common practice to make replicas of the great Italian violins, even to the point of duplicating the pattern of worn-finish coloration. Gibson's first shaded finish was on a mandolin, and it was more in the style of these violin finishes. Only a few years later, the coloration was given much more lively tones and a symmetrical pattern. The "sunburst" finish had been born!

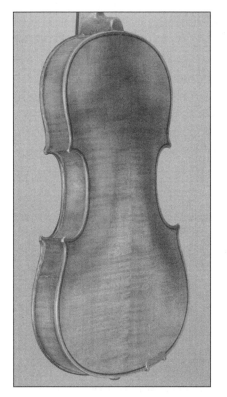 

Violins may have been the inspiration for color or sunburst finishes. Gibson first used a sunburst finish with its early mandolins.

The first sunburst finishes were colored stains applied directly to the wood by rubbing, followed by a hand-applied varnish or French-polished clear coating. Before long, the red gave way to a dark walnut brown; and as soon as nitrocellulose lacquer became the standard spray finish, the hand-rubbed coloring was

A Gibson sunburst finish.

changed to a spray technique. Various layers of tinted lacquer were applied to develop the sunburst shading, and then clear lacquer was applied over the entire instrument in the conventional manner.

Around 1930, the sunburst finish had become such a standard that most guitar companies offered such colored guitars as standard models, or at least made them available on special order. When solid-body electric guitars became a force in the guitar industry, a whole new revolution in color followed. Les Paul had asked Gibson to make an instrument with a top of metallic golden lacquer. Fender offered guitar bodies in various automotive paint colors. In subsequent decades, there have been brief periods of popularity of colored guitars, including special commemorative instruments.

8 Body Hardware

Pickguards (Scratchplates)

Due to their original popularity as pure rhythm instruments played with a flatpick, the majority of steel-string guitars feature some kind of pickguard. The pickguard serves an important function by protecting the instrument's top from getting scratched, or even worn through, by a pick whose attack goes beyond its intended target.

Although some form of top protection can be found on very early guitars, pickguards as we know them today first came into widespread use on Italian mandolins during the 18th century. Played exclusively with a flatpick, these instruments were subject to far more abuse than the tenderly strummed guitars of the day. Often covering the entire area between the soundhole and the bridge, and featuring ornate decorations such as flowers, cherubim, and butterflies, these pickguards (often made from tortoise shell) were as much a blank canvas for the maker to add his original touch as they were a way of protecting the top. While rare on European guitars of the era, American luthiers began using similar pickguards on their guitars in the late 19th century. Because the preferred playing technique of the day involved planting the little finger of the picking hand on the top, these also became known as "finger-rests."

With the development of steel strings and subsequent changes in guitar design and playing styles, pickguards began covering a greater area around the treble side of the soundhole, and away from places were it wasn't really needed, such as directly under the strings. Martin began using this type of asymmetrical pickguard as a stock feature on its OM model, which, as its name implies (Orchestra Model), was originally intended to hold down the rhythm in large bands.

Besides protecting the instrument, the pickguard also gives the maker of the guitar an opportunity to identify his or her signature style. Just like the shape of a headstock, a pickguard will often have a distinctive look that identifies a manufacturer or model. Good examples of this are found in Taylor's trademarked design, as well as the small teardrop identifying a Martin OM, or the elaborately decorated pickguard of a Gibson Hummingbird.

Pickguards give the instrument's maker a chance to deliver a personal statement. Early mandolins in particular offered highly decorated pickguards.

Pickguards on Flattops

Most flattop guitars feature pickguards that are glued directly to the top of the instrument. Originally made out of celluloid, pickguards are now most often made out of a more modern form of plastic. Due to the fact that celluloid easily gets very brittle and warped with age, plastic is really a better material in the first place.

Many vintage guitars—in particular Martins built before 1985—feature pick-guards that are glued directly to the top's bare wood, prior to finishing. Unfortunately, this method often leads to problems as the instrument ages. The most serious of these is a tendency for the wood at the pickguard's edge to develop cracks due to different rates of expansion between the wood and the celluloid in various climates. Because the older celluloid pickguards also tend to shrink as they reach a certain age, they often result in an outline of bare wood showing around their perimeter, necessitating a partial refinishing of the instrument. A few guitar companies who build exact copies of pre-war Martins still attach their pickguards in this manner, even though it offers no sonic benefits and is virtually guaranteed to result in necessary repairs down the road.

Most manufacturers today use plastic pickguards that feature a self-adhesive backing made by 3M. These are very easy to install (even at a later time if a guitar didn't come with a pickguard); and the fact that their glue isn't ultra-strong turns out to be an advantage, as the pickguard will usually come lose before causing cracks or other damage.

Some flattops feature "double" pickguards, one on each side of the soundhole, with Gibson's Everly Brothers model probably being the most famous example. However, while double pickguards certainly protect a larger area of the top from even the wildest Pete Townsend–inspired strumming, their weight and rigidity can also have a deadening effect on the sound. Double pickguards are also sometimes found on guitars that have been converted for left-hand use. In this case, possible problems with the removal of the existing guard are avoided by simply adding a matching second one in the opposite location.

If you feel that protection of the top is important, but aren't fond of the way most pickguards look, then you might want to check out clear pickguards. Used extensively by companies such as Larrivée and Lowden, these pickguards are barely visible, allowing the beauty of the wood's grain to show through.

*Distinctive pickguard from various builders: (clockwise from top left):
Martin dreadnought, Taylor, Gibson Hummingbird, Guild.*

The Gibson Everly Brothers double pickguard (shown here on an Epiphone copy).

Pickguards on Archtop Guitars

Because it is difficult to glue a pickguard directly to a top with multiple curves and interfering *f*-holes, most archtop guitars use a "floating" pickguard. As a leftover from the days when players routinely rested their little fingers on their guitars, archtop pickguards are also sometimes called "finger-rests." Usually mounted to the end of the fingerboard and a metal bracket attached to the waist of the instrument, these pickguards don't touch the top at all. Similar to the pickguards on flattop guitars, these guards were originally made out of celluloid (and sometimes tortoise shell); but today, plastic or hardwood (such as ebony) is the preferred material. If wood is used, it often matches the fretboard and a wooden tailpiece. Because floating pickguards aren't glued to a supporting surface, they tend to be fairly thick: a 1/8-inch for wooden examples not being unusual. Although many of these pickguards are nothing more than a piece of the chosen material cut to shape, in some cases they become pieces of art in their own right. Multiple binding (similar to the way a body or headstock might be bound), and elaborate inlays can contribute significantly to the appearance of the guitar, as well as to its asking price.

In the case of archtops that are equipped with floating pickups, the pickguard becomes the platform to which the electronics are mounted. Although the pickup itself is often attached directly to the end of the fingerboard, the pickguard will generally hold volume and tone controls, and sometimes even the output jack.

Floating pickguards on a Benedetto (left) and a vintage Gibson (right).

Floating Pickguards on Flattop Guitars

There are a few instances were archtop-style floating pickguards are used on flattop guitars. Although unusual on contemporary instruments, this style was popular with certain makers and models in the past. Many old Stella guitars, some Gibsons, and even resonator instruments such as National's Trojan can be found with this style of pickguard. Because of the way a flattop's geometry differs from an archtop (mainly a much smaller distance between the strings and the guitar's top), many players find that this design gets in the way of their picking technique. For this reason, flattops that were originally built with floating pickguards have often had them removed or replaced with more standard designs.

Golpeador on Flamenco Guitars

Due to the rhythmic strumming style employed by flamenco players, the guitars used for this music are protected by a *golpeador*. Similar to the pickguard on flattop steel-strings, the golpeador is usually made from a sheet of thin plastic that is glued to the top (some contemporary luthiers also use thin hardwood veneers). Traditionally, the golpeador covers a large area ranging from the space between the soundhole and the bridge, as well as both sides of the soundhole. Many less aggressive players find that it's sufficient to only cover the treble section of the guitar, leaving a greater area of the top uncovered to vibrate freely. Many classical players also add a smaller version of a golpeador on their instruments if they occasionally venture into flamenco techniques.

Most flamenco guitars are protected by a golpeador, which is often made out of clear plastic.

Temporary Pickguards

In certain instances, it's impractical to install a permanent pickguard. Reasons for this could include wanting to avoid altering a vintage instrument, or a fear that a pickguard will affect the sound of the guitar. In these cases, a temporary pickguard is the ideal solution. Made from ultra-thin, clear Mylar, these pickguards can be easily cut to size, and cling to the instrument via static electricity. Because some guitars' finishes will react to the prolonged contact with Mylar, it's important to not leave this type of pickguard in place during periods when the guitar isn't played.

Adding or Removing a Pickguard on a Flattop Guitar

If your flattop guitar didn't come with a pickguard, then it's usually an easy matter to add one should you find it necessary. Most guitar stores sell a variety of shapes and styles, and it's generally a matter of simply removing the pickguard's adhesive backing and sticking it into place. It's important to make sure that the area where the pickguard is to be mounted is absolutely clean, as it won't stick well to a dirty or greasy surface.

Sometimes it becomes necessary to remove a pickguard. This could be because the size or style isn't what's desired, or because a section has come lose and warped on its own, making a replacement necessary. If the pickguard in question is on a guitar that used the older method of gluing the guard directly to the bare wood, then this job is best left to a professional to avoid damage to the top. However, on most modern guitars, it's reasonably easy to remove a pickguard that's glued to the finish. Generally, a little heat from a hairdryer is all that's needed to make the glue soft enough to gently pull it off. In some cases, it's also possible to use a solvent, such as naphtha or lighter fluid (which is safe on most finishes), to loosen the adhesive.

Besides the obvious fact of reduced protection, there is another consideration if you plan to remove a pickguard altogether. Unless the guitar in question is brand new, it's quite possible for the finish that was covered by the guard to have aged differently than the areas exposed to light. This usually results in a "tan line," were the space previously occupied by the pickguard is visible due to a much lighter color. If there is only a slight difference, then the colors will eventually blend; but on many older guitars, it's impossible to remove the pickguard's outline, leaving an undesirable shape of a different color on the guitar.

While the removal off an archtop's pickguard usually involves nothing more than the extraction of a couple of screws, adding one to a pickguard-less guitar can be a bit tricky. Unless the guitar already has pre-drilled mounting holes, and you have found a perfect-sized match, it's probably best left to a professional, as there are too many available shapes and sizes to offer a generic fit.

Strap Buttons

If you're planning on playing your guitar standing up, then you'll need some hardware to attach a shoulder strap. Traditionally, most steel-string guitars feature an endpin made out of hardwood, plastic, or ivory in the endblock of the body. Usually held in place by way of friction, this pin (which looks a bit like an oversized bridge pin) allows the attachment of one end of the strap—the other end of which was originally tied to the headstock of the guitar. In more recent years, most players have discovered that the guitar hangs in a more comfortable position if both ends of the strap can be fastened to the body. For this purpose, a strap button is mounted to either the heel of the neck or the bass-side of the upper bout of the body. Some contemporary manufacturers (such as Seagull) have stopped using traditional endpins completely, and are installing a strap button at the end of the guitar as well.

On guitars that are equipped with a pickup, the rear part of the strap is usually attached to an *endpin jack* (more on these in the "Pickups and Electronics" chapter of this book). Designed to replace a traditional endpin, an endpin jack allows the installation of a jack for the pickup with minimum modifications to the instrument.

Players who are concerned about their straps coming lose during a performance sometimes use "strap locks" on their guitars. Available from companies such as Schaller and Dunlop, strap locks use a simple mechanism that can't be removed unless a small button is pulled (on the Schaller) or pushed (on the Dunlop). While these systems are very popular with electric players, they're only occasionally seen on acoustics, as they don't work with endpin jacks, and often have an awkward fit if one of the buttons is attached to the heel of the neck.

Two options for attaching a second strap button: Next to the heel in the side (top), and the most common placement right into the heel (bottom).

Installing Strap Buttons

Installing a strap button is easy, but there are several factors to consider. If the guitar in question doesn't already have an endpin (such as most nylon-string guitars), then it usually makes more sense to install a standard screw-on type strap button, rather than taking the more complicated route of fitting a traditional endpin. The most important thing to check for this kind of installation is to make sure that the guitar's endblock (the piece of wood that reinforces the inside of the guitar where the two sides meet) is strong enough to support the weight of the instrument hanging off its strap. It's rare for this to pose a problem (mostly in the case of some classical guitars), but if there are any doubts, it would be a good idea to have a luthier check it out. To install the button, all that's necessary is to drill a pilot hole, slightly smaller in size than the wood screw that's used in the fastening. A few pieces of masking tape should be used to protect the surrounding area from being scratched by an accidental slip of the drill. Screwing in the button completes this simple procedure. For a really slick job, a small washer made out of leather or felt can be placed between the button and the wood.

Mounting the second button follows the same procedure, but there are more factors to consider when choosing the exact placement. The most common location for the button is on the treble side of the neck's heel. Mounted in this place, the button allows the guitar to hang well-balanced, and provides a secure anchoring point for the strap.

Sometimes the strap button will be mounted into the heelcap of the guitar. Some players feel that this location is less distracting for playing in the upper neck positions, but this benefit is offset by the fact that the guitar may then have a tendency to fall forward when attached in this manner. Another disadvantage of this placement is that the exposed button tends to chew up the inside of the guitar's case over time.

Another possibility for mounting the strap button is directly into the guitar's side, adjacent to the neck's heel. There are no disadvantages to this placement, but mounting the button in this manner requires reinforcement inside the body, as the thin sides don't provide enough support for the mounting screw. On some guitars, the width of the neckblock extends into the sides, in which case it can provide a secure base for the button.

If the guitar in question has a bolt-on neck, it is important to make sure that drilling the pilot hole doesn't interfere with the bolts, as hitting one of them will cause irreparable damage. Most manufacturers will be able to provide a template or measurements for secure drilling, and the bolts can also be found using a strong magnet.

Tailpieces

While most flattop guitars fasten the strings directly to the bridge, archtops generally use a *tailpiece* for this purpose. Similar to the concept of attaching the strings on bowed instruments such as the violin or the cello, a guitar's tailpiece is mounted to the instrument's endblock, and extends approximately halfway toward the bridge.

In the early days, the majority of archtop tailpieces were either made out of thin sheet metal, die-cast metal, or welded from several pieces of thick steel wire. Fancy models include a hinge that allows the tailpiece to automatically assume the perfect angle for holding the strings at tension, while more basic designs feature a fixed attachment. Metal tailpieces are usually mounted to the guitar's endblock with three or four screws, using a centered endpin for additional support.

On the left, the fancy cast tailpiece of a Guild Artist Award. On the right, the simple wire tailpiece on a vintage Gibson archtop.

Starting with the late Jimmy D'Aquisto, many contemporary archtop builders have started using tailpieces made out of ebony—going back to the design originally used on bowed instruments. Lighter in weight, these tailpieces can result in a warmer sound, and their appearance often matches that of the fingerboard. Luthier Bob Benedetto even attaches his tailpieces to the guitar's endpin with cello gut, as he feels that this design contributes to the sound of his highly acclaimed instruments.

Luthier Dale Unger with one of his American Archtop models featuring an ebony tailpiece.

Tailpieces on flattop guitars were once popular on inexpensive instruments, but are rarely seen today. While the use of a tailpiece virtually eliminates the risk of the bridge coming loose, it also results in the strings *pushing* onto the top, rather than *pulling* on it, as is the case with a pin bridge. This has the effect of completely changing the sound of the guitar, usually accompanied by a loss of volume. In some cases, this "inferior" sound has become a classic in the context of certain musical styles, making it desirable for some players. Leadbelly's Stella 12-string is a prime example of this phenomenon, making the guitar a candidate for copies by various modern manufacturers.

The stamped metal tailpiece on a flattop 12-string by Dell'Arte.

Mario Maccaferri designed a fairly simple tailpiece to be used on Selmer guitars. The tailpiece was stamped out of brass, and had an insert of ebony, rosewood, or

237

Bakelite to make it lighter. The tailpiece was set up with six posts which had holes drilled in the middle of them, which allowed the use of either ball-end or loop-end strings. Because the tailpieces were made at the Selmer factory, they were only found on real Selmer guitars. In the 1950s, Bilardi made a rough copy of the Selmer tailpiece that was used by Favino and other builders working in the Selmer tradition. These days, there are a number of people making accurate reproductions of the Selmer tailpiece.

A Selmer/Maccaferri–style tailpiece.

Resonator guitars also use tailpieces to attach the strings. The majority of these instruments use a design that's stamped from sheet metal. In most cases, it is possible to mount the strings either from the top of the tailpiece or the bottom, enabling the player to choose how much pressure the strings exercise on the guitar's cone.

Armrests and Guitar Supports

Although not usually found as standard equipment, armrests and guitar supports are frequent accessories that are added to an instrument.

While there are other designs, the John Pearse Armrest (named by and after the British guitarist-turned-string-and-accessory-manufacturer) is by far the most popular. Mounted to the bass-side of the lower bout with durable, double-stick tape, the armrest is designed to keep the player's right arm (or left arm for left-handed players) from touching the top, allowing it to vibrate more freely.

The John Pearse Armrest.

Guitar supports that attach to the treble-side of the instrument are popular with many classical players. Elevating the guitar into the playing position without the use of a footstool, these supports often allow for a more ergonomic sitting position, which is especially beneficial for people with back problems. Attached with rubber suction cups, the support is easily removable for fitting the guitar in its case.

Pickups and Electronics

9

History

Due to the fact that the acoustic guitar is a comparatively quiet instrument, amplification is a topic that most players have to tackle eventually. Although classical guitarists often perform in large concert halls with no electronic help (made possible in a large part by a well-behaved audience), most steel-string players find that they need more volume than the instrument itself can offer if they venture out of anything but the most intimate venues.

In some situations, a good microphone will be all that's needed to make the link between the guitar and the loudspeakers. Under ideal circumstances—a good PA, a great-sounding room, a performer that sits still while playing, relatively low stage volume requirements—a microphone is clearly the first choice for capturing the instrument's true acoustic voice. Most sound engineers use a small-diaphragm condenser microphone for acoustic guitars, and with a little skill at the mixing board, the results can be outstanding.

However, as any seasoned performer will attest, there are many situations that are far from the ideal we just described, and often a microphone alone will lead to less than desirable results. Feedback, poor sound, and lack of consistency from one venue to the next are just a few of the problems often faced when using microphones alone, any one of which is reason enough to look into ways of joining the ranks of players who plug their guitars in.

With the cornucopia of dedicated acoustic-electric guitars and after-market pickups available to modern players, it's easy to forget the arduous journey it took to get this technology to the advanced stage we enjoy today. Not wanting to take modern convenience for granted, let's take a quick look at the early history of amplified guitars.

Although there is no doubt that others experimented with different ways to electrify the instrument, some of the earliest developments can be traced back to Lloyd Loar's electrostatic pickups of the early 1920s. Working for Gibson at the time, Loar installed his invention in various L-5 archtops (which he also designed); but the company felt that there was no future in the electric guitar, and his efforts received little support. After leaving Gibson, Loar eventually marketed a new magnetic pickup design on his own line of instruments (including an electric viola!) under the ViviTone brand in the 1930s.

However, credit for the first commercially successful electric guitars generally goes to Rickenbacher's (the spelling was later changed to Rickenbacker) early lap steels of the same period. Made for playing the era's popular Hawaiian music, these guitars featured solid bodies and magnetic pickups—the same basic technology that electric guitars use to this day.

Rickenbacher (later spelled Rickenbacker) lap steels were the first widely successful electric guitars.

Because lap-steels are designed to be played horizontally with a slide, their versatility for different kinds of music is limited, and soon players sought ways to install pickups in their regular guitars, thereby creating the first crude acoustic-electrics.

Having developed its own pickup system after Loar's departure, Gibson introduced the ES-150 in 1936. Based on the company's popular 16-inch archtop shape, it had a large magnetic pickup fitted into the top, and controls for volume and tone allowed the player to shape the guitar's sound. Charlie Christian was one of the first players to see the instrument's potential (and today, the Gibson ES-150 is often

Gibson's early ES-150 with a pickup.

called the "Charlie Christian" model). Playing with Benny Goodman, Christian used his amplified guitar to play single-note lines and solos in a way only horn players had been able to before, forever changing the perception of what a guitar is capable of. Gone were the days in which the guitar was relegated to strumming rhythm parts and accompanying folk singers. Electricity gave way to a radical new era.

Having seen the possibilities that amplification offered, countless guitarists were now looking to add electronics to their existing acoustic guitars. Because most jazz cats already played archtops, it was this instrument type that first benefited from after-market pickups. DeArmond introduced what would be by far the most popular choice with its "Guitar Mic" pickup in the 1940s. Mounted to either the end of the fingerboard or the guitar's pickguard, the unit required almost no permanent modifications to the instrument, and its sound became synonymous with jazz guitar. Although the electric guitar obviously made large strides since the introduction of the DeArmond pickup, similar designs are still the standard for acoustic-electric archtops, and original units often sell for sky-high prices on the vintage market.

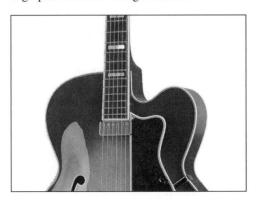

Epiphone Emperor Regent, with a "floating" magnetic pickup.

243

Gibson's J-160E (shown here as a copy by Epiphone) was one of the very first acoustic-electric flattops.

Despite the electric guitar's campaign to revolutionize popular music, successful amplification of flattop and classical guitars proved to be a bigger challenge. Although DeArmond was quick to adapt its archtop pickup to fit into the soundhole of a flattop guitar, it soon became clear that the resulting sound was a far cry from the instrument's complex acoustic voice. Still, as music in general became louder and louder, soundhole pickups became a popular accessory, enabling flattops to hold their own next to screaming Les Pauls and Telecasters.

Both Gibson and Martin made efforts to offer electrified acoustics early on. Introduced in 1951, Gibson's CF-100E featured a modified version of the company's P-90 pickup (the same design used on early Les Pauls and various electric archtops) mounted between the fingerboard and the soundhole, as well as featuring volume and tone controls mounted into the top at the lower bout. As it was also the first Gibson flattop to have a cutaway, the guitar was perhaps too radical for its time, and slow sales caused the model to be discontinued by 1959. However, another acoustic-electric Gibson model would have an impact lasting long after its introduction in 1954. Known to many guitarists as the "John Lennon guitar," the J-160E used the same electronics found in the CF-100E, but offered a more traditional appearance. Built with a thick, ladder-braced, laminated top, the guitar was able to withstand rock 'n' roll volumes without a wince. The reissue J-160E that Gibson started making after 1991 featured solid spruce tops and X-bracing.

Martin followed suit by offering an electric D-18E in 1959. However, while Gibson had found an elegant way of mounting the pickup in such a way that only a small portion showed through the top (the large coils were inside the body), Martin crudely mounted a pair of DeArmond pickups, effectively killing the acoustic sound of the instrument. Although the company would eventually add a 00-18E and D-28E, its questionable aesthetics and poor sound led to a tough sell, and the instruments were discontinued in 1964.

Even though it would take another decade for the technology to be refined, Gibson once again showed a pioneering spirit when it introduced the C-1E in 1960. As a nylon-string guitar, the instrument was already unusual for the company, but it really broke new ground with a new piezo pickup that was mounted in the bridge. Produced until 1967, the model became informally known as the "Charlie Byrd model," due to the fact that it was used for some time by the late bossa nova star. Another early piezo-equipped nylon-string was made by the Baldwin piano company. Played by country stars such as Chet Atkins and Jerry Reed, the guitar quickly gained widespread recognition. Willie Nelson had the Baldwin pickup installed in his Martin nylon-string guitar, and uses this setup to this day.

It took a completely new guitar company to take acoustic guitar amplification to the next level. Founded in 1966, Ovation is a subsidiary of Kaman Aerospace, a company famous for its innovative helicopter designs. Using a fiberglass bowl in place of a traditional wooden back and sides, Ovations were radical even before the company used its advanced electronics know-how to effectively invent the modern acoustic-electric guitar. Besides utilizing a new piezo-electric pickup mounted in the saddle, Ovation also moved the volume control to the side of the instrument, allowing the top to move freely.

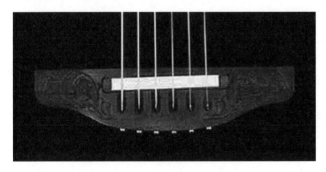

Ovation's original pickup is integrated into the saddle, and uses six individual piezo crystals.

Ovation's concept struck a chord with the market. Continually updating its models, the company practically owned the amplified acoustic market throughout the 1970s, and it remains popular today. While most purists will argue that Ovation's sound is far-fetched from true acoustic timbre, it is undeniable that the guitars offer hassle-free performance, and a sound that is immediately identifiable as that of an acoustic guitar.

Players who didn't adapt to the first wave of factory-built acoustic-electric guitars had few options for retrofitting their existing guitars with a pickup. Barcus Berry had considerable success with its soundboard transducers throughout the 1970s, and several manufacturers (including Bill Lawrence and Schaller) made sound-hole pickups; but in stark contrast with other vintage accessories, most players who remember these units would just as well forget the sonic results of their use.

The next big step in acoustic amplification would arrive in the form of pickups that mounted under the guitar's saddle. Similar in their functionality to the earlier designs by Gibson, Baldwin, and Ovation, these new pickups could be retrofitted to most existing guitars. Requiring minimal modifications to the instrument, these pickups provide reasonably accurate sound, a high feedback threshold, and relatively easy installation (which, however, is best left to a professional to achieve optimum results and avoid damage to the instrument). Although this type of pickup is sometimes criticized for a harsh attack (often referred to as "quack"), it remains to be the most popular choice available. Available from numerous man-ufacturers, this is the kind of pickup found in the vast majority of contemporary guitars that leave the factory with electronics installed.

Active or Passive

One of the distinguishing features to be aware of with electronics for acoustic guitar is whether the system is *active* or *passive*. Active electronics make use of an internal preamp, which buffers the otherwise weak output of most pickups to usable levels. Although there are some pickups that work well without being boosted by a preamp, most offer such a low signal if used alone that they hardly drive the amp or mixing board they're plugged into. Worse yet, many passive electronics offer a poor impedance match to the amps they're plugged in to, and as a result, lose much of their signal's integrity, especially if long cables are used. Both factors result in compromising the sound's warmth and bass response. In order to make a passive system sound its best, it is generally necessary to route the signal though an external preamp before feeding the final destination.

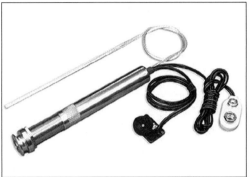

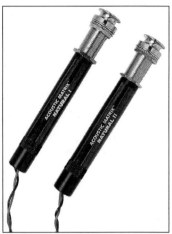

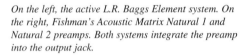

On the left, the active L.R. Baggs Element system. On the right, Fishman's Acoustic Matrix Natural 1 and Natural 2 preamps. Both systems integrate the preamp into the output jack.

If you're not sure which kind is installed in a guitar you're looking at, check whether there is an internal battery (usually a nine-volt type). Many guitars with factory-installed electronics will have a special compartment for this purpose, while others provide access through the soundhole.

Under-Saddle Transducers

Pickups that are installed under the guitar's saddle are generally referred to as *under-saddle transducers*. Pickups of this type all share a common design in that they consist of a thin element that fits between the saddle and the bottom of the bridge's saddle slot. While there are exceptions, most of these pickups rely on *piezo* technology to sense the strings' vibrations. Consisting of ceramics or actual crystals that convert pressure into electric current, piezo technology is also used for such things as doorbell buzzers. First-generation pickups embedded individual (one or two per string) piezo crystals in the under-saddle element (and in the case of Ovation guitars, in the saddle itself). This approach leads to relatively high output, but because the crystals have to line up exactly under the strings, problems with certain strings being louder than others occur.

Several manufacturers continue to offer pickups using this older design, and some players are attached to their sound. Shadow's Bridge Pickup, Fishman's AG-125, and L.R. Baggs's LB-6 (which has the pickup element permanently glued to a replacement saddle) are all examples of this type. SC Labs offers a piezo-based undersaddle pickup that places the crystals *between* the strings.

Most modern under-saddle pickups circumvent the problems associated with individual crystals by using a continuous piezo film instead. Various manufacturers use different approaches to turn the film into a usable pickup element. In Fishman's Acoustic Matrix, it is embedded in a rigid sandwich of film, metal foil, and conductive cabling. On the other hand, L.R. Baggs's Ribbon Transducer uses the piezo foil inside a flat, rubber element, which offers excellent flexibility.

Yet another type of under-saddle pickup uses a coaxial piezo cable for its sensing element. Borrowed from applications such as monitoring vehicle traffic, this is the technology found in Headway, Highlander, and Duncan/Turner D-TAR pickups (Fishman also offers similar designs in packages that are installed directly by guitar manufacturers, but they're not available as after-market products), as well as the L.R. Baggs Element (which uses a flat, braided cable).

The L.R. Baggs Dual Source system consists of a pickup, a preamp (with battery), a control unit, a microphone (installed in a block of foam), and an output-jack.

As implied earlier, a few under-saddle pickups don't use piezo technology at all. B-Band's UST relies on a patented electret film, charged with what the company compares to "microscopic gas-bubbles," which also create an electrical charge under pressure. The company claims that this design produces a more natural attack than most piezo-based pickups, and many players find that it does indeed result in excellent acoustic tone.

Schertler's Bluestick also mounts under the saddle, but relies on an actual miniature microphone to reproduce the guitar's sound. Connected to the center of an element that looks very similar to other under-saddle pickups, the Bluestick aims to merge the convenience of a pickup with the sound of a microphone.

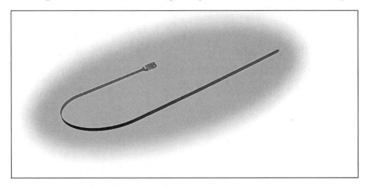

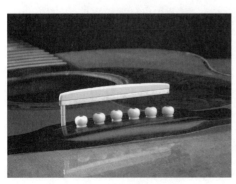

From top to bottom: B-Band's UST pickup consists of a thin plastic strip that installs under the saddle. The visible plug is used to connect with the onboard preamp.

Fishman's Acoustic Matrix is one of the most popular pickups for acoustic guitars.

The L.R. Baggs LB 6 is permanently glued to a replacement saddle.

Hexaphonic Pickups

Another type of pickup that's related to under-saddle designs is found in the *hexaphonic* models made by L.R. Baggs, RMC, and the Swiss company Paradies. Instead of placing an element under the saddle, these systems use individual metal saddles for each string with the piezo crystals built right in. Advantages of this approach include a very hot output signal, no problems with string balance, and the possibility to drive MIDI devices such as guitar synthesizers. However, hexaphonic pickups can also have a tendency to sound very bright, and their installation involves elaborate modifications to the guitar's bridge. Godin has long used the RMC units in its MIDI-ready Multiac guitar, and the L.R. Baggs pickups are standard equipment in Taylor's Doyle Dykes signature model. Additionally, hexaphonic pickups are used for the saddles of otherwise electric guitars (such as the Parker Fly) in order to offer a sound resembling that of an acoustic instrument.

Piezo Pickups for Archtop Guitars

Although magnetic pickups are the most common way to amplify an archtop, some players prefer bridge-mounted piezo pickups on this instrument type as well. Some luthiers simply adapt an under-saddle pickup made for a flattop guitar by installing it in an archtop's floating bridge. However, it is more common to replace the entire bridge with a unit that has piezo elements built right into its saddle. Fishman and Shadow are the two leading manufacturers of this pickup type as an aftermarket option, and Yamaha offers it in its AEX-1500 model guitar, which the company developed in collaboration with jazz player Martin Taylor.

How Are Under-Saddle Pickups Installed?

One of the reasons for the popularity of this pickup type is its relatively easy installation. Necessitating only minor modifications to the instrument, under-saddle pickups are virtually invisible; and if you decide that you'd like a different pickup at a later time, it's easy to reverse the installation.

At its most basic, installing an under-saddle pickup involves drilling a small hole through the bottom of the saddle slot, lowering the saddle by the height of the pickup, and enlarging the guitar's endpin hole to fit the output jack. If the system is active, then a battery clip needs to be fastened to the inside of the body (usually at the neckblock); and if the preamp isn't mounted to the endpin, it will also have to be glued or Velcroed to the inside.

There are several possible issues that may require additional work. If the saddle slot isn't deep enough, it will have to be routed to accommodate the combined depth of both the pickup and the saddle. As a general rule, it's a good idea to have no more than about 50 percent of the saddle sticking out from the bridge. Most manufacturers of pickups that use a coaxial cable also recommend that the bottom of the saddle slot be routed to a half-round shape for the pickup to rest in. This procedure allows the pickup to sense the bottom of the saddle and the bridge, as well as the sides of the bridge, which is one of the benefits of this pickup design. Some makers (including Rick Turner and Lakewood) feel that it is beneficial to install the saddle at a slight angle toward the bridge pins, as this method can provide more pressure on the pickup.

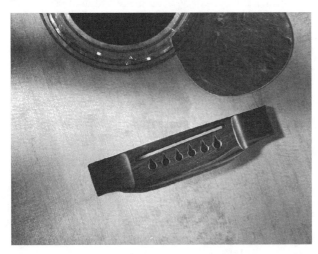

This picture shows an under-saddle pickup (in this case, an L.R. Baggs Ribbon Transducer) installed in the bridge, with the saddle removed.

If the angle of the strings crossing the saddle is very shallow, it may be necessary to "ramp" the bridge. This technique refers to cutting slots into the front of the bridge-pin holes, allowing the strings to move closer to the saddle, resulting in a steeper usable angle.

One of the most common complaints about under-saddle pickups is related to problems with string balance (when some strings are louder than others). In most cases, these issues are related to a saddle that is either too tight or too loose in its slot, or an uneven bottom on the saddle itself. If both of these potential culprits have been corrected and there are still problems, then an experienced luthier will be able to use a number of tricks to still create an even sound. This may involve shaping the bottom of the saddle in such a way that it puts more pressure on certain strings than others, or shimming areas under the saddle or pickup. Overall, these kinds of issues are the reasons why it's best to leave the installation of an under-saddle pickup to a professional, as it can be difficult to determine the cause of less-than-perfect performance without a lot of experience.

Soundboard Transducers

Soundboard transducers (also called *stick-on pickup*, *contact pickup*, or *contact microphone*) are pickups that attach to the guitar's top. Sensing the way the top vibrates as the strings are plucked, this pickup type has the potential to very accurately reproduce the instrument's acoustic sound. Because some models simply attach to the outside of the top, this type of pickup can be used to amplify all kinds of instruments, including those that aren't compatible with under-saddle or magnetic designs.

The basic design of a simple soundboard transducer is very similar to sensors used in many industrial applications, such as measuring seismic activity or triggering burglar alarms. As such, it was this pickup type that pioneered the use of piezo technology for guitar amplification. One of the first soundboard transducers designed specifically to amplify acoustic guitars was the Barcus Berry pickup, which was introduced in the mid-1970s. Although few people would still consider the original Barcus Berry to be a competitive design by today's standards, another early soundboard transducer has achieved cult status. Used by players such as Neil Young, Jackson Browne, and the late Michael Hedges, the FRAP pickup utilized a sensor that functioned on a three-dimensional axis to capture not only up-and-down movement of the top, but vibrations in all directions. Although FRAPs can sound incredible (one listen to Neil Young's amplified sound should be enough to dispel any doubts), they are difficult to install; and combined with poor marketing, the company eventually went out of business. Recently, a company called Trance Audio has come out with a pickup design very similar to the original FRAP.

One aspect that's shared by all soundboard transducers is that they are very sensitive to the exact location in which they're installed. Every guitar has a "sweet spot" in which the pickup sounds its best, and finding this location can be a time-consuming process of trial and error. Although good-sounding locations can be found anywhere in the lower-bout area of the top, the most consistent choice for placement tends to be directly under the bridge area (on steel-strings, the pickups are usually attached to the bridge plate).

The simplest soundboard transducers consist of a coin-sized pickup with an attached cable and ¹/₄-inch plug to connect directly to an amplifier. Although they can be modified for internal installation, most of these units are designed to attach to the outside of the instrument by way of easily removable sticky putty. Examples of this type are the Dean Markley Artist and the Shadow Quick Mount, but many other manufacturers also offer similar designs. With proper placement and the addition of a good external preamp, these units can lead to acceptable results in amateur situations, but few professional players would rely on one of these pickups as their primary source.

More sophisticated designs have recently enjoyed a surge in popularity among players looking for alternatives to the ubiquitous under-saddle pickups. With improved sound, onboard preamps, and simplified installation, the latest generation promises to offer microphone-like sound with plug-and-play convenience. Examples of these new systems include B-Band's AST, L.R. Baggs's iBeam, McIntyre's Feather, and offerings by Pick-Up The World. B-Band has applied its proprietary sensor material (described in the "Under-Saddle Transducers" section) to a thin rectangular pickup that attaches to the guitar's bridge plate with double-sided adhesive tape. Designed to be used with the company's endpin-mounted preamp, the system can be expanded with an internal microphone or B-Band's under-saddle pickup to create a variety of tonal possibilities. L.R. Baggs's iBeam uses piezo material inside an I-beam–shaped, lightweight plastic enclosure that also attaches to the bridge plate. Available in active and passive versions, the pickup enables a variety of installation scenarios. For players who'd like to retrofit an existing acoustic-electric guitar, L.R. Baggs even makes a model that includes an onboard preamp designed to replace the Fishman Prefix series units found on many guitars.

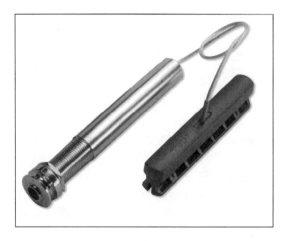

The L.R. Baggs iBeam (shown with its preamp) mounts to the underside of the top.

McIntyre's Feather and Pick-Up The World's designs use an ultra-thin sensing film to pick up the guitar's sound. One of the advantages of this approach is a minimum of weight added to the top, resulting in less of an alteration of the instrument's acoustic tone, and possibly less risk for feedback at higher volumes.

A couple of high-end soundboard pickups are made by AKG and Schertler. AKG's C411 Micro Mic is a miniature condenser mic (which requires phantom power) mounted in a plastic housing that sticks to the instrument with adhesive putty. Schertler's DYN transducer uses a moving coil coupled to a magnet inside its coin-sized housing. It also attaches to the instrument with putty, making it quick to install and remove. Both of these units terminate in XLR plugs, making them ideal for interfacing with professional-level equipment.

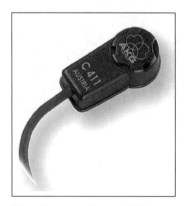

Microphone manufacturer AKG's C411 Micro Mic.

It's difficult to make a generalized statement about the tonal qualities of soundboard transducers. In contrast to other types of pickups (under-saddle or magnetic) which often have an inherent sound of their own, no matter which guitar they're installed in, the instrument in question can make or break the success of a soundboard transducer. For example, a very stiff top may not give the pickup enough vibration to work with, while an ultra-resonant instrument may overwhelm its available frequency response. The player's style also figures prominently into the equation. Someone playing soft classical or fingerstyle music will be more likely to be happy with a soundboard transducer than a player who strums at high volumes in a rock band. Additionally, the remaining equipment used to interface with the pickup will greatly affect its performance. Because of the pickup's sensitivity to feedback and boominess, it's a good idea to have a good EQ or notch filter available in order to give the sound the desired shape.

Schertler's DYN mounts to the top using special sticky putty.

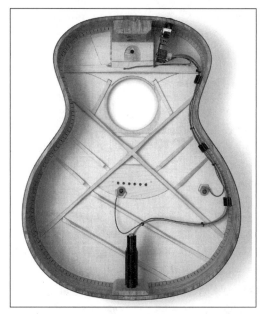

Although many soundboard transducers work with virtually any stringed instrument, some are limited to certain bracing patters. With proper installation and processing, many players find that soundboard transducers are excellent alternatives to using a microphone. Whether in performance or noisy home-recording situations, these units are worth a try.

Taylor uses two top-mounted transducers as part of its proprietary Expression System.

Magnetic Pickups

As their name implies, magnetic pickups work by magnetically sensing the strings' vibrations. As such, it comes as no surprise that this pickup type only works with steel-string guitars; nylon-string players will have to look to other types of technology to amplify their instruments.

Consisting of an actual magnet (some models use multiple magnets) surrounded by a coil made up of copper wire, this type of pickup features the same basic design found on most electric guitars. Although different models' sounds vary quite a bit, most magnetic pickups can't hide their heritage, and as a result, a bit of an electric guitar's edge tends to be part of the sound. Some magnetic pickups feature active electronics built right into their design.

Humbucker vs. Single-Coil

Magnetic pickups are available in *single-coil* and *humbucker* versions. While the single-coil's name explains itself (the design uses one coil to produce its sound), the humbucker features a second coil, which is used to suppress unwanted noise ("hum") and outside interference. Although singe-coils are very popular with electric guitars for their brightness and "twang," most acoustic players prefer the humbucking design due to its quieter operation, more robust bass, and generally fatter sound.

Magnetic Pickups for Flattop Guitars

Magnetic pickups made for flattop guitars are generally installed in the instrument's soundhole (which is why they're also called *soundhole pickups*). Although looks haven't changed drastically, a lot has happened since the first designs became available more than 50 years ago. While early efforts simply retrofitted pickups made for electric guitars, contemporary designs are carefully voiced for use with bronze strings, and take the tonal ideals of acoustic players into consideration.

Magnetic pickups for flattop guitars are available in many price ranges. Entry-level models, such as Dean Markley's Pro Mag, Seymour Duncan's Woody, or Fishman's Neo-D use a passive single-coil design, and their low price and ease of use make them attractive to amateur players who don't want to invest a lot of money and only occasionally have the need to plug in. Although these pickups don't tend to offer the more natural and sophisticated sounds of more expensive units, they can be a great choice to amplify an existing guitar without having to go through much trouble installing a more elaborate system. Designed to plug directly into an amp or PA (although the use of a preamp will generally improve their sound), these basic pickups are truly plug-and-play.

The Sunrise has long set the standard for magnetic pickups.

For many years, the high-end market for magnetic soundhole pickups was dominated by one single model. The venerable Sunrise pickup was introduced in the early 1980s, and due to its use by players such as Michael Hedges, Ben Harper, Leo Kottke, Keith Richards, and others, it developed an almost cult-like following. The fact that it was only available in very limited quantities (and in the beginning, only directly from its California-based manufacturer) added to its mystique. Using a passive stacked-humbucker (which arranges the two coils on top of each other, rather than side by side) design, the Sunrise does indeed offer a highly three-dimensional and rich sound which, when paired with a good preamp, continues to be the benchmark for the competition. However, the pickup is also quite heavy and large, which many players feel affects the acoustic sound of the guitar it's installed in. Additionally, while the Sunrise will work without a preamp, it really needs to be boosted to reach its full potential—a fact that should be considered if the player is trying to keep his or her rig simple.

The first serious competition for the Sunrise came in the way of the British Mimesis pickup. Featuring super strong neodymium magnets, the design allows for a very small size and light weight, despite its active nature, greatly reducing the effect the pickup has on the guitar's acoustic sound. Licensed by Fishman, the pickup is now made in the U.S. under the Rare Earth name, and it's available in several different configurations. The Rare Earth line starts with a single-coil model, moves on to a humbucker, and continues with two models that include added miniature microphones. The microphone-equipped Rare Earth Blend pickups are of particular interest, as they allow the blending of the gutsy magnetic sound with

Fishman's Rare Earth pickup features a very narrow design, and is available with an optional microphone.

Seymour Duncan's MagMic combines a magnetic humbucking pickup with an internal microphone.

the more delicate but natural microphone, resulting in a tone that could be considered the best of both worlds. Attached to the pickup with a flexible gooseneck, the microphone goes on the *inside* of the guitar with the standard Rare Earth Blend, and on the *outside* of the soundhole with the Rare Earth Custom Blend. The mixing of the two signals can either be accomplished with a small dial on the pickup itself, or the pickups can be wired for true stereo operation using a tip-ring-sleeve–type cable. All active Rare Earth pickups use a small three-volt, button-type battery to power their built-in preamps.

Seymour Duncan has added to the field of high-end magnetic pickups with its Mag Mic model. Featuring an active humbucking design that's in between the size of a Sunrise and a Fishman Rare Earth, the Mag Mic—as its name implies—also features a built-in microphone. Rather than using a gooseneck, Seymour Duncan decided to simply integrate the microphone into the bottom of the pickup, facing into the soundhole. Although there is no way to move the microphone in order to find a sweet spot inside the guitar, many players find that mixing just a touch of the microphone's sound to the magnetic is enough to "naturalize" the overall sound, and that the location is more than adequate for this purpose.

Most recently, L.R. Baggs has come out with the M1 magnetic pickup. Featuring a design that suspends one of the humbucker's coils, the M1 offers a high degree of body sensitivity (similar to a pickup/microphone combination) in a very simple passive design.

One trait that's shared with all magnetic pickups is that they're a great choice if modification of the guitar is of concern. Although permanent installation with a standard endpin jack is possible, these pickups can also be used with a long cable that's directly attached, hanging out of the soundhole. In this scenario, the pickup can easily be installed and taken out again without altering the instrument at all, which can be a major factor with the use of collectible or vintage instruments. It is also conceivable to use one pickup for several instruments, or to only install it for performances, leaving the guitar untouched by electronics for use at home or in the recording studio.

Magnetic pickups are also great at capturing radically lowered tunings and harmonic slap-style playing techniques, making them a favorite choice among many modern fingerstyle guitarists. Although magnetic pickups can have a tendency to sound more "electric" than other acoustic guitar pickups, they offer an undeniable warmth and smooth attack, providing a sanctuary for players who are frustrated with the sometimes harsh and bright sounds of the ubiquitous under-saddle pickups.

Flattops with Built-in Magnetic Pickups

Although magnetic pickups are usually an after-market affair, there are a few acoustic-electric flattops that feature this pickup type as an integrated design. The most famous of these is undeniably Gibson's J-160E, which was described at the beginning of this chapter. Featuring a single-coil pickup that's cleverly integrated into the end of the fingerboard, the guitar had its glory days as John Lennon's favorite acoustic. More recently, Ibanez has begun using a similar concept on its MASA Series guitars. With a pickup installed between the soundhole and the end of the fingerboard, the guitar also features a built-in preamp and EQ in its side. Washburn is using a modified Fishman Rare Earth pickup on its thin-body NV-300 guitar, and Taylor used a similar system in its limited edition Chris Proctor signature model. Most recently, Taylor has included a magnetic pickup (mounted invisibly underneath the fingerboard) as part of its proprietary Expression System.

Ibanez uses a built-in magnetic pickup for its MASA series (left). On the right, a Gibson J-160E John Lennon edition.

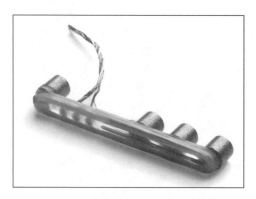

The magnetic pickup used by Taylor as part of its Expression System.

Magnetic Pickups for Archtop Guitars

Magnetic pickups for archtop guitars can be divided into two categories: electric guitar-style units that install into the top of the guitar (along with their volume and tone controls) and "floating" pickups that mount to the end of the fingerboard or the pickguard. The type of archtop that uses the former is really more of a hollow-body electric instrument than an acoustically functional guitar, so for our purposes, we'll focus on the latter design.

Originally designed to be an easy retrofit for existing acoustic archtops (an option that remains today), floating pickups require only minimal modifications to the guitar. Additionally, they have virtually no effect on the instrument's acoustic sound. Floating pickups differ from their purely electric cousins in that they are much thinner in order to fit into the narrow space between the strings and the body. This usually requires the use of smaller internal magnets, which often leads to slightly lower output and not quite as fat a sound as what's possible with a full-sized humbucker. Floating pickups usually also feature a mounting bracket that attaches to the sides of the fingerboard. In order to keep the top vibrating as freely as possible, a floating pickup is typically accompanied by volume and tone controls that are mounted to the pickguard, rather than directly into the guitar's body. Older guitars that have been retrofitted with electronics often even have the output jack fitted to the pickguard, but most modern luthiers have found an endpin jack to be more practical.

In stark contrast to pickups for flattop guitars, most magnetic pickups designed for archtops really haven't changed much since the 1940s. Companies such as Seymour Duncan, EMG, and Shadow have certainly helped to refine the tone these units offer, but many players continue to hold original-issue DeArmonds in high regard.

Internal Microphones

It would seem that simply placing a microphone inside the guitar's body would be the most logical way to amplify the instrument. Eliminating the complaints brought on by quacky under-saddle pickups, electric-sounding magnetics, and the inability to move around when using an external mic, it may come as a surprise that very few performers find an internal mic alone to be capable of delivering satisfactory sound. Put simply, the main reason for this is the fact that the inside of a guitar usually doesn't produce a good sound—while a guitar's tone is able to fully unfold and develop once it leaves the instrument, the inside tends to be a boomy place, lacking many of the delicious frequencies we associate with good acoustic sound.

However, while an internal mic alone may not cut it for most players (although there are exceptions, such as Martin Carthy, who uses nothing but a modified Radio Shack mic in his famous Martin 000-18), many find that it can enhance their sound when used in addition to a pickup. The kind of microphone usually used for this application is a miniature electret mic, similar to those designed to clip to a tie or a shirt collar.

Fishman was one of the first manufacturers to offer a pickup/mic combination with its original Blender system. Using the company's Active Matrix pickup and a miniature microphone made by Crown, the system offers stereo output on the guitar, and requires an external box called the Blender (many other brands' two-channel preamps will also work) to combine the two signals. More recently, Fishman has introduced its Prefix Blend system, which has become the most popular pickup/mic system to be installed directly by guitar manufacturers. With the microphone built into the unit's onboard preamp, the system allows the mixing of the two sources right on the guitar, eliminating the need for external blenders or stereo cables.

Not surprisingly, L.R. Baggs also offers several internal mic/pickup combinations. The most unique is the Dual Source model. Adding a mini mic to the company's Ribbon Transducer pickup, the Dual Source features onboard blending of the signals with a clever control unit that clips in the soundhole. B-Band, Highlander, and K&K Sound are some other companies that offer internal mics, each differing slightly in their approach to its use.

Many guitarists successfully use modified lavalier mics (the type designed to clip on a tie or shirt collar) in their instruments. Although it will usually take some experimenting to find a reliable way of mounting and powering these units, surprising results are often possible with these sometimes very inexpensive mics.

Mounting of Internal Mics

There are several ways to mount a mic inside the guitar. Most manufacturers—such as B-Band, Fishman, and Highlander—use a spring-loaded clip to attach the mic to an internal brace. L.R. Baggs places the mic in a small cube of rubber-foam, which is then stuck inside the guitar with double-stick tape. Yamaha has a preamp that features the mic on a small gooseneck that sticks into the body. No matter how the mic is attached, it's a good idea to experiment with its placement, as the sound can vary drastically within mere inches.

Phantom Power

Electret mic capsules feature almost microscopic built-in FET preamps, which require power in order to be functional. Usually ranging between 6–15 volts, this current can either be delivered by an onboard preamp, or externally via low-level phantom power (this is not to be confused with the 48 volts of phantom power used by full-sized condenser mics, which is delivered by most mixing boards). The kind of power needed is provided by most two-channel blenders made specifically for use with internal mic/pickup combinations, such as Fishman's Blender, L.R. Baggs's Mixpro, or Raven Lab's PMB II. Traveling on the same lead as the mic's signal, low-level phantom power works with a standard guitar cable.

Preamps

As described earlier in the *Active vs. Passive* section, most acoustic guitar pickups—and especially piezo designs—benefit greatly from being used with a preamp. The reason for this comes from the fact that the pickup's own output signal is often too low in impedance to effectively drive the relatively high-impedance input of an amplifier or mixing board. Besides the most obvious result of being quiet, a more serious issue is the fact that these differences tend to result in being incapable of producing the full fidelity needed in amplifying acoustic instruments. What musicians tend to describe as "thin" or "weak" tone is actually a poor match of impedance in electronics terms. Measured in ohms, impedance describes an electric circuit's opposition to alternating current, which, in the case of many pickups, needs a little help to equal the level at which an amplifier's input stage functions.

Preamps for acoustic guitars can take on various shapes and forms. The simplest type is connected directly to the inside of the guitar's endpin jack; and besides the addition of a battery clip, no further modifications are necessary to the instrument. Other designs combine the preamp and battery holder in a single unit (usually not much bigger than a box of matches) that gets installed inside the guitar's body. Some of these designs include a channel for the pickup they come with, and another

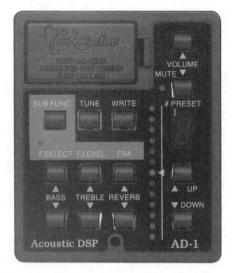

Takamine's AD-1 preamp features built-in digital effects.

channel for stereo operation with a second pickup or internal mic.

A type of preamp that's particularly popular with guitars that have their electronics installed at the factory includes controls for volume and various tone-shaping options. Mounted in the side of the guitar, these units put the ability to control the sound right at the player's fingertips. Some even include built-in microphones to add to the pickup's sound, and Shadow's MT-8 goes as far as featuring built-in digital effects.

The internal preamp of this L.R. Baggs Dual Source system is clearly visible through the soundhole. The system also features a volume and mix control that clips into the soundhole.

Onboard Controls

As described in the section above, knobs are a frequent addition to acoustic-electric guitars. Let's have a look at what the various pots and sliders found on the side of many guitars do.

Ovation's OP40 offers EQ, a built-in tuner, and other functions.

Volume

Onboard controls usually start out with a knob or slider labeled *volume*. As its name implies, this feature allows the adjustment of the instrument's loudness by changing the strength of its output signal, making it easy to match your volume with that of other musicians in a band. Having a volume control can also be helpful if you're using several guitars with different electronics, as it allows you to select a similar output level for all of them, keeping your stage volume at an even level. Finally, a volume control can act as a kind of a "panic button." If you're suddenly experiencing feedback, noise, or other abnormalities, then being able to quickly cut the guitar's volume can be very handy.

Takamine's GT-40 preamp also has a built-in tuner.

Equalization

The function of *equalization* (also called EQ for short) is to cut or boost specific frequencies. EQ can be as simple as a single knob that makes the guitar's sound more bassy or trebly (similar to the tone control on your car stereo), or get as complicated as a channel on a mixing board. Although a good pickup and preamp should sound great "flat" (without the addition of EQ), some playing situations call for an adjustment of the basic sound due to different-sounding amps, room acoustics, or to make the instrument more audible in a mix.

While most electric guitars get by with a simple "tone" knob, the majority of acoustic-electrics

265

feature a more elaborate setup. The reason for this is that dividing the available range of frequencies into smaller sections—such as bass, mids, and trebles—allows a more surgical alteration of specific areas of the sound. The example just mentioned would be called a *three-band EQ*, with each control allowing the player to select more or less of the frequency range that the button or slider is assigned to.

Some EQs allow the user to select the frequency that is being boosted or cut. This kind is referred to as a *parametric EQ*, and it is often used for the midrange control of preamps used for acoustic guitar. Systems such as Fishman's Prefix series will have set frequency controls for bass and treble, but parametric mids, resulting in a system that may look as if it has four bands (due to its four sliders), even though it's only a three-band system with one slider for the selection of the midrange frequency.

Notch Filter

A notch filter is a type of EQ that boosts or cuts an extremely narrow range of frequencies. In the case of acoustic guitar amplification, it is a powerful tool for fighting feedback at high volumes. By finding and cutting the exact frequency-causing problems, it is possible to eliminate feedback with a minimum of tonal loss.

Phase

Some onboard electronics include a switch labeled "phase" (sometimes called "invert"). This function reverses the preamp's polarity, allowing an ideal match with the phase of the amp or PA. Because phase affects the way the guitar's signal interacts with the sound waves produced by the loudspeakers, it can be used to optimize tone and fight feedback.

Blending

If the electronics in the guitar consist of a combination of a pickup and an internal microphone, then its controls are likely to include a "blend" or "mix" control. A blend control will either add the microphone signal to the sound of the pickup, or allow a complete sweep between the pickup and the mic (one end of the control is 100% pickup, the other 100% mic). Because the pickup tends to be used as the primary source for the overall sound, the former setup is more commonly found.

Do I Need Onboard Controls?

While it's easy to be seduced by the convenience of onboard controls, it's a good idea to take a critical look before committing to their use. Some players (often those with a background in electric guitars) feel that having control over their instrument's sound without having to reach for external equipment is crucial. In certain situations—such as playing in a loud band that doesn't have a dedicated sound engineer—being able to tweak one's sound directly from the guitar is, without a doubt, a godsend. However, there are also situations in which a player's desire to constantly change his or her sound on stage will actually make the sound worse for the audience. As a matter of fact, some players who perform on large stages have their guitars' onboard controls disconnected, leaving the shaping of their sound to the engineers instead.

However, perhaps the most significant reason to carefully evaluate the need for elaborate onboard controls is the fact that anything electrical tends to become outdated much quicker than the guitar itself. Because acoustic guitar amplification hasn't evolved and developed as fully as other areas of the guitar, what's hot today will be more than likely to be undesirable ten or twenty years from now, sometimes even sooner. Because most onboard controls involve drastic modifications to the guitar (usually a square or rectangular hole in the side), it's not a simple matter to remove or replace them when a different system is desired. (There are exceptions to this rule, such as L.R. Baggs's iBeam Onboard system, which fits into the same-sized opening as Fishman's Prefix model). Simply put, a fine guitar will outlast its owner, and in many cases, it's best to make additional equipment as removable as possible.

If you feel that you need basic onboard control, but don't want to chop up your guitar, then you might want to look at a system that installs the necessary components inside the soundhole. L.R. Baggs's Remote Control is part of the company's Dual Source system (where it offers adjustments for volume and pickup/mic blend), and it's also available for pickup-only systems (in which case the controls are for volume and tone). Cleverly clipping onto the edge of the soundhole, the Remote Control is securely mounted, yet it's easily removable. Schertler's Bluestick system also includes a simple volume control, which mounts inside the soundhole with double-stick tape. Shadow's Megasonic features full control for volume, EQ, and blending capabilities. Including the entire preamp assembly, this is a rather larger unit, yet it mounts easily accessible via Velcro.

Output Jack

In order to plug in a standard guitar cable with a $1/4$-inch plug, the instrument needs to be equipped with an output jack. Although some acoustic-electrics and many archtops use standard electric guitar jacks mounted in the lower bout (necessitating a reinforcement of the area), most manufacturers and players now prefer to use an *endpin jack*. Replacing the standard strap button found on the endblock of most guitars, this kind of jack only requires minimal modifications to the instrument (a slight enlargement of the endpin's hole).

There are a few different methods for securing the jack in the guitar. Most endpin jacks feature a threaded barrel, held in place by a nut on each end. Some kinds require tightening from inside the guitar's body, which can be difficult without the proper tool. A better design features the tightening nut on the *outside*, generally followed by another nut in the shape of the actual strap holder. Yet another kind of endpin jack features very coarse threads (similar to those on a sheet-metal screw), and this type is designed to screw directly into a pre-drilled hole in the guitar. Eliminating the need for an inside nut, this type of jack is perfect for instruments with limited inside access.

If even the minor modification of enlarging the existing endpin hole is out of the question, then there are some alternative options. Many archtop guitars have a mini-jack (smaller than a standard guitar plug) mounted to the underside of their elevated pickguards, making modifications to the body unnecessary. Similarly, some flattop players who use magnetic soundhole pickups choose to have a short cable with a mini-jack hanging out of the guitar's soundhole. In most cases, this cable will be secured with a loop over the endpin, or with a piece of Velcro on the body. There are also mini-jack-equipped endpins that fit into a standard-sized endpin hole. None of these mini-jack options are as secure as a standard $1/4$-inch jack installed somewhere in the guitar's body, so most frequently performers decide to go ahead and modify their instruments in favor of plugging in without hassles.

Most pickup systems use an output jack that is integrated into a strap-button.

Mono vs. Stereo Jacks

One-quarter-inch jacks are available in *mono* and *stereo* designs. The difference between the two is that a mono jack only has two available contacts—one for the tip of the plug, one for the sleeve—while a stereo jack offers three: tip, ring, and sleeve. A mono jack is all that's needed for a standard passive pickup, but even if you don't plan to actually run your sound in stereo (which, by definition, features different signals coming from the left and right speakers), there are reasons for using a stereo jack. The most common use for a stereo jack on acoustic-electric guitars is that the third contact gets used to automatically turn active electronics on and off as a plug is inserted or pulled out. This eliminates the need for an additional switch on the guitar, but it also means that the electronics are always on if the guitar is plugged in (so it's a good idea to pull the plug if you're not playing for a while in order to save battery power).

The other reason for using a stereo jack is to run two pickups—or a pickup and an internal microphone—with one cable. In this scenario, the two sources will share the plug's sleeve for their ground connection, while using the tip and ring for their individual hot wires. This is the easiest to accomplish with two passive sources, as the second pickup or mic will use the connector otherwise required to switch active electronics on and off. Special preamps with integrated jacks can resolve these problems (for example, Fishman's Active Matrix preamp can accommodate the also active Rare Earth magnetic pickup for use with one jack), but the solution will depend on the individual setup.

A relatively new kind of stereo jack includes a *fourth* contact as a dedicated battery switch for active electronics. With this design, it is possible to run a stereo setup (using both the top and ring contacts) in an active format, greatly improving the flexibility available when matching components.

It goes without saying that a dual-signal system relying on stereo output needs a matching stereo cable to function properly. While it may look identical to a standard cable at a first impression, closer inspection will reveal two rings near the tip of the plug rather than one, indicating the additional available contact (this is the same kind of plug used on most headphones). Stereo cables can either have a tip-ring-sleeve (TRS) plug on each end, requiring an amp or preamp with dedicated stereo *input*, or feature a Y-split on one end. A Y-cable terminates in two mono plugs, allowing the use of two standard amp or mixer channels to access the guitar's double signals.

Outboard Gear

While most acoustic-electric players don't go as crazy as their purely electric counterparts when it comes to plugging into little boxes, there are a few accessories that are worthwhile additions in order to accomplish good plugged-in tone. Rather than modifying the sound with a lot of effects (although some acoustic-electric

players certainly use effects such as reverb, chorus, compression, etc.), most plugged-in acoustic players find that a good preamp, EQ, and a direct box (which turns the guitar's high-impedance output into a low-impedance signal to interface with PA systems) can make a big difference in the quality of their sound. As a result, several companies have developed boxes that do all three of these functions in one unit. Fishman's Pro EQ Platinum and L.R. Baggs's Para DI are among the most popular boxes of this kind. Additionally, some acoustic guitar preamps feature two channels for the mixing of two signals, often also providing low-level phantom power for internal

Outboard units such as this Fishman Pro EQ allow further tonal adjustments.

microphones. This category includes Fishman's Blender series, L.R. Baggs's Mixpro, Rane's AP-13, Raven Labs's PMB II, and PreSonus's AcoustiQ.

If passive electronics are used in the guitar, then one of these units will practically be a necessity in order to get the sound that the pickup is capable of. However, even those who have active electronics in their instruments will find that using a good preamp/EQ allows for greater flexibility, as well as the ability to tickle the equipment to its utmost capabilities.

10 Care and Maintenance

Cleaning the Guitar

Procedures for Different Finishes

A clean guitar does not necessarily sound better than a dirty one, but it certainly *looks* better! Left on the surface, a heavy coating of dust, dirt, grime, oil, sweat, or drips of sticky beverages will tend to damage almost any finish. As a dirty guitar is handled, the finish is abraded under the gritty surface. Many guitar finishes can be seriously damaged by the chemical action of the dirt itself as it sits there year after year. While Willie Nelson has made a career of "accidentally" abusing his guitar, a dirty instrument does not project the image most of us appreciate. If an instrument is really dirty, it may be difficult to detect cracks in the wood, or looseness of parts such as the bridge. So, a clean guitar is more likely to be a healthy one, because it gets a regular visual exam each time it is wiped down, and the player is more likely to notice any impending trouble.

An acoustic guitar may be finished with one of a variety of different materials, and the composition of a given finish may not be obvious. It is wise to be conservative in cleaning or treating the finish to avoid doing any damage while trying to maintain it. In general, the best procedure is to avoid the need for cleaning and polishing by simply wiping the guitar with a soft cloth after each playing session. While this may seem a bit "basic" it is amazing how much good it can do. Most finger oils, dust, perspiration, and other dirt can be eliminated by a simple light wipe with an old, soft cotton cloth. A piece of flannel or an old T-shirt will make a fine guitar cleaning cloth. Many different commercially available guitar cleaning cloths are available on the market, and any one of them will serve you well.

The biggest advantage of this simple maintenance is that you don't need to know anything at all about the finish. A light wipe with a nonabrasive cloth will do wonders for any kind of instrument finish and will go a long way to keep it from getting dirty, dull, and oxidized. Paper towels can be rather abrasive, and can scratch sensitive guitar finishes.

Modern instruments with solid, intact finishes can handle a more vigorous cleaning than ones with very old, cracked, and oxidized finishes. If your guitar is very old, or if the finish is seriously damaged it would be worth your while to seek some professional advice before using any cleaning products on it. Old finishes can absorb the water from commercial guitar polishes.

These cracks have absorbed oil.

Oils can run into finish cracks, causing stains and/or lifting the finish from the surface. Any kind of contamination can make cracked instruments more difficult to repair.

Guitar polishes come in a number of different varieties, including water- and oil-based varieties, and many of them are designed to leave a bit of shiny residue or wax on the surface. The creamy, slightly abrasive guitar polishes will leave a high shine on many types of finish, but they may damage a French-polished finish, and they will often leave a white residue in any tiny cracks, which can be particularly annoying on a dark finish. If you use a wax-type polish on your guitar, you may end up with a slight coating of wax on the surface. In itself, the wax does no harm, but it is a very difficult surface coating to maintain. Waxed surfaces are prone to becoming sticky and showing fingerprints, and they are notoriously susceptible to water spotting. All in all, it is best to avoid waxy polishes because, in an attempt to keep the instrument looking shiny, you will tend to build up more wax each time you use it, and maintaining that waxy surface is really difficult.

Just as it is the most sensitive to scratching and wear, a French-polished finish is very delicate when it comes to using any kind of cleaning agent. In fact, it is best to avoid the use of most guitar polishes altogether if you have a French-polished guitar. If a simple wipe-down is not sufficient to clean your French-polished instrument, then you could try spraying a light mist of water on the cleaning cloth, NOT on the instrument. Then, a light wiping might be a bit more effective in removing water-soluble surface dirt. A very small amount of naphtha and/or lemon oil on the wiping cloth will help to pick up oils from the surface without injury. Bear in mind the dangers of working on a damaged finish.

Nitrocellulose lacquer is usually a bit less sensitive to water, but it has some peculiarities. One of the most important is the tendency for the lacquer to become softened where the player handles the instrument repeatedly. The back of the neck and the face of the guitar where the playing arm touches are areas where the finish is likely to have become more or less softened by contact with skin. If you are cleaning your guitar and just can't seem to get those areas to buff up to the same high shine as the rest of the guitar, it would be best to leave them alone. In fact, as you rub or polish vigorously you may be removing more finish and still not achieve the result you are after. There is no way to polish a softened finish.

Fortunately, most of us do not have to worry about this kind of trouble. In general, you can use pretty much any kind of guitar polish on a nitrocellulose lacquer; and if your guitar has fine scratches, you might get good results polishing it with one of the commercial creamy guitar polishes.

Again, as with French-polished finishes, lacquer finishes respond well to a periodic wiping and cleaning with a slightly damp cloth. Lemon oil will not harm any unbroken lacquer finish, and will do a good job of getting off oily grit and grime, as well as some of the residue that may be left by pressure-sensitive tape. Many musicians have a habit of taping song lists to the sides of their guitars, and the tape may leave a nasty residue behind. Owners of nitrocellulose-lacquered guitars would be wise to take such lists off after each performance to avoid long term damage to the finish. (I hope you wouldn't tape anything to a French-polished guitar!) Naphtha will clean more aggressive tape residue or other oil-soluble dirt without damaging the lacquer.

Here's where the catalyzed polymer finishes really shine! Any kind of commercial guitar polish, and virtually any kind of plastic or automotive polish, will work well on polymer finishes. In fact, these finishes are so nearly inert that they can handle a wide variety of aggressive-solvent cleaning agents or regular household cleaners. Polymer finishes are so hard that they can handle being wiped with paper towels—and it is common for guitarshop personnel to polish instruments with this kind of finish using the same cleaner they use on their glass display cases.

Strings, Frets, and Fingerboard

Care of the fingerboard is a source of confusion among guitarists. All that dirt and grime that can build up under the player's fingers will not harm a rosewood or ebony fingerboard. In fact, those tropical hardwoods are so dense and resinous that they really need no special care at all. Remember that in years past, rosewood was the standard material for kitchen-knife handles that could survive many trips through the dishwasher without damage. But it is so easy to clean a fingerboard, there's really no excuse for leaving it dirty. A simple rubdown after each playing session will do wonders for the fingerboard and frets. It is extremely easy to clean the strings at the same time by gripping them individually through the wiping cloth and rubbing them over their full length. This simple procedure is an effective way to prolong string life and it keeps dirt from building up on the strings themselves. Strings that get dirty or rusty enough can start to play severely out of tune due to the mass of the dirt attached to them!

Frets become oxidized and can start to feel rough or sticky, particular as the player's fingers slide from fret to fret. Keeping the fingerboard wiped down will not only clean the wood, but also prevent the oxidation on the frets. Once a year, it is a good idea to take all the strings off the guitar to allow good access to the fingerboard for cleaning. That's the time to get out the bottle of lemon oil. Using the lemon oil just as you would any other cleaning agent—wipe the fingerboard with a cloth vigorously until it is nice and clean, then remove as much of the surface oil as you can with a clean cloth. The small amount of oil that remains on the wood will give it a good, fresh look. With all that wiping, you'll have cleaned the frets as well. If the frets are really oxidized, you can use a bit of #0000 steel wool to polish them, being very careful not to snag the ends of the frets with the steel wool. You don't want to lift a fret out of alignment!

Cleaning the frets with steel wool.

It is best not to use natural vegetable oils, such as linseed oil, for cleaning instruments or for oiling fingerboards because these oils polymerize and thicken as they oxidize over time, becoming sticky and gummy on the surface. Likewise, it is best not to think of the lemon oil as a means of "feeding" a dry fingerboard, but rather to consider it as a cleaning agent. Adding lots of oil may make a fingerboard look "well fed," and may make it feel slick, but the oil will tend to collect in the fret slots, and may make future fret work difficult.

Adjusting the Truss Rod

If there's one aspect of an acoustic guitar that causes the most confusion, it is the adjustable truss rod. The truss rod has only one job to do, and that is to control the straightness of the neck. Before the invention of the adjustable truss rod, guitar builders relied on the stiffness of the neck to hold it straight against the pull of the strings. Even today, most classical guitar builders use no adjustable truss rod because the classical guitar neck is quite heavy and stiff, and the string tension is relatively low.

A hundred years ago, the first steel-string guitars had rather large, heavy necks that were often made with hardwood laminations for extra stiffness. As popular guitar playing techniques started to demand instruments with necks of a slimmer profile, the Gibson company developed and patented the first adjustable truss rod, which is still a standard of the industry. The first adjustable truss rod was an internal straining device that compressed the back of the neck slightly to counteract the external tension of the steel strings. Over the years, many different styles of truss rods have been developed, but their purpose and action are still the same: to bend the neck, counteracting the forward pull of the strings.

With an adjustable truss rod, the neck can be adjusted to compensate for the differential tension of various gauges of strings and even the tension changes of different tunings. Despite the somewhat mysterious action of the device, adjusting a truss rod is generally an easy proposition. The classic method of determining proper truss rod adjustment consists of holding a string (usually the third string) down at the first fret and at the fret where the neck joins the body, and observing the clearance between the bottom of the string and the top of the frets in the center portion of the neck. This clearance is called "relief," and the ideal measurement may be different depending on the player's style and "attack." A good starting point is about .010" of relief. A bluegrass player with a vigorous, hard attack is likely to need more relief, where a light fingerstyle player might well be able to handle a neck with nearly no relief at all. In all cases, the truss rod affects only the flexible shaft of the neck, which is why all measurement of relief must be done "outboard" from the body.

Inspecting neck-relief.

If this test is performed and the string lies right on top of the frets, the neck could well have a "backbow," or reverse curve. Such a backbow will be certain to cause serious buzzing at the low-fretted positions. In this case, the truss rod should be loosened a bit to provide just a bit of clearance. Clearly, if the relief is well over

.020", the truss rod may need to be tightened to achieve a more appropriate measurement. The "feel" of a truss rod adjustment may be deceptive. A truss rod nut that is difficult to turn might be working against an inappropriate amount of friction due to rust or corrosion of the screw threads. If the truss rod is a "single action" type, as seen on Martin, Taylors, and Gibsons, it may be wise to remove the nut entirely and lubricate the threads and the bearing surface with some white grease or heavy oil. Then, when adjustments are performed, there will be far less chance of the rod breaking when the nut seizes and twists the threaded portion. Almost all truss rod breakage is caused by twisting a seized nut.

Although its adjustment has an effect on action, the truss rod is not there for the purpose of making action adjustments. An adjustable truss rod has no effect on a guitar's eventual need for neck resetting. Many musicians fear that the adjustable truss rod will cause damage to the neck if all the strings are removed at once, but it is impossible to damage any guitar neck by simply taking off all the strings!

Adjusting Action

The first step in adjusting the action is to verify that the truss rod adjustment is correct, that is, to check the neck relief.

Checking and/or correcting the action at the nut comes next. The nut occupies a position that might be thought of as a "zero" fret position. Some instruments are made with a fret in the nut position, often called a "zero fret" so that action adjustment at the nut is automatically determined when the frets are installed. Most guitars are made with a conventional nut that must be set to the correct height. Determining nut action is a very simple procedure. By pressing the tuned string between the second and third frets, you can easily see the nut action as the clearance between the bottom of the string and the top of the first fret. If the string actually touches the fret, the nut is too low. It's simple as that—there should be just a bit of clearance under the first string. The amount of clearance is usually very small—just enough to see, about .002", or the thickness of a page of a telephone directory. Unlike the test for neck relief, the nut action must be checked individually for each string.

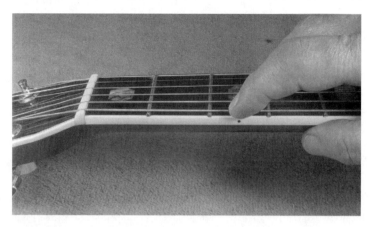

Check the action-height at the nut by fretting at the third fret.

If the nut action is too low, it may be necessary to make a new nut or to raise the existing one. Most of the time there is no harm in raising a nut by adding a thin shim underneath and gluing the nut back in place. It is customary to shim the nut a bit high and to file each nut slot individually to the correct depth to achieve the proper action for each string. If only one or two strings are too low, it may be possible to fill the corresponding nut slots with an appropriately hard material and to recut them to the correct depth.

If the nut action is too high, the nut slots for each string need to be filed down until the desired action height is reached. As the nut slots are filed, it is important to maintain the correct angle of the slot, so the highest point is where the string "exits" on its way toward the bridge. Also, the nut slots should have a profile that roughly matches the diameter of the strings so that the strings are held firmly but not pinched. A too-loose nut slot can cause buzzing, where a too-tight slot will make tuning difficult.

Once the proper nut action is reached, all future action adjustments may be made at the bridge saddle. It's fair to say that the nut action is a relatively permanent adjustment, where neck relief and bridge action may vary with time, player preference, and string gauge.

Action is measured and described as the clearance between the top of the twelfth fret and the bottom of the string, usually the first and sixth strings. For most players, this works out to somewhere between .060" and .085" at the first string and between .090" and .012" at the sixth. Specifically, an action of .0625" (2/32") and .0938" ($^{3}/_{32}$") is known as "standard low action" in many guitar shops, and in the U. S., is often referred to as setting up a guitar to "3 and 2." The other strings are generally set to heights that increase gradually between the first and sixth, although they might be set differentially to address certain playing styles, tunings, or other difficulties.

It's easy to adjust the bridge of an archtop.

Raising or lowering the saddle is a trivial matter for the player of an archtop guitar. Most of these instruments have screw-adjustable bridges, and a player can easily raise or lower the action without assistance.

Steel-string flattop and classical guitars usually have removable saddles that can be cut, filed, or sanded to accommodate lower action. Many older instruments, and some modern replicas, have saddles that are glued in place, so these must be cut lower without being removed. Lowering the action is always easier than raising it. If the action must be raised considerably at the saddle, it is best accomplished by replacing the saddle. Slight upward adjustments may be made by adding thin shims underneath the saddle, but for the best structural integrity, it is best to replace the saddle. Here, it is a matter of a luthier's experience and judgment. As the saddle is raised, the amount of forward pull exerted by the strings is increased. A very high shimmed saddle is likely to crack the bridge.

Even a low-tension classical guitar has enough forward thrust on the saddle from the angle of the strings crossing over it that if the saddle is raised by adding thick shims, it may tip forward and cause the bridge to crack.

Adjusting Intonation

Intonation, or the ability of a guitar to play accurately, is a topic of increasing concern for acoustic guitar players. These days, most guitar players can easily afford an electronic tuner capable of detecting even slight variations in tuning. Many guitarists record their own performance in order to distribute their music, to improve practicing, and as an aid in composing. There's nothing like hearing yourself on a recording to make you notice every little flaw in your playing, including any intonation difficulties.

Once again, the archtop guitar player has it easy. Intonation is customarily adjusted by moving the bridge and/or saddle. Since the archtop guitar's bridge is readily moved, the player can simply change its position to improve intonation. Striking the harmonic note at the octave position above the twelfth fret, and comparing that note to the note produced when the string is fretted at the twelfth, the player can determine whether the fretted note is sharp or flat. If the fretted note is sharp, the bridge needs to move closer to the tailpiece, effectively lengthening the vibrating string. After repeating this test on different strings, the archtop-guitar player can set the bridge in a more or less ideal position. As the strings age, or if the player changes to a different gauge or tuning, the bridge can be relocated to suit the new situation.

Checking intonation at the 12th fret.

Life is not so simple for the other acoustic guitarists who usually must rely on luthiers to make intonation adjustments. In this situation, the luthier is likely to make the same tests, and calculate the ideal position for the saddle. If the intonation does not need much correction, it may be possible to reconfigure the top of the saddle so that the string bears on a point closer or farther from the fingerboard. Often, it is necessary to remove a saddle, inlay the bridge with the appropriate hardwood, and relocate the saddle within the bridge. In the most serious situations, it may even be necessary to relocate the entire bridge.

Alternate tunings can have a profound effect on intonation. A steel string player who switches from standard tuning to DADGAD, for example, may need to have the saddle position moved more than $1/8''$ to accommodate that tuning.

All in all, intonation can be just about the most frustrating of all problems confronting a guitarist. As a stringed instrument with fixed fret positions, a guitar simply demands that the player and listener make some compromises in the quest for perfect intonation. It's a given that perfection does not exist for guitar intonation, and it is important to recognize that in today's music recording industry, it is possible to readjust or substitute "bad" notes at almost any point. So, the "perfect" intonation you hear on recordings may not indeed be all that normal.

Tuning Difficulties

Getting a guitar in tune is one of the hardest parts of learning to play. Whether a player uses an electronic tuning aid, or uses "relative" tuning from one string to the next, there's nothing more irritating than a guitar that simply won't tune up.

By far the most common tuning difficulty comes from not having the strings anchored properly at the tuner posts. A string may be wound around the post several times and still slip gradually, making it impossible to tune up correctly. Take a look at the illustrations and read through the stringing information to see one very positive way to eliminate this problem.

Winding the strings around the tuning posts too many times can make tuning more difficult.

On a flattop steel-string guitar, if the string windings catch between the bridge pins and bridge-pin holes, it is possible for the string to feel tight, but the ball-end can slip slowly for days as it seats itself under the bridge. Unwound classical guitar strings are incredibly slippery and can slide through the bridge in much the same way as a string can slip on the tuner post.

If the nut slots are too tight, the strings will stretch between the tuner and the nut, and then jump with an audible "ping" as they are tuned up. This may well feel like a problem with the tuner itself because when the string jumps, the guitarist will feel a change in the tension on the tuner button.

Guitar tuning machines come in a wide variety of qualities and styles. They do share some basic characteristics, and with very few exceptions, all of them will hold a string in tune just about equally well. That's because the "worm gear" mechanism can't actually run backwards, as it's driven by the string tension. It is important to keep open gears oiled so they will work smoothly without excessive wear. A drop of light household oil on each of the moving parts once a year is more than sufficient lubrication to help even the most modest tuner to last a lifetime!

In all cases, it is critical not to tune "down" to the note. It is important always to tune below and then slowly up to the correct pitch. In that way, the backlash is automatically taken up in the gear mechanism, so the string tension will keep the tuner locked in place. Also, if there is excess friction at the nut, tuning up in this way will ensure that the string will be most likely to stay at pitch.

Buzz Diagnosis

All acoustic guitars make some extraneous and unwanted noises. That's a fact of life we simply can't escape. There are lots of causes for undesirable "buzzing" that can be corrected, and some of these causes can be symptoms of more serious problems. Here's a list of some of the major causes, and some suggestions for remedies:

Low Action – A prime cause of buzzing is when the string simply bumps into the fret because the action is too low overall. The classic situation is a guitar that plays very well for a light touch, but buzzes at almost all fret positions when a heavy attack is used. In this situation, the logical cure is to raise the action until the buzz is not a problem.

High Action – This buzz is counterintuitive, but actually rather common. If the action is too high, it might be difficult to hold the string tightly against the fret, and a buzz will result. This particular buzz is one that beginners may face if their instruments are not set up properly.

Relief – Too little relief may cause the strings to buzz against the frets when the guitar is played in the low positions. At the first few frets, the string is vibrating in a wider arc because it is longer than when fretted high up the neck. Players with a hard attack will generally benefit from more neck relief to alleviate this situation. A truss rod that is too tight is the most common cause of this problem.

Light Strings – If the strings are too light for a player's style, they may vibrate in too wide an arc, and may hit the frets. Rather than raising the action, it may be more appropriate to change to a heavier gauge of string. That's why most flatpickers like medium gauge.

Low Nut - If the nut is too low, it will cause buzzing *only* when the strings are played in the "open" position. Once fretted, the string is no longer affected by nut height.

Nut Slots – Nut slots that are too wide can provide enough lateral movement of the string to cause a buzz. Likewise, a nut slot that does not angle downward toward the tuner post will be a likely candidate for buzzing.

Back Buzz – A special, sympathetic buzz can occur when a fretted string just touches the frets between the nut and the fretted position. If the nut is a trifle too low, or the truss rod just a little too tight, it is possible to generate a buzz that occurs on the section of a string behind the fretting hand, only when certain notes are played on a *different* string.

Low Saddle – If the saddle is too low within the bridge, the string may not make a good contact, and may bounce up and down against it when played. The resulting "sitar" tone is really annoying and tends to affect every fretted position. A simple bit of reconfiguring of the bridge will typically take care of this problem.

A saddle that's too low will cause buzzing, because it doesn't provide the strings with enough angle.

Flat Saddle – On a classical or steel-string guitar, the top-edge saddle must either be rounded or angled downward away from the fingerboard, so that the string "exits" from a single point on the top of the saddle. If the saddle is flat on top, it is very likely to cause a subtle, but annoying buzz. This is a particularly common cause of buzzing because the top of the saddle is often the target of inexperienced repairers seeking lower action.

Deeply Notched Saddle – Classical and flattop steel-string guitars are not supposed to have notches in their saddles. Inexperienced people sometimes try to lower the action by cutting such notches, which can easily generate nasty buzzes. Similarly, the notches in the top of an archtop guitar bridge may also cause buzzing if they are improperly cut, or not angled downward toward the tailpiece.

Notches in the saddle of a flattop or classical guitar are a poor way of dealing with high action.

Uneven Frets – Uneven frets will cause buzzing in isolated areas. If a guitar buzzes only in certain positions that are not adjacent, the chances are that some frets are uneven. Frets can become loose with time and migrate upward a few thousandths of an inch, or they may not have been level in the first place. Either way, it will be necessary to correct the problem by leveling the frets, or, in the worst case, by replacing them.

Low Frets – Frets that are too low will allow the player's fingers to start to touch the fingerboard before the strings make solid contact with the frets. As a result, it is possible for the string to buzz against the actual fret against which the player is pressing. The only logical remedy is to replace the frets with ones of a higher profile.

Flat Frets – Frets are commonly leveled by filing, and the leveling process leaves them flat on top. If they are not rounded afterward, they may be so flat on top that they cause a very subtle buzzing or slightly dead note when the string is played. Flat frets are most often seen as a result of repair, but are also a problem on inexpensive or poorly made new instruments.

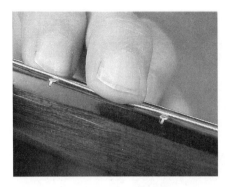

Frets that have been worn flat can lead to buzzing.

String Interference – Twelve-string players know this problem. When the pairs are hit too hard, or when the strings of each pair are too close together, the strings actually bump into each other, buzzing like crazy. Widening the pairs may require making a new nut.

Stray String Ends – Leaving the excess free end of the string dangling from the tuner post may have a casual, "folksy" appearance, but it can be the cause of really nasty buzzes. It's best to trim those strings and get them out of the way. At the bridge, the ends of classical guitar strings should similarly be trimmed so they can't touch the face of the guitar where they will rattle and buzz.

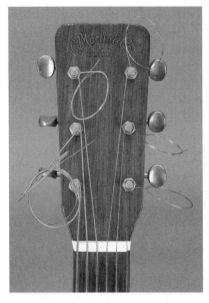

Loose strings might look cool, but often cause rattles.

Damaged Strings – The strings themselves can become damaged and can buzz. If the windings become loose, a string will make a dead, "sizzling" kind of sound. If the string is accidentally bent downward near the nut, it can buzz violently against the first fret. Either by excessively heavy capo use or by accident, a string can be bent downward around or over a fret. Such a bent string will buzz only at that one fretted position, making it appear that the fret is at fault.

Loose Parts – Loose parts can cause a rattle or buzz on an acoustic guitar. It's a long list, but if the cause of a buzz is to be found, it may be necessary to check out everything. Generally, loose parts will rattle when the instrument is tapped or "rapped" with the knuckles. Sometimes, you can even pinpoint the rattle by the area in which it appears to originate. More often, though, the body transmits these noises or rattles. Buzzing caused by loose parts is often generated "sympathetically" as certain notes are played.

Anything that is attached to the guitar with screws can become loose and rattle, including tuner bushings, the tuners themselves, elevated pickguards, tailpieces, pickup parts and controls, or even a truss rod cover. Most of the time, these items can simply be tightened to eliminate the buzzing. The truss rod itself can become loose within the neck, and rattle. A very slight adjustment of the rod may silence it, or it may be necessary to inject some resilient filler through the fingerboard to insulate the rod.

On steel-string guitars, the ball-end of the string may not be fully seated up against the bridge plate, and the ball can rattle within the string itself. This little problem is more common than one might expect, and a quick look under the bridge is a good early diagnostic step.

If a ball-end isn't properly seated at the bridge-plate, it may be the cause of a rattle.

289

Broken Parts – Any part of the guitar that is broken can rattle. Big cracks in the body are an obvious cause of buzzing, but a loose or rattling part may be quite obscure. A top or back may become slightly loose from the sides, a pickguard can be lifting ever so slightly, braces can be loose or cracked, and there can be an internal separation between the layers of veneer that form the tops of inexpensive guitars. Virtually all these problems require professional attention.

Technique – Some players simply can't play without excessive buzzing because of their technique. The angle of pick attack is crucial to the way in which a string vibrates. Hitting the string with a flatpick held at a 45-degree angle will cause the string to jump straight up and down, hitting and buzzing against the frets. Held at a 90-degree angle to the plane of the fingerboard, a pick will cause the string to vibrate sideways, allowing for far more powerful strokes without buzzing.

Troubleshooting Electronics

Most acoustic guitar pickup systems are relatively simple electronic units, and are remarkably trouble-free considering the constant movement and vibration of an acoustic guitar as it is played. After a few years of jostling around, the various wires inside the body have the potential of working loose where they are connected to the pickup unit, a preamp, controls, or the output jack. In addition to a diminished output, a common symptom of a loose wire is a constant electronic "hum" through the amplifier.

Many of the most popular systems, such as the Fishman Matrix, have piezo electric sensing units that are installed directly under the saddle within the bridge. These are very delicate strips that can be very easily injured when saddles are installed and removed. There is often a thin foil shielding surrounding the piezo strip, and this foil can be scratched as the sharp corner of a saddle is dragged across it. Even the smallest break in the shielding foil can result in a nasty electronic hum. Generally, these elements cannot be repaired once they are injured.

When an "under-the-saddle" pickup is installed, care must be taken to ensure that each section of the saddle presses equally on the sensing element. It may be necessary to mill the bottom of an uneven saddle slot to assure a good surface against which the element will rest. Likewise, the luthier will make sure that the bottom of the saddle is also quite flat and even. Additionally, it's important that the saddle fit the bridge loosely enough to allow microscopic movement as it presses against the pickup element, yet tightly enough to have full mechanical support against the string tension. A saddle that fits tightly at one end is likely to produce low output for the corresponding strings. The only practical way to adjust the output of individual strings is by reconfiguring the bottom of the saddle to redistribute the downward pressure. The appropriate small area of the bottom of the saddle may be scraped to lower the pressure beneath a string, and tiny bits of metallic or other tape may be added to similarly increase the output of a given string.

Cold or broken solder joints will cause an intermittent or constant failure in a pickup's output, but the most common cause for an intermittent connection is a failure of the output jack. The pulling and twisting of the cord and plug that connect the guitar to an amplifier will often result in a failure within the output jack itself. The contacts become corroded or no longer bear firmly on the plug, so that there is a "crackling" noise as the plug is moved around, in or out. Because the plug and cord are even more likely to be damaged, it is very important to check them before suspecting a pickup-jack failure. Most serious acoustic-electric players have several cords of various lengths, so they will find it easy to check to see if the guitar or cord is at fault by simply switching cords to see if the problems persists.

If an amplifier is not properly grounded, an electronic hum can result when a guitar is plugged in. So, it's important to make sure the electrical supply to the amplifier is appropriately wired and grounded. Sometimes, an amplifier and pickup will hum only when plugged into certain wall sockets, indicating that the problem is not within the pickup or amplifier system.

If an acoustic guitar has an "active" pickup system—that is, one that is powered by an onboard battery—it is a good idea to change the battery regularly, say once a year, even if it seems to be working satisfactorily. As the battery ages, the voltage eventually drops to the point where it can't power the preamp. When this happens, the symptom is a really nasty distortion through the amplifier. Since there's no warning when this may happen, keeping the battery fresh will insure that it won't be right as you step onstage at an important gig!

Installing Strings

Piano strings last a long time without needing replacement, but guitar strings start to sound "dead" after only a short while because they are constantly being handled by the player. Fortunately, guitar strings are relatively inexpensive and easy to change. Unlike a pianist, a guitar player can retune the instrument at each playing session, and can change the strings easily. Frequent string changing is the simplest method a player can use to keep a guitar sounding its best. All guitarists should learn to change their own strings so they can be in control of their instrument's sound.

Before installing new strings, you'll have to remove the old ones. Despite the old wives tale that strings must be changed one at a time, it is perfectly safe and reasonable to remove all the strings so you can give the fingerboard a good wipe-down with a cleaning cloth to remove built-up dirt and grime. With all the strings off, you can take a good look at the tuners and spot any loose washers, buttons, or bushings. But, if you are more comfortable changing the strings one at a time, then that's what you should do. It is much easier to maintain the position of the moveable bridge on an archtop guitar if you change the strings one at a time.

Removing the strings is the easy part—you just detune each string until it is slack and then unwind it from the tuning post and remove it from the bridge or tailpiece. Since you should have a pair of diagonal wire cutters handy for trimming the new strings, you may want to use it to cut the strings to make them easier to take off.

Steel Strings

Most steels string guitars have "pin bridges" where the string is inserted into the bridge, followed by a bridge pin.

- The first operation is to insert the ball-end of a new string into the hole, and hold it so the ball hangs well down inside the guitar body.

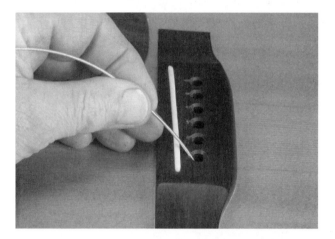

- Then, insert a bridge pin with the groove facing the string, simultaneously pulling lightly on the string, so the string's ball will catch on the bridge plate.

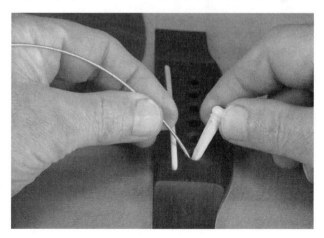

- The bridge pin holds the string aside so that it grips the inside of the guitar and is held against the bridge plate.

- Then, maintaining pressure on the bridge pin, pull the string firmly until you can feel that the end is held tightly in place.

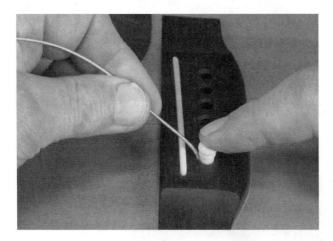

- Run your fingers up along the string, aligning it along the neck, and feed the end of the string through the appropriate tuner post. Holding the string about 1.5" above the fingerboard, pull the free end all the way through the tuner post.

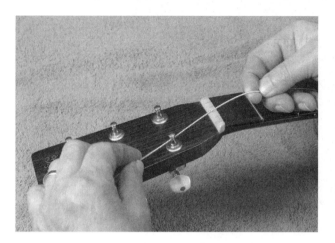

- Next, bring the free end around the post down the center of the peghead between the rows of tuners.

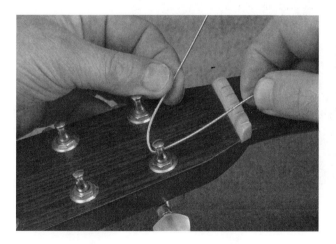

- Then pass the free end of the string under the portion of the string between the tuner post and the nut.

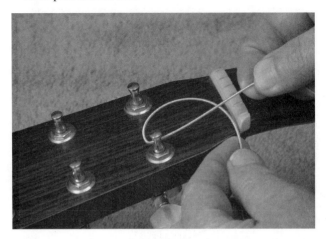

- Fold the string up and over and start to turn the tuner button to wind the string around the post, maintaining finger tension on the string as it winds up.

- You'll notice that the free end of the string is tightly held against the tuner post so that there's no chance that it can slip as it reaches the tension necessary to bring it to pitch. As soon as you tune the string up, you can clip the free end as close as possible to the tuner post.

That way, there won't be a loose bit hanging that can rattle, and there won't be a long enough piece sticking out to be dangerous. These cut strings are sharp!

With the strings attached in this manner, it is impossible for them to become loose at the tuner, so it is not necessary to have them wind around the post a lot of times. While it doesn't harm anything to wind a lot of turns around the post, a large clump of windings can look messy and cause instability in tuning until the windings seat themselves on the post.

Some steel-string guitars have "pinless" bridges, which have simple holes though which you'll thread the strings. They are even easier to string than the pin-bridge style; but since all the string tension is held entirely by the glue joint of the bridge, there's reason to think that the pin bridge is a more sturdy design.

Some steel-string guitars have slotted pegheads that may look as though they require a different stringing technique. In fact, you can use exactly the same procedure.

• Pass the string through the post.

- Bring it back up through the peghead slot behind the tuner post and down in front.

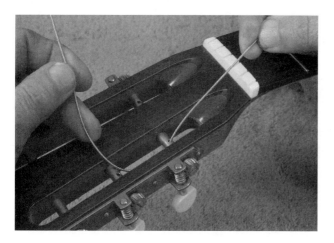

- Then pass the string under.

- And back over, so it will lock as it is wound up.

- Once the string is brought to pitch, clip the free end so it won't tangle in the slotted peghead.

Nylon Strings

When you restring your classical guitar, you have to pay special attention to those slippery nylon strings.

- The bass strings often have a special flexible area right at one end. This is for attaching to the bridge. Pass the string through the hole in the tie block.

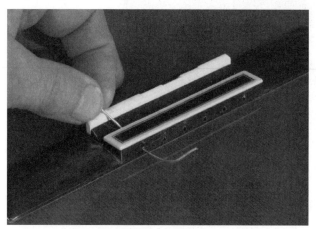

- Loop the end under the string behind the saddle and around back toward the back edge of the bridge.

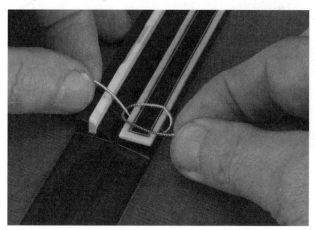

- On the bass strings, it is conventional to make a single loop under, making sure that the free end of the string is held around the back corner of the tie block.

- Run your hand along the string and bring it up to the nut, holding the string about 1.5" high away from the fingerboard.

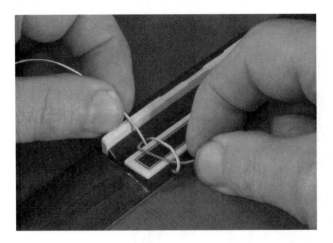

- Pass the end of the string through the tuner roller.

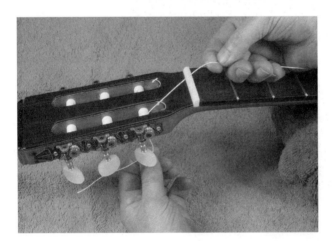

- Bring the end of the string back up behind the roller and pass it under the string between the roller and the nut.

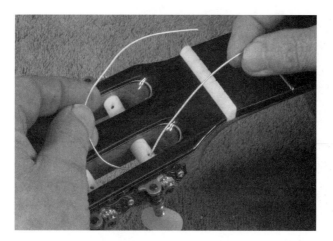

- Pass the free end under the string.

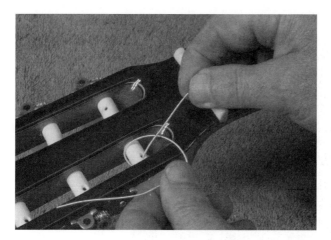

• Then back up over the roller.

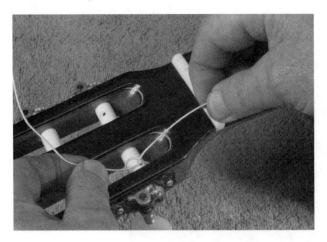

• Now you can wind the string up and tune it to pitch safely without fear of it becoming loose. Clip the loose end after you have tuned the string.

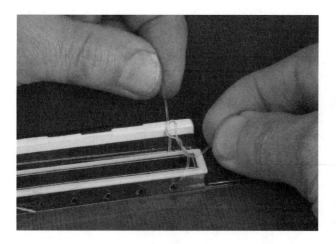

- The unwound nylon strings are far more likely to slip than the wound ones. As you tie the string onto the bridge, be sure to wind it under and through a couple of extra times to make sure it won't come loose, being careful to make sure that the free end of the string is held against the back of the tieblock. The first string is very likely to slip if that last turn doesn't go over the back corner of the tie block.

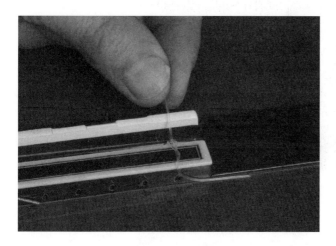

- The same thing goes for the tuner roller. Pass the free end of the unwound string over and around the string an extra time to help generate the necessary friction as it is tuned to pitch.

Archtops

Archtop guitars have tailpieces and moveable bridges. Other than that you can string them just as you would a flattop steel-string instrument.

- Most archtop tailpieces accommodate ball-end strings and have holes or slots to hold them.

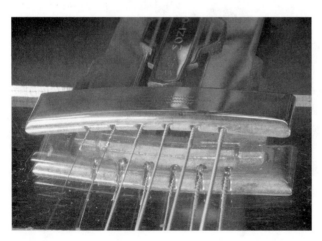

- The popular Selmer/Maccaferri–style guitars have an unusual tailpiece that requires a loop end string.

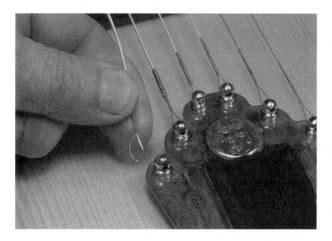

- In almost all situations, the tailpiece is very easy to deal with and requires no special care.

- Securing the strings at the peghead is just the same for archtop guitars as flat-top steel-string instruments.

But, the moveable bridge can be a bit of a trial. If you change the strings all at the same time, you'll notice that the bridge just falls off. That may be handy for cleaning, but it will require some knowledge of bridge placement to get it back where it was. There's usually a scuffed area or a scar where the bridge had been, so it is very easy to get it put back approximately right.

A useful procedure to align the bridge is to install just the first and sixth strings, and tune them to pitch. Then by comparing the harmonic at the twelfth fret with the string fretted at the twelfth, it's not too difficult to get the bridge situated correctly. If the fretted note is sharp, move the bridge toward the tailpiece and test the intonation again. Once you've done this kind of adjustment a few times, it will become an easy routine.

A Brief Introduction to More Serious Repairs

Some instruments may last a very long time before repair is needed, but eventually every acoustic guitar will need professional attention. Whether from accident, extremes of temperature and humidity, relentless string tension, or the wear of playing, there will be a time when a luthier's attention is required to maintain the integrity of the instrument.

Acoustic guitars are made of thin pieces of hard and soft woods formed into complex shapes and elaborately braced to withstand the pull of strings tuned to pitch for very long periods. As a general rule, the more expensive an instrument, the more delicately it is built, and the closer it comes to that "dividing line" between structural stability and the flexibility that allows for the greatest volume and tone.

Cracks in the Wood

Most cracks are quite visible; and while they may not immediately endanger the life of an instrument, they should be repaired. Serious cracks with splinters and missing pieces are the kind of damage that everyone can notice and understand.

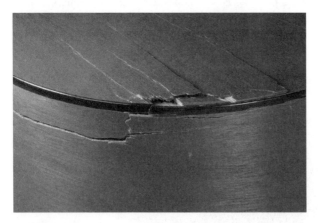

Splintered cracks such as this should be repaired as soon as possible.

Further damage is likely to occur if cracks are left unattended. Because the body of an acoustic guitar is not designed to come apart, most repairs must be done with specialized tools and clamps, using the soundhole as the primary access to the interior. Some body damage may look catastrophic but may be easily repaired, and certain subtle cracks may look insignificant but may have great structural consequences, and may require sophisticated repair techniques. An experienced luthier is the one who can easily distinguish the difference.

Cracks come in an amazing variety of shapes, sizes, and causes. It's the luthier's job to analyze each crack in order to choose the most effective method of repair. Sometimes, it is perfectly sufficient to introduce some glue into the crack, clamp it in to alignment, and allow time for the glue to set. Often, it is desirable to reinforce the inside of the crack to avoid future damage. It's logical to think that a crack that resulted from the instrument being dropped is not likely to recur except in the case of a similar accident. Such a crack may not need reinforcement. A side crack that results from the pressure of the guitar on the player's leg is an example of a crack that usually does need reinforcement. Such pressure is going to be present each time the guitar is played, and because the repaired area will flex a bit, it is likely to crack again unless reinforced from the inside.

Broken Headstocks

The long neck of an acoustic guitar can exert a lot of leverage at the body and can be the source of serious damage in the event of a fall even if dropped when in a substantially sturdy case. By far the most common damage that occurs inside a case is the result of the inertia generated by the mass of the peghead and tuners. Right at the area behind the nut, the neck is the thinnest and the angle of the peghead cuts through the longitudinal grain of the neck. With the shock of an abrupt blow, that "short grain" area of the neck can snap. This is particularly liable to happen in a forward fall, such as occurs when the guitar tips from a guitar stand to the floor.

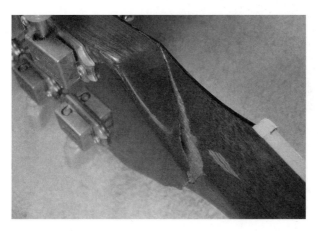

If a guitar falls, then the headstock is often the first thing to break.

Unglued Bridges and Fretboards

Parts that become unglued need to be reglued. Although it sounds simple, regluing a loose part, such as a bridge, may be problematic because of the changes that occur as the parts separate. A loose bridge may allow serious deformation or cracking of the bridge plate, which can result in very serious damage to the guitar's top. What seemed like a simple job will have become a major restoration. A loose fingerboard can result in a serious amount of forward-bending of the neck, causing high action and/or the appearance of a loose truss rod. Over-tightening of the truss rod is an example of the kind of mistake an inexperienced repairer might make in an attempt to correct the problem caused by a loose fingerboard.

Broken Truss Rods

A broken truss rod is a very serious condition, and is almost always caused by an attempt to adjust the rod. Over-tightening or twisting a seized nut can break a truss rod, which may require major surgery to correct. The standard repair is to remove the fingerboard, excavate and replace the rod, and reglue the fingerboard. Refretting and refinishing might also be required to complete a very expensive job.

Refrets

Refretting is most commonly an operation used to renew frets that are worn out from years of playing. As certain notes are played repeatedly, the frets under the strings are worn excessively in those positions, making the action difficult and resulting in buzzing.

Frets that are this worn should be replaced.

Removing all the frets allows the luthier a golden opportunity to level and correct the surface of the fingerboard, compensating for years of subtle "settling" of the neck, and returning the neck to the playability it had when new.

When new frets are installed, the luthier can use frets that fit more tightly to make the neck more rigid and stiff, or more loosely to allow a bit of forward flexibility. This is the mechanism by which the stiffness and relief of a neck is controlled when there is no adjustable truss rod. Martin instruments made before 1985, and most classical guitars, are part of a substantial population of instruments without adjustable rods.

Neck Resets

There is one particular serious repair that has received a lot of attention in the last few decades—neck resetting. All acoustic guitars are under a lot of strain caused by string tension, and while they may be well-built, they all respond to this strain with subtle changes in their bodies, particularly in the upper region where the neck is attached. Flattop steel-string guitars are the most susceptible to these body changes because they have very light construction and high string tension. The tension of nylon strings will cause changes in classical guitars, but much more slowly because the tension is quite low compared to steel strings. Archtop guitars have bodies that are generally a lot heavier than flattops, and the arched top and back are more resistant to the pull of the strings.

At this point, most experienced players realize that there will come a time when their steel-string guitar will need to have its neck reset to correct the change brought on by string tension. As the strings pull the neck forward, the back flattens just a bit, the top sinks a little around the soundhole, the "belly" increases in the area of the top around the bridge, and the neckblock rotates forward, resulting in high string action. Over the years, as the action rises, the saddle may be cut lower to accommodate the player's needs. Eventually, though, the saddle would become too low to work properly, and at that point, it's time to reset the neck.

Most neck resetting is accomplished by removing the neck from the body, and cutting the joint precisely to allow it to be refitted to the body at the correct angle for ideal action. Traditional dovetail neck joints can be released by injecting steam to soften the glue.

Modern necks are often a bolt-on design allowing for ease of separation from the body, and reducing the effort and cost of the neck reset operation. Unfortunately, there still are large numbers of steel-string guitars made with non-removable necks. Most of them are inexpensive Asian imports and will be discarded without having their necks reset. A technique sometimes used to reset the neck of a guitar built with such construction is to saw the neck free from the body and convert it to a bolted joint.

Special Considerations

It is up to the owner of the instrument, in partnership with a luthier, to determine the proper course of action for major repair work. Certainly, the owner is the boss and can choose the fate of the guitar, but the luthier has a responsibility to educate the owner as to the cost-effectiveness of any repairs. Consideration must be given to the style and quality with which the instrument was originally built. The current value of the guitar may be a big factor, as will the player's sentimental attachment.

Temperature and Humidity

Ambient temperature and humidity are facts of life that we can't escape. In some parts of the world, it may be nearly impossible to control the humidity in one's living environment. Just as we humans may be uncomfortable in very high or low extremes of temperature and humidity, it's safe to say our guitars suffer right along with us. In a very general sense, it's logical to treat a guitar as though it were alive. The same conditions of high heat that would kill an animal will also cause very serious damage to your guitar. For both animals and guitars, the most common source of such high heat is an enclosed parked car, where the temperature can reach 175 degrees Fahrenheit or more—certain death for cats and dogs, and big trouble for guitars. In high heat, the glue simply loses so much strength that stressed glue joints can come apart completely. Bridges come loose, fingerboards slide—allowing the neck to warp catastrophically—necks come loose, top and back center joints open up, and braces pull loose, especially under the bridge where the stress of string tension is concentrated.

Very low temperatures may cause a guitar's finish to crack as it shrinks, but there are no structurally serious difficulties that arise directly from exposure to low temperatures. Musicians often worry about sending or traveling with their guitars if they are to be stowed in the hold of an airplane. In fact, the only problem that might arise would be a matter of cold checking of the finish. It takes long enough for the temperature inside the aircraft to equilibrate to the low outside temperature at high altitudes that in most situations, this isn't a problem. Leaving the guitar out on the runway in a blizzard is more likely to provide the cold shock necessary to crack the finish. The baggage compartments of aircraft are not pressurized, and fortunately, acoustic guitars don't mind the low atmospheric pressure, so no damage is likely from that source.

Excess heat can lead to parts becoming unglued, such as with this loose bridge.

It is much easier to avoid extremes of temperature than to escape high or low humidity. In fact, we simply couldn't survive in the temperature range that completely destroys guitars, but we can easily tolerate the kind of humidity that can cause real trouble for fine acoustic instruments.

Any consideration of humidity requires some understanding of the way in which atmospheric moisture affects wood, and a knowledge of the ambient humidity in which the guitar was made. As wood gains and loses moisture from the air, it changes dimensionally, but only across the grain—so a board will get wider and thicker, but not longer, when it absorbs water. The most sensitive parts of an acoustic guitar are the top and back, which are glued to the sides all around edges. Since the sides that define the perimeter and the braces on the inside of the top and back can't get longer in high humidity, the top and back will buckle upward and outward. In extreme cases, the upward movement results in a guitar with very high action and a distinctly swollen appearance. The sides also gain moisture, but since they can expand without the same constraints, a guitar might become a bit deeper from front to back; but that won't be noticed as a deformation, and generally won't cause any problem.

In the worst cases, a fingerboard will swell so much that the ends of the frets no longer reach the edge of the fingerboard, and the fingerboard might actually start to overhang the neck a bit. Most of the effects of high humidity can be reversed by returning the guitar to an atmosphere similar to the one in which it was made; and doing so can often reverse all the apparent damage done by excess moisture. Then, the guitar will equilibrate to its surroundings and return to its original dimensions and configuration.

Low humidity does more damage to acoustic guitars because the wood shrinks as it loses moisture. Since the perimeter of the top and back are rigidly defined, the wood develops a lot of tension as it loses moisture. The top is usually most vulnerable, and typically sinks inward, sometimes to the point of being obviously concave. As the tension increases, the wood eventually cracks along the grain lines. Sometimes the dryness causes so much shrinkage that the wood can't actually return to its original size and shape after it is returned to normal humidity, and the top remains somewhat concave for the life of the instrument. Cracks may be so wide as to require inlay of new material.

Because low humidity can accompany high heat, the real disasters come as a combination of the two forces. The high heat of a parked car is once again a major culprit, with the heat driving out moisture; the instrument is subjected to both the effects of high temperature and low humidity. The top not only sinks, but the center glue joint comes apart from glue failure as well.

One of the first signs of low humidity may be the shrinkage of a fingerboard, where the frets start to stick out from the edge. Virtually no new instrument is made with frets that protrude, so if the ends of the frets feel bumpy and sharp along the edge below the surface of the fingerboard, it is a certainty that the fingerboard has shrunk since the guitar was made. Sometimes, this shrinkage is a matter of unseasoned wood shrinking after construction, but most of the time, it is a clear sign of low humidity.

How to Store a Guitar

The safest place to keep your guitar when you aren't playing it is in its hardshell case. Inside the case, the guitar is protected from obvious mechanical damage, falling books, children, or whatever. The case will give some protection from momentary changes in humidity and temperature, but eventually, the conditions inside the case will equilibrate to those outside. In a hot, parked car, for example, the guitar can easily be heated way beyond the temperature necessary to break down the glue and crack the wood in just a few hours. If the case is in direct sunlight, that time will be reduced to a few minutes. The same thing goes for instruments sitting in a room if they are subjected to direct sunlight or the output of a room heater.

The best location for a cased guitar is in an interior closet, where it will be out of the way and further insulated from variations in temperature and humidity. It makes no difference whether the case stands on edge, or lays flat, or even if it is upside down. The guitar will have excellent support at any angle.

But to quote Act 1, Scene 2, of Shakespeare's *Timon of Athens*, " . . . sweet instruments hung up in cases, . . . keep their sounds to themselves." Often, a musician likes to have an instrument handy for a moment of inspiration or practice. Digging out a case, finding a place to open it, and reversing the procedure after playing may impede inspiration before it begins. So, while keeping a guitar sitting out on a stand may be convenient, it is also a good way to risk damaging it. The vinyl or rubber pads on some stands can eat right into a sensitive lacquer or shellac finish. Stands are often at a level where they can be kicked or bumped,

Hanging a guitar on the wall is a safe place to keep it.

denting or sending the guitar flying to nearly certain damage. Luthiers spend a fair amount of time repairing broken headstocks that were the result of a stand being knocked forward, and filling dents and scratches that occurred when a housekeeper's vacuum cleaner collided with a guitar in a stand.

A much safer method of keeping a guitar on display, ready for use, is to hang it on the wall. The same kind of hook commonly used to hang pictures will work quite well for a guitar. Simply tie a leather thong or bootlace around the top two tuning machines, and you have a perfect guitar hanger! Hung on the wall, the guitar is about as safe as it can be without actually residing in its case.

315

Naturally, it pays to use good judgment as to the choice of location where a guitar is to be hung. Directly above a heat radiator or in direct sunlight would be about the worst choices. On an interior wall away from obvious heat sources, a guitar is not only safe and ready for use, but is a great decorative element for any room!

How to Travel with a Guitar

We've all heard stories about people who have lost their luggage when traveling by air. Likewise, musicians have their horror stories about instruments damaged by baggage handlers. Year after year, it has become increasingly difficult to carry a guitar on board any aircraft, and there is every sign that the situation will tighten up even more in the future.

A hardshell case is good protection for travel—after all, that's what they are made for, aren't they? For most travel situations, a solid hardshell case is just the thing. It will protect a guitar from being squashed by other luggage in a car, and it can bump its way safely through any doorway. But, a conventional hardshell case is somewhat vulnerable to mishandling by airline personnel and equipment. There are a number of "flight" cases available, which are quite popular among professional musicians who travel by air. Unfortunately, these cases are quite heavy and very expensive.

The greatest single danger to a guitar in a hardshell case is a matter of "whiplash" at the peghead. As the case is dropped, the inertia of the peghead with its heavy tuners is often enough to break the neck near the nut. Often, a case may be left standing on its end, only to tip and fall flat on the ground. Such a fall never injures or even scratches the case, but it can certainly break a peghead right off. This kind of injury is particularly common among guitars handled by airlines. And, the airline baggage claims office is likely to deny responsibility because, if the case was not injured, they can call that proof that they did not mishandle it.

Crumpled newspaper can be used for extra protection of the headstock.

Packing the peghead, then, becomes the most important simple task a traveler can do to insure the safety of a guitar. If the peghead is held rigidly within the case and prevented from moving, it will not be likely to break if the case takes a substantial fall. Packing material must be resilient and must be very tight. Regular urethane or rubber foam is *not* sufficient. Clothing, or balled up newspaper will suffice, if enough is used. It's a good idea to pack both the top and back of the peghead so that it takes a good deal of force to close the case at that end.

Covering all the latches with duct tape to keep them from snagging along the conveyer completes the job to ready the case for air travel.

For nearly complete security, the case can then be packed in a regular guitar shipping box filled with resilient material, just as though it were to be shipped by a freight carrier. A single hole in the side of the box can make it as convenient to carry as a large piece of luggage.

Packed in its case and then a padded shipping box is a safe way for shipping or checking a guitar with an airline.

317

What to Look for When Buying a Guitar

Buying a new guitar can be incredibly fun and scary at the same time. On one hand, the anticipation of acquiring a finely crafted instrument is enough to make most people become weak in the knees. On the flipside, spending a considerable amount of hard-earned cash tends to raise feelings of doubt. Especially for those who are new to the guitar, finding the right one is often a matter of going with what looks good and putting trust in the sales person at the local music store. In order to minimize the risk of disappointment, it is important to carefully examine what the expectations of the instrument in question are.

What's the "Best?"

The first notion to get out of the way is that there is such a thing as "the best" guitar. Although the chances of getting a high-quality instrument increase with the amount of money you spend, a high price alone is no guarantee that you'll get a guitar that matches your style of music, your tonal preferences, or the "feel" that you like. For example, you could get a beautiful dreadnought by a famous maker, only to find out later that you prefer a wider neck and that the guitar isn't quite responsive enough to the fingerstyle playing you're learning. The very same guitar may be a perfect match for a lead player in a bluegrass band, but as it is, you find yourself playing much better on your friend's laminate-top OM-sized guitar that cost a fraction of what you spent.

The same advice of caution rings true when looking up to musical heroes in choosing an instrument. Just because a guitar sounds good on a famous player's recording or during a concert doesn't mean that this quality will translate into the picking you do in your living room. There are simply too many factors involved in the studio or onstage to know for sure whether the guitar alone is what sounds so good. Maybe the player uses a certain pickup that ends up having a greater impact on his or her sound than the choice of the instrument. Maybe they're running through a rack of effects that will make almost any guitar sound good. Perhaps the most discouraging factor is that they might have a unique touch or playing technique that gives them their signature sound, regardless of the instrument or equipment they use. Think about how you will use the instrument. In the case of a classical guitar, someone who plays a large concert stage will have very different tonal requirements than someone performing in front of a few people in his or her living room. If your style is indeed similar to another player who you like, and you find yourself playing in similar situations, then by all means, check out the gear they use—but don't get hung up on thinking that if it works for them, it must also work for you.

Having a good idea of what you're looking for in a guitar will make it much more likely that you'll end up with a good match. Think about the kind of music you'll use the guitar for. Do you need an instrument for loud strumming? Delicate fingerstyle work? Flamenco? Latin styles? What kind of a neck do you like? What gauge strings do you use? Will you need to amplify? Do you need a cutaway? Finally, you should have a clear idea of how much money you want to spend. All these questions will help you keep a focus while you look at your options, and ultimately avoid disappointment.

How Much Do I Have to Spend?

Unless you are one of the lucky few who doesn't have to worry about such minor matters, price is likely to be an important factor in your search. The less you have to spend, the more careful you have to be in making sure that you're getting a maximum degree of quality and tone; but even if you can afford a guitar at the upper ceiling of the spectrum, it pays to think about what you're getting for your money.

Budget Instruments

At the time of the writing of this book, it is possible to find new nylon-string guitars for as little as $100, and steel-strings for under $150. Even after adjusting one's expectations for quality to the undeniably attractive price, there usually isn't much to be recommended about these ultra-cheap instruments. While we can excuse the low-grade laminated woods and questionable craftsmanship, it's difficult to ignore the often unbelievably poor playability. Generally caused by details such as a bad neck angle, shoddy fretwork, or lack of a setup, these guitars have taken the desire to play out of more than one beginning picker. If you absolutely have to keep your spending at a minimum, then it will probably be better to look into a good used instrument. While finding the right guitar might take some help from an experienced friend or teacher, it will generally be possible to end up with one of greater quality than if you bought a new one.

Spending about $100 more than the bare minimum just mentioned is likely to result in a quantum leap of quality. At this price, you'll begin to encounter entry-level models from some of the major manufacturers, which often feature playability similar to the more expensive instruments. Although most instruments under about $300 will still be made out of all laminated woods, these guitars tend to have a much better fit of parts, superior finish, and carefully executed setups. Some brands to look for in this range include Alvarez Yairi, Epiphone, Takamine, and Washburn for steel-strings, and Aria, Cordoba, and Yamaha for nylon-strings. There are no archtop guitars available at this price.

The next jump in value generally accompanies guitars with price tags that pass the $300 mark. The magic words here are "solid tops," which are beginning to appear on instruments in this range. As described in chapter 5, a solid top is made from a solid piece of wood rather than a laminate, leading to a greater ability to vibrate, and thus almost always resulting in better sound. The majority of instruments in this category are made in Asia, but you can also start to find some Spanish-made nylon-strings and American-made steel-strings. This is an excellent price range to look in for beginning players. With a sound that can be surprisingly mature, these guitars won't make you feel like you need to upgrade as soon as you've learned to play a few chords, yet the initial investment is low enough that you're not going to loose too much money if you find out that you need a different type of guitar or that you're not as interested in the instrument as you thought you were. Many accomplished players keep an inexpensive solid-top guitar around as a back-up to their more expensive, main guitar; and equipped with a pickup, these instruments can make fine stage guitars.

In order to get the best sound in an inexpensive guitar, it can't be overstressed how important it is to avoid being seduced by features that you don't need. As a general rule, the fancier a cheap guitar looks, the more likely it is that the manufacturer put more emphasis on appearance than on tone. Elaborate inlays in the fingerboard, or pearl binding, probably means that corners had to be cut elsewhere to keep the price affordable. Similarly, it's best to stay away from features such as cutaways and pickups, unless you absolutely need them. Most guitarists would agree that they'd be glad to forego a cutaway for superior tone, and a pickup (perhaps even one better than what comes stock on an inexpensive instrument) can always be added as the need arises. Good examples of guitars that offer a maximum of tone and playability without breaking the bank include Godin's line of Seagull guitars and Taylor's Big Baby.

Taylor's Big Baby (left) offers the company's famous playability and tone at a lower price-point. Canada's Seagull guitars (right) are also well-made, affordable flattops.

Mid-Level Steel-String Flattops

Particularly in the world of steel-string flattops, the last decade or so has seen amazing strides in the $500 to $1000 range. While spending this kind of money may seem like a lot for someone who's still uncertain of their commitment to the instrument, most experienced players and retailers agree that this is perhaps were the greatest overall value can be found.

With today's enormous selection, it's easy to forget about the once rampant gap between inexpensive entry-level guitars (usually made in Japan or Korea) and high-end instruments (particularly those made in the U.S.). The key to shrinking these differences can be attributed to greater efficiency in the building process, much of it due to CNC (Computer Numerical Controlled) machines and less labor-intensive UV–cured finishes (see chapter 7). Although American companies such as Gibson and Guild had previously offered relatively inexpensive versions of their popular models, this market was virtually replaced by Japanese instruments during the 1970s and 1980s. Pioneering the use of CNC machines for carving necks and manufacturing parts, Taylor shook up the industry when it introduced its 410 dreadnought for under $1000 in 1991. Although the guitar featured simplified appointments, a satin finish, and slightly lower-grade (but all solid) woods, it provided much of the same tone, feel, and quality as the company's more expensive guitars. Not surprisingly, the guitar became a huge success, leaving other manufacturers scrambling to follow suit. Within a year or two, Martin was offering its 1-Series, Gibson came out first with an updated Gospel model and then the Working Musician's Series, and Guild was making an economy version of its classic D-25 called the D-4. At a time when several of these classic guitar companies were struggling to adapt to a changing market, these new lower-cost instruments allowed a new generation of players to own a guitar made by Gibson, Guild, Martin, or Taylor.

These first examples of modern all-solid-wood guitars available at an affordable price triggered what can only be called a domino effect. Not only do all of the well-known American manufacturers now offer this type of instrument, but several Japanese companies, such as Alvarez Yairi and Takamine have joined the ranks.

It is fair to say that in many cases, these mid-level guitars offer very similar performance to the more expensive models made by the same companies. Bob Taylor has been known to say that his entry-level 300 series offers 90% of the sound of the high-end 900 series at less than a third of the cost. This kind of a statement illustrates that it is the design and construction of the guitar that accounts for a much greater part of its tone than the woods it uses. To continue using Taylor as an example, while an entry-level 310 model uses sapele (an African wood similar to mahogany) back and sides, a Sitka spruce top, partial satin finish (for its back and sides), and simple appointments, it's built exactly the same as the 910 model, which uses high-grade Indian rosewood and Engelmann spruce. For many players, the decision comes down to preferring a certain look or wood combination or a need for features which aren't offered in the lower-end models (such as cutaways, electronics, or custom options).

Guitars such as Taylor's 300 series (left) and Guild's D-4 (right) represent inexpensive versions of the manufacturers' more upscale models.

Mid-Level Nylon-String Guitars (Classical and Flamenco)

Classical and flamenco guitars in the $600 to $2000 range differ from their steel-string cousins in that they haven't experienced the same revolutionary changes in construction techniques. This can primarily be attributed to the fact that very few of these instruments are made in the U.S., where a high cost of labor has made efficiency in the building process a top priority. The vast majority of mid-price nylon-string instruments are manufactured in Spain and Japan, with other Asian and European countries also participating in the market share.

As with nylon-strings at any price, the basic look, design, and internal construction of these instruments doesn't vary nearly as much as it does with steel-string guitars. Mostly based on Antonio de Torres' design from the mid-1800s, these guitars usually feature similar body dimensions, a fan-braced top, and a wide neck with a slotted headstock. Because of these superficial similarities, the quality of materials, craftsmanship, and attention to details become the factors that make some examples better than others.

At the lower end of this range, one can find models made by companies such as Aria, Alvarez, Cordoba, Takamine, and Raimundo. Generally featuring a solid top (either spruce or cedar) with a laminated back and sides, these guitars are ideal for student-level players and those for whom the guitar is mostly a casual hobby. Despite their low price, these guitars should offer tone that, while not as mature as on more expensive instruments, doesn't give the impression of a compromise, and their playability shouldn't limit the player in executing difficult techniques.

At the higher end of this range, one can find instruments, which, at their best, are very close to concert-level guitars. With the exception of some acoustic-electric versions, these instruments should be made from solid woods all around and exhibit a high degree of craftsmanship. Although the majority of guitars fitting this description still come out of factories, a few will represent the entry-level offerings of some smaller shops and individual luthiers. These instruments are ideal for advanced students and hobbyists, as well as those who are beginning to play concerts but can't afford a more expensive guitar.

Many manufacturers offer versions of these models with cutaways and pickups. With a reasonably good acoustic sound, excellent playability, and worry-free plugged-in performance, these guitars are great for using a nylon-string sound in a band context and for working musicians who need maximum versatility.

Yamaha's GCX31C (left) is a typical example of an acoustic-electric classical guitar. The guitar on the right is a mid-level Hanika 1 APF.

High-End Guitars

With guitars that surpass the $1500–$2000 range, a lot of the differences will be more about what the individual player prefers than a simple questions of quality. In the case of steel-string flattops, many of the famous models by major manufacturers—such as a Martin D-28 or a Gibson J-45—are available for not too much above the threshold for this class. These upper-level factory guitars, which would also include most models by Avalon, Guild, Lakewood, Larrivee, and Taylor, among others, are excellent utility instruments, and represent the type of guitar that most professionals play. Although these instruments often share a similar design with mid-level models by the same manufacturers, and they're generally made on the same production line, they also feature better quality woods and greater attention to detail.

Martin's D-45 is made with premium woods, and features rich ornamentation.

Above a price of about $3000, most factory guitars begin differentiating more in terms of decoration than in the actual quality of materials or sound. Guitars in this category include models such as Martin's classic abalone-bound D-45, Gibson's J-200 Vine, or Taylor's Presentation Series. Certainly, these models feature premium quality woods, extensive inlays, and stunning quality throughout, but from a purely utilitarian perspective, they won't surpass their standard-model siblings by the same amount that their prices increase.

Many connoisseurs of acoustic tone find that instead of going with a top-of-the-line factory guitar, they prefer an instrument made in a smaller manufacturing environment. Building in much smaller numbers (about 500 to 3000 instruments annually, as opposed to as many as 60,000 that the largest builders produce), companies such as Collings, Goodall, Lowden, and Santa Cruz are seen by many as the next step in quality. Operating on less of a production line, but offering more skilled luthiers doing more than a few steps of the building process, these companies are able to offer a greater degree of individual attention than bigger manufacturers. This will manifest itself in more careful selection of materials, tops that are individually voiced by hand, and the possibility for a myriad of custom options.

Popular guitars from smaller shops: A Goodall RGC (left) and a Lowden O25 (right).

At the upper end of the available spectrum of acoustic guitars are instruments that are made one at a time, by a single luthier or a handful of luthiers working in a very small workshop. In the steel-string world, these kinds of guitars tend to be primarily for those who either have specific needs that aren't addressed by a factory instrument, or who simply like to be certain that they're getting the ultimate in quality. With the majority of professional players using high-end factory guitars, it could be argued that there are few tonal reasons for choosing an individually made steel-string, even though their beauty and "vibe" are undeniable. The last twenty years have seen an abundance of new luthiers specializing in making custom steel-strings, and their names are too many to list. In the U.S., some of the top-level examples would include James Olson, Kevin Ryan, Jeff Traugott, and Froggy Bottom, but European makers such as Albert & Müller in Germany, Stefan Sobell in England, and Maurice Dupont in France are not to be ignored.

Guitars such as this Froggy Bottom M (left) and Albert & Müller S6 (right) are made individually and almost completely by hand.

Among classical guitarists, there is no question that an individually made guitar is an object of desire for any advanced player. Although high-end factory instruments such as those by Hirade (Japan), Hanika (Germany), or some of the Spanish manufacturers like Rodriguez or Ramírez offer excellent tone and playability, they really aren't used by any professional concert-level players. With the ability to use the highest quality materials, and utmost attention to detail, luthiers such as Paulino Bernabé in Spain, Thomas Humphrey in the U.S., Matthias Damman in Germany, or Greg Smallman in Australia are able to continuously advance what the instrument is capable of.

The process of buying a small-shop or luthier-made instrument generally differs from the way a factory guitar would be acquired. Due to the limited numbers that these makers produce, most of these instruments are either sold directly by the maker or in very specialized guitar galleries. In many cases, the guitar will have to be special ordered, with waiting lists of several years not being uncommon for some of the top luthiers. An individual consultation with the maker is often an integral part of choosing all the details of the instrument to be made, resulting in a guitar that—at least in theory—will be a perfect match for its future owner.

A high-end Albert & Müller CL4 classical guitar.

Archtop and Selmer/Maccaferri–Style Guitars

Because acoustic archtops and Selmer/Maccaferri-style guitars represent a rather small niche in the overall market, their availability differs from steel-string flattops and classical guitars. As these guitars are really part of a past era, their appeal to the instrument-buying masses is limited, resulting in the fact that there are virtually no really inexpensive options to choose from.

In the case of archtops, the entry-level is found in instruments such as Epiphone's Emperor Regent or Aria's FA-71, both of which reside around the $1000 mark. With a good setup, these guitars can make fine instruments for players who only play an archtop occasionally or who are just starting out, but their laminate tops keep them from being able to truly compete with more expensive examples of the genre. In many cases, the most cost-effective way to get a good archtop at a reasonable price is to hunt down an instrument that was made during the acoustic archtop's glory days between the 1930s and 1950s, as the jump to higher

Aria's FA-71 is an entry-level archtop.

quality new models tends to be an expensive one. Gibson's 1920s style L-5 reissue, Guild's Artist Award, and the current crop of Japanese-made D'Angelicos are good examples of high-end factory archtops; but with list prices for these guitars hovering in the $6000–$8000 range, it's also worth looking into what individual luthiers have to offer. American luthiers such as Steve Andersen and Dale Unger have begun making plain-looking versions of their individually made creations, often competing with the prices of good factory-made instruments.

The upper end of the archtop spectrum features some of the most expensive guitars of any style. Luthiers such as Bob Benedetto, Linda Manzer, Tom Ribbecke, and John Monteleone constantly redefine the fusion of function and beauty, elevating the genre to new heights.

A modern Steven Andersen Streamline archtop (left) and a vintage Gibson L-12 (right).

While archtops had the benefit of being produced by several major manufacturers, Selmer was the primary maker of guitars based on Mario Maccaferri's design during the instrument's heyday. Even though it provided a major factory setting, the company built less than 1000 guitars between 1932 and 1952, making surviving originals a rare commodity. However, several "vintage copies" as well as offerings by contemporary manufacturers, are available to players seeking the original Django sound.

In the 1950s, shortly after Selmer stopped their guitar production, Jacques Favino began making a guitar inspired by the classic Selmer that was slightly wider across the lower bout and slightly deeper. In the 1970s, more and more luthiers began to build guitars in the Selmer style to meet the demand created by a resurgence of the style. In England, John LeVoi, Doug Kyle, and David Hodson, and in Scotland, Ron Aylward, have all gained reputations for making fine guitars in the tradition. The current crop of luthiers offering Selmer-style guitars also includes Germany's Stefan Hahl, whose instruments are used by Gypsy jazz star Bireli Lagrene. In France, Maurice Dupont makes what most players consider to be the most accurate reproductions, while Jean-Pierre Favino carries on the tradition of his father Jacques. North American builders include individual builders Michael Dunn and Canadian Shelley Park. Dell' Arte in California offers a wide range of models based on both Selmer and Favino designs. In the 1970s, Maurice Summerfield began having Selmer reproductions made in Japan by Ibanez and later Saga. In the late 1980s, Saga offered a line of five different Selmer copies, including both 12- and 14-fret models. They discontinued production by 1990, but they recently revived it with the

Two Selmer-style guitars by Klaus Röder.

introduction of the Chinese made Gitane Models that feature both 12-fret neck/ D-shaped soundhole, and 14-fret/oval soundhole models.

New vs. Used

Just as is the case with most things we buy, the majority of guitars sold in music stores come fresh from the factory. Buying a brand new guitar will give you that special feeling of being the first one to play it, put your own set of scratches and dings in it, and begin your relationship with the instrument with a clean slate. A new guitar will also have a warranty from the manufacturer (often for the life of the original owner). There will also most likely be a greater selection of similar instruments to choose from, and in the case of a newly introduced model, it may be the only way to find the instrument in question. However, there are just as many—and maybe more—reasons to consider buying a previously owned guitar. Clearly the most common reason for going this route is to save money. With the exception of certain rare and vintage guitars (more on these later), a used guitar will generally sell for one-half to two-thirds of the price that was on its tag the first time it got sold. If you're starting out, this can mean the difference between only being able to afford a guitar made entirely with laminated woods, and finding out that you can get one with a solid top. At the higher end, you may be able to get a model that's higher up in the manufacturer's line, or you might save enough money to afford a pickup installed and buying an amp. Because a properly cared-for guitar doesn't really "wear out" (although certain part such as the frets, tuners, or the nut and saddle may have to eventually be replaced), the money saved comes without any compromises in tone, playability, or longevity.

Another reason for considering a used guitar is because the guitar you're looking for isn't available as a brand new instrument. In the most drastic example, a company may have stopped making a certain model altogether, making the hunt for a used one the only choice. It's also possible that the model you're after is still being made, but that the specs have changed, and you prefer the older style. Esoteric vintage specifications are the most obvious example of this, but there are also many instances of more recent changes to certain guitar's designs. For example, Martin began using Micarta (a very dense synthetic material) bridge and fingerboards on its 16 series guitars in 2001. If you feel that the previous choice of real ebony was superior, then you might want to try to find one that was made prior to the switch.

Another example is found in the fact that many manufacturers have started to auto-matically include side-mounted preamps and pickups in all their cutaway guitars. Unless you want to go through the trouble and expense of a special order, the only way to get certain cutaway guitars without electronics is to find an older one.

Finally, many players feel that older guitars simply sound better than new ones. Although a certain amount such sentiments may be hearsay, there is no doubt about the fact that most quality guitars "open up" with age. As the wood ages, the glue and finish hardens, and the entire instrument "settles" under the prolonged tension of the strings; so you'll often find that an older "played-in" guitar will offer superior volume, a greater dynamic range, and better frequency response than a new one of the same kind.

Conditions and Repairs to Watch Out for with a Used Guitar

As with anything you buy used, it's a good idea to make sure that there's nothing wrong with the guitar you're considering. If the guitar in question is being sold by a store with a good reputation, then you probably have little to worry about; but if you're buying from a private individual, you should use some caution.

After looking the guitar over for any signs of obvious damage or visible repairs, you should give it a playing test. How does it sound? Do all the tuning machines work smoothly? Is the action at the height that you like? Are there buzzes in cer-tain areas of the fingerboard? How's the guitar's intonation? Does it play in tune throughout the fingerboard? Are the strings old and worn out? If you're serious about the purchase, then it might be a good idea to restring the guitar with your preferred set in order to form a better opinion.

Check whether the guitar's neck is straight. If you hold the guitar up and look down its fingerboard, you will be able to see whether it's flat or curved. Most steel-string guitars are equipped with adjustable truss rods, which can be used to straighten a slight bow; but on a classical guitar, you may be faced with an expensive repair. If the guitar does have a truss rod, then you might want to make sure that it works. Broken truss rods are rare, but stripped nuts or frozen threads can make it very difficult to use it for its intended purpose.

What is the condition of the guitar's frets? A little bit of wear will be normal, but if you see deep divots under the strings, then it might be time for a fret-mill, or even a re-fret. See whether any of the fret-ends are lifting, necessitating a repair. While you're at it, check for poorly done re-frets. Are the ends of the frets nicely crowned? Some less-than-stellar repair people will cut into a fingerboard's binding during a re-fret, resulting in a crude appearance, and greatly reducing the instrument's value.

Next take a look at the bridge. On a steel-string flattop or a classical guitar, check whether the bridge is lifting by trying to push a piece of paper under it. If the paper is able to slide between the top and the bridge, then it will have to be reglued, which often involves a complete removal. Make sure there are no cracks between the pins or on either side of the saddle. These can sometimes be glued, but often it's best to replace the entire bridge if this turns out to be an issue. Check whether the area behind the bridge is bulging, causing a dome-shape in the top. A little bit of this is normal with an older guitar, but severe cases may indicate internal problems, such as loose braces.

On an archtop (or any guitar with the strings attached to a tailpiece), make sure that the bridge hasn't caused the top to cave in under the tension of the strings. If the bridge is an adjustable design, make sure the mechanism works.

Check whether the saddle has been lowered to the point where it's hardly exposed. Not only will a low saddle make it difficult to further reduce the height of the action if necessary, it could also indicate a neck that's been pulled forward by the strings, necessitating an expensive neck reset. Spotting this kind of potential problem requires a certain amount of experience, so if you have any doubts, you might want to get a second opinion.

Give the guitar a good shake (but be careful to not hit anything!). This will indicate if there are any loose parts, particularly on instruments with onboard electronics. If you lightly tap on various areas of the top and back, you should be able to determine whether there are any loose braces inside the guitar's body. As with a loose bridge, braces whose glue has come undone may be an indication of the guitar having been exposed to very hot temperatures, which could have other adverse consequences.

Look for cracks in the wood. Cracks that are the result of impact can usually be glued and are merely a cosmetic issue. However, some cracks—such as split between the two bookmatched halves of the top—may be caused by a lack of humidification, and a proper repair may be more involved than a simple glue job.

Look for a crack or repaired break at the back of the neck in the area behind the nut. This is one of the guitar's weakest areas, and breaks are common. Although a good repair will restore the headstock's original strength, any issues in this area should greatly reduce the instrument's selling price.

If the guitar has a pickup, then make sure it's in good working condition. Check whether the strings have even output, whether there is any distortion, and whether all the controls do what they're supposed to.

Finally, make sure the guitar's serial number is intact. Most quality guitars have the number printed on a label inside the body, or stamped onto the neckblock or the back of the headstock. The seller of the instrument should be able to explain the reason for a missing serial number, as it could indicate stolen property.

If the guitar you're looking at passed all these tests, then its time to start negotiating. If it looks like it needs repairs, then they should be taken into consideration. Use common sense in deciding whether the guitar is worth buying. If it's a model that's widely available, then you might be able to find one in better condition for the same or only slightly higher price. However, if the guitar you're looking at is a rare model, then it might be worth going through a certain amount of repairs, even if it means spending a little more than originally planned.

Guitar shows can be good places to see custom and used guitars.

Vintage Guitars

At a certain point, old guitars go from simply being "used" to becoming "vintage." Age is certainly one deciding factor (it seems as though at least 25 to 30 years have to go by before the term is appropriate), but availability, historical significance, and associations with famous players also figure into whether a guitar can wear the vintage badge of honor.

Vintage guitars are interesting from several perspectives. Just like with anything else that's old and rare, collecting vintage instruments has become a hobby for some, and, with prices for certain examples exceeding $100,000, a lucrative business for others. Instead of being played, these instruments often end up in glass showcases, creating controversy among musicians who feel that they're being deprived of functional tools for their musical expression.

Indeed, certain vintage guitars provide tonal qualities that are difficult, if not impossible, to find in newly made examples. Experts love to argue about the specific reasons for this vintage mystique, but most agree in several areas. The most important myth to get beyond is the notion that old guitars are better because they have simply "aged." While it's true that a good instrument will likely get better as it gets older, this process alone won't turn an average instrument into one that's superb. Accordingly, the guitars that we lust after 60 or 70 years after they were built probably started out with excellent tone, only to "mature" even further as the years went by. Interestingly, it is often the guitars that show obvious signs of having been played a lot that sound the best. Whether this is because people wanted to play them because they always sounded good, or that they sound good because they've been played is another issue that's up for debate.

Particularly in the case of steel-string flattops, one difference between many old guitars and newer versions of the same models is that chances are that the older example was built a lot lighter. Because the use of steel-strings was still relatively new in the 1920s and 1930s, manufacturers hadn't come to terms with how strong a guitar needs to be built in order to keep it from collapsing over time. While these early guitars often sounded spectacular, a growing amount of warranty claims ended up causing many companies to build their steel-string guitars stronger. A prime example of this phenomenon is found in Martin's move from scalloped braces to non-scalloped braces on its D-28 model in 1945, which reduced the amount of necessary repairs, but also took away some of the volume and bass response that the older design was revered for. However, thanks in part to the fact that few players still use strings that are as heavy as what was once common, many of the lightly built originals have survived the test of time better than expected.

Another often-cited reason for the superior sound of many old guitars is that they utilized better-quality woods than what's available today. Particularly with varieties such as the Brazilian rosewood and Adirondack ("red") spruce used on many high-priced Gibsons and Martins, this is a point that's hard to argue with, as the supply simply isn't as available as it was 50 years ago. However, many players and luthiers alike feel that the quality of the wood alone is a relatively minor factor in a guitar's overall performance. To substantiate this claim, all one has to do is point out that there are as many poorly sounding instruments made out of the highest grade of woods as there are instruments made from less-than-perfect materials that sound spectacular by any definition of the term.

With acoustic archtop guitars, the vintage market looks a little different. Because production of these instruments experienced a drastic decline after the introduction of electric guitars, a much larger segment of the "used" market happens to be "vintage." Because of this, Gibson, Epiphone, or Guild archtops from the 1950s can be a wise choice for players who simply want a good-sounding guitar and have no interest in becoming collectors. With most high-quality contemporary archtops being custom creations, these instruments should even be considered as cost-effective solutions. In order to get a good deal on a "player's" guitar, it helps to keep a few points in mind. Blonde (natural finish) models will cost more than sunburst versions. Although the only real difference is in the color of the finish, collectors almost always prefer blonde guitars, as they display the wood's grain and possible flame patterns (particularly in the case of maple back and sides). Additionally, cutaways tend to fetch higher prices than non-cutaways. For some players, there is no question that a cutaway is necessary, but others may be able to save a considerable amount by asking themselves whether they really need easy access to the higher frets. If all you do is play rhythm in a swing band, chances are that a cutaway is nothing but an expensive feature with little practical use. If finding a good utility instrument is the primary goal, then it will also be a good idea to look beyond famous models associated with particular artists of the past. For example, don't expect to find many bargains on mint-condition 1934 Gibson L-5s, but plainer models such as the L-7 or L-12 may turn out to be excellent-playing and -sounding instruments costing hundreds or even thousands less.

Curiously, classical and flamenco guitars are virtually untouched by the vintage craze that often surrounds older American steel-strings. While historically significant instruments—such as an original Torres, Hauser, Ramírez, or Fleta—will be sought after by collectors, they tend to have little appeal to contemporary players. In the case of flamenco guitars, the reason for this is found in the fact that few of the instruments survive decades of the abuse posed by the aggressive playing that's typical for the style. While many older classical guitars continue to sound great, incredible strides have been made in the construction of the instruments. In a constant quest for greater volume, dynamic range, and overall tone, it appears that most contemporary players prefer modern classical guitars.

Two vintage classics: A Gibson L-00 (left) and a Martin 0-15 (right).

Vintage Reissues

With an increased demand for vintage instruments, many manufacturers have started making models that promise to offer the tone and feel of their designs of the past. It goes without saying that a true vintage reissue can only be offered by companies that were around when today's vintage guitars were new, which in the world of acoustic guitars essentially means Martin and Gibson. The vintage phenomenon hasn't caught on with makers of classical or flamenco guitars, which tend not to advertise the fact that many of their designs are virtually the same as they were 50 years ago.

Introduced in 1961, Martin's 0-21NY may have been the first example of a new model that clearly resembled an earlier discontinued design. With the folk music boom introducing a new generation of players to the small-bodied, 12-fret guitars Martin had made 30 or 40 years earlier, the company was quick to develop a relatively inexpensive instrument to meet the demand. However, the aspect of vintage specs wasn't really a plan of the company's marketing until the introduction of the HD-28 dreadnought in 1976. Having stopped the use of scalloped bracing and herringbone purfling on its guitars in the mid-1940s, this was the first model that reintroduced these pre-war features on a new guitar. Without a doubt, the decision to bring back the older design was spurred by the fact that, in an attempt to achieve the much praised tone of older Martin dreadnoughts, more and more luthiers were reaching inside guitars to scallop their braces after the fact.

Gibson didn't begin offering vintage reissues until the company moved its acoustic division to its current home in Bozeman, Montana in the early 1990s. Under the leadership of luthier Ren Ferguson, it didn't take long for the company to reintroduce J-45s, J-200s, Hummingbirds, and other models that were true to their original designs.

Both Martin and Gibson continue to build reissues of many of their most popular vintage models. In both cases, the resulting instruments are very close to the originals, but usually take the contemporary availability of materials and certain improvements into consideration. For example, while the Martins built prior to 1969 featured Brazilian rosewood as a standard, the more affordable Indian rosewood is used on the majority of reissues. Martin reissues also feature adjustable truss rods in their necks, even though the company didn't start using them until 1985. It is also logical that while most of the guitars are true to those of the past, today's instruments are built with contemporary construction techniques. This includes modern glues and finishes, and parts that are often carved by CNC machines rather than by hand.

If you want a guitar that's a closer copy of a vintage instrument than what the original companies are offering today, then a number of smaller builders are happy to oblige. Using the best of what vintage guitars have to offer as a template, builders such as the Merrill Brothers, Schoenberg Guitars, or Lynn Dudenbostel create instruments that don't have to fear comparison with their inspirations in any way.

On the left, a Gibson Advanced Jumbo reissue. On the right, Martin's HD-28CW.

Factory-Built or Custom-Made

The majority of guitars are manufactured in large factories. With its high level of efficiency, this type of environment is ideal for creating instruments that offer a very favorable ratio of quality vs. price. Although the thought of a factory dispells the romanticism many associate with acoustic guitars, one shouldn't forget that, particularly in the history of flattop steel-strings, many of the most highly regarded instruments have come out of factories. To serve as an example, Martin was already a large operation building several thousand instruments annually when it produced what are now considered its "Golden Era" guitars during the 1920s and 1930s.

Today, manufacturers such as Martin, Taylor, and Larrivée are continuously raising the bar on the quality and consistency that high-volume production can achieve. Considering that the output by these companies is close to 200 instruments *per day*, each, during peak production periods, it quickly becomes clear that no single craftsperson can complete an entire guitar from beginning to end in the same time frame. Nevertheless, due to stringent quality control, careful selection of materials, and striking attention to detail, for many players, the resulting instruments often represent the finest available in terms of sound, playability, and functionality.

Some players have different requirements of their guitars than what stock models offer. Reasons for this might include a need for different neck dimensions, particular tonal ideas, or a desire for an instrument that has a distinct look. Because of this, many manufacturers offer custom shops where it is possible to special order variations of standard models. Although prices can be significantly higher than on stock models, and delivery often takes several months, special ordering a guitar from a large manufacturer often results in very special instruments that are perfectly tailored to their owners.

If more individuality is desired than what can be achieved by slightly altering an otherwise mass-produced guitar, then it is possible to order a completely unique instrument from one of many smaller shops. Most independent luthiers will work with the customers to choose exactly the right body size, combination of woods, and visual elements, creating instruments that are truly one-of-a-kind. Besides getting unique specifications and looks, many players also find that, because of the additional attention to detail, an individually made custom guitar also results in better tone and general performance.

While steel-string players have differing opinions about whether factory- or custom-made guitars suit them better (and top-level professionals can be found playing either), there are virtually no professional classical or flamenco guitarists who use factory-made instruments. Perhaps due to the nylon-string guitar's association with classical music (a classical violinist wouldn't consider a factory-made instrument either), but also because of an undeniable jump in tone quality between factory and individually made instruments, practically all high-end nylon-strings are made in relatively small numbers by independent luthiers. Of course there are large numbers of nylon-string guitars in the lower- and medium-price ranges made in factories around the world, but the majority of these instruments remains aimed at student-level players, hobbyists, and those who play acoustic-electric.

Archtop guitars have traditionally been split relatively evenly between being made in factories and small shops. Many of the world's most famous instruments of this category came out of the Gibson, Epiphone, or Guild facilities, where they were churned out alongside hundreds of other instruments. On the other hand, makers such as John D'Angelico and his apprentice Jimmy D'Aquisto where among the first wave of American luthiers building ultra-high quality instruments. Today, this tradition is continued by makers such John Monteleone, Tom Ribbecke, and Linda Manzer, whose instruments fetch some of the highest prices of any non-vintage guitars.

Although there is a large number of relatively inexpensive factory-made electric archtops available, it is difficult to find good examples made primarily for acoustic playing. Epiphone's Emperor Regent, Aria's line of D'Aquisto copies, and some of Eastman Strings' archtops are some of the few choices available.

Jean Larrivée and his son Matthew in the Californian Larrivée factory (top). Smaller shops, such as that operated by the Santa Cruz Guitar Co., still rely on a lot of steps being done by hand (bottom).

343

What Does "Handmade" Mean?

Whether a guitar is made in a large factory or made in a one-person shop, it is quite likely that the word "handmade" is found on its label or as part of its description in a catalog. Naturally, this word has various meanings among different instruments. Given how there's no such thing as a machine that turns raw materials into a finished guitar, all guitars feature a certain amount of hand-work in their manufacturing process. Necks are carved, sides are bent, lacquer is sprayed, etc., but in the case of a large factory, it's likely to be dozens, if not hundreds, of hands that touch the guitar before it is completed. On the other hand, a growing number of small-scale manufacturers are beginning to use power tools and even CNC machines in their shops, resulting in the fact that their instruments aren't completely made by hand, if held to a strict definition of the term.

Because of these confusing issues, most people familiar with acoustic guitars prefer to distinguish between *factory-made*, and *individually made* instruments. An

In a really small shop (in this case at Albert & Müller), each guitar gets lots of individual attention.

individually made guitar from a small shop will not only differ from one made in a factory in the amount of machinery used in the building process, but chances are it was also conceived as a unique piece of work, rather than one of many. Smaller shops will also be able to pay more attention in order to voice each instrument according to the particular set of woods used. For example, while a factory is likely to use the same pre-cut braces no matter what the stiffness of a particular top is like, a luthier in a small shop may carefully shave the braces of each guitar until it reaches the exact sound he or she is striving for. While invisible from the outside of a finished instrument, these are the kinds of details that can squeeze the last bit performance out of an instrument, and it is here that a luthier's real skills come to light.

Amount of Ornamentation ("Appointments")

Looking at a selection of guitars, it quickly becomes clear that some are very plain looking, while others are downright gaudy. Strangely enough, the selling price of the instrument tends to have little to do with the amount of decoration it receives, as there are examples of austerity and beyond-kitsch to be found at all price ranges.

Over the years, different kinds of guitars have gone through various stages of ornamentation. French and Italian guitars of the 18th century often featured elaborate inlay, binding, and rosettes, as did many American flattop steel-strings made for the cowboy singers of the 1930s.

In the case of the classical guitar, the instrument began taking on a more utilitarian look around the time Torres conceived of his groundbreaking designs. While earlier makers had used pearl rosettes and purfling, luthiers now followed suit and limited themselves to designs made out of dyed wood, often using intricate mosaics to display their individuality. Undoubtedly influenced by Andrés Segovia's conservative aesthetics, this approach has remained to be the standard for classical guitars to this day. An occasional exception to this rule can be found in the carved bridges and headstocks of guitars made by luthiers such as Jerónimo Peña Fernández.

With flattop steel-strings, the story looks a little different. Traditionally, a maker's line of guitars will feature more elaborate appointments as the level of quality goes upward. Martin is a good example of this approach, with the company's entry-level style15 featuring nothing but simple dots in the fingerboard, while the top-of-the-line style 45 is completely bound in abalone pearl and sports matching inlays in the fingerboard. At the same time that the appearance gets more dressed up, Martin also reserves its premium-quality woods for the upper end of the line, theoretically resulting in these guitar's having superior sound.

As with virtually all other things related to steel-string guitars, Martin's model designations are now being used to describe other makers' levels of ornamentation. For example, a "style 45" will generally refer to a rosewood body that's completely bound with abalone pearl, while people might refer to a "style 18" when talking about a plain looking guitar made out of mahogany. Taylor and Gibson have similar structures of appointments relating to the quality—and price—of a model. For example, Taylor's 800 series and 900 series are both made with Indian rosewood back and sides and spruce tops; but while the 800s use relatively simple binding and inlay, 900s feature abalone-bound tops, more elaborate inlay in the neck, and higher-grade woods that make an obvious visual difference. Gibson has traditionally reserved fancy inlay work for its high-end Hummingbird, Dove, and J-200 models.

Many times, appointments that rival those found on the expensive models by a famous maker are found on surprisingly cheap Asian imports. Made possible by inexpensive labor, and in many cases, fake materials, such as imitation pearl, these instruments will give inexperienced buyers the impression that they're getting more value than they would with a less expensive model by the same maker. However, this impression often turns out to be false, as many guitars matching this description are really the exact same instruments as those costing much less, but simply feature gussied-up looks. Especially with inexpensive guitars, it is therefore important to look beyond appearance when trying to get the best sound for the money. A plain-looking instrument by a manufacturer that also makes high-end guitars is almost always preferable to a fancy one at the same price that represents the maker's top-of-the-line.

It is interesting to note that among small-shop custom guitarmakers, the trend has been overwhelmingly toward instruments that show restraint in their appointments. In most cases, this is not a step to save money, but rather an attempt to truly show the elevated quality of the materials and craftsmanship without unnecessary distractions. Archtop makers such as Jimmy D'Aquisto and Bob Benedetto were among the first to choose austerity over ostentation, essentially following the direction taken earlier by classical builders.

The D-50 is Martin's top-of-the-line stock model (left), and Taylor's standard line peaks with the Presentation series, such as this PS-55 (right).

Should I Get an Acoustic-Electric If I Don't Really Need It?

These days, many guitars come with built-in pickups and preamps whether you ask for these features or not. Particularly steel-string flattops that feature a cutaway are increasingly difficult to find without electronics. While some players welcome this trend, many others find that they never have a need to plug in. As the years go by and new electronics become available, it becomes apparent that what once seemed like "added value" has suddenly turned into an obsolete accessory that may even *reduce* the amount the instrument's worth. Even players who do intend to amplify their guitars often find that they would prefer a different manufacturer's system than the one the guitar company decided to include at the factory. If the onboard electronics involve a hole cut into the guitar's side, then it is often difficult to replace the system with another, as sizes vary. For all these reasons, it can be a good idea to look at stock electronics with a critical eye. If you don't need them when you buy the guitar, consider finding a completely acoustic instrument, even if it means placing a special order. If the need for electronics arises later, they can easily be added, often surpassing the tone and quality of standard equipment.

Buying Online and Through Mail Order

Although it has been possible to buy musical instruments through the mail for a long time, the proliferation of Internet sites has made this option more common than ever before. With a virtually unlimited selection and generally low prices, simply clicking on a website is an attractive way to buy a guitar for many people. Besides the already-cited obvious benefits, there are other advantages to buying online. It is now possible to easily shop at renowned stores, even if they are hundreds, or even thousands of miles away. Want to buy a rare vintage guitar from Gruhn's in Nashville, Tennessee? No problem, as long as you have a credit card and you're willing to pay for shipping, it doesn't matter where in the world you're located. In the case of unusual and rare instruments, this is a huge plus, as it exponentially multiplies the possible outlets for purchasing an instrument. At a less drastic level, perhaps the manufacturer whose instrument you're interested in doesn't have a dealer in your area, and you don't want to drive several hours just to buy a guitar.

As enticing as buying a guitar on the Internet might sound, it also creates a vast array of potential problems. Probably the most important issue to deal with is the fact that it's impossible to actually play the guitar in question. With the possible exception of the few available instruments made from composite materials, guitars simply vary enough from one example to the next that most players will prefer one to the other. Although large strides have been made in achieving greater consistency, every piece of wood still has its own unique qualities, resulting in the fact that no two guitars are 100% the same. Accordingly, the chances are pretty good that if you play more than one example of the model you've decided to buy, you'll discover slight preferences. With used guitars, these problems multiply.

Even with the best intentions, it can be difficult for the seller to accurately describe the condition of the instrument. Worse yet, what if the guitar has a serious flaw that doesn't show in the digital picture that you had the good sense to request before typing in your payment information? If the guitar is in imminent need of a neck reset, has loose braces, or a bridge that's starting to lift, it may be impossible to spot these problems until the instrument is in your hands. Even worse, the guitar you're pulling from the giant shipping box may not even be the exact model that it was advertised to be. In the best case of these scenarios, you'll only have to pay for shipping the guitar two ways; it doesn't take much imagination as to what the worst case scenario might bring....

For all these reasons, it is absolutely crucial to understand what the terms for a return of the instrument are if you're not completely satisfied. If you're buying from a reputable store, this should not be much of an issue, as most will allow for a 24-hour evaluation period before committing you to the purchase. However, in the case of unknown sellers or auction-based websites such as eBay, these kinds of arrangement can be more difficult to make. As with anything that you're buying sight-unseen, it's a good idea to ask lots of questions to avoid surprises. If you're not satisfied with the response you get via email, then don't be shy to call the store or seller on the phone. Unless they have something to hide about the instrument they're trying to sell you, they will probably welcome an in-depth dialogue, as it is likely to save both parties trouble later on.

Speaking about online auctions, be absolutely sure that you know what you're bidding on. Especially if you're shopping for a vintage instrument, don't go by the seller's word alone when determining whether it is indeed rare and worth that they're asking for it. Do some prior research, and know what the typical value of the guitar in question is. Too many eBay customers get so swooped up in the bidding excitement that they don't realize they're paying far above market value. Once you add a few repairs that you didn't know the instrument needed, what looked like a good deal may suddenly have turned into something you'd rather not talk about.

These warnings aside, great deals can certainly be found online, and it is up to the individual to decide whether the potential risks are worth taking.

An example of a guitar shop's detailed website.

Do I Need More Than One Guitar?

This is a question that can only be answered by the player. Some professionals play one guitar exclusively for years, while many amateurs find they enjoy owning multiple guitars as much as they do actually playing them. Collecting habits aside, there are good reasons to own multiple guitars. The most obvious reason is that you may need radically different sounds for playing various kinds of music. The dreadnought you got for playing bluegrass won't sound too good for flamenco, for example, so if you like the entire palette of possible tones, you'll need several instruments. But there are also less obvious reasons for owning more than one guitar. You might want a different guitar for playing at home or in the recording studio than what you use on stage. One may be acoustically very strong, while the other is excellent to amplify. If you use a lot of alternate tunings, then having more than one guitar on stage can make the difference between boring the audience with lengthy retunings between songs and quickly moving through your set. Some players aren't comfortable traveling with their primary instrument, and buying a second, preferably less-expensive model, provides the best solution. No matter what your reason for deciding that you need more than one guitar, rest assured that you're not alone. Acquiring guitars can be addictive, and many aficionados find that the buying and selling and comparing of instruments is an essential part of their guitaristic existence.

12 A Look Into the Future

With the vast majority of acoustic guitars deeply rooted in designs that are at least 70 years old, and vintage reissues experiencing greater popularity than ever, it could seem downright silly to predict what the future may hold. However, while certain aspects of the instrument have probably reached their peaks of development, others are likely to continually have their envelopes pushed. With the risk of embarrassing ourselves down the road, let's have a look at some of the trends that are already on the horizon.

Alternative Woods

One of the most impending issues facing the production of acoustic guitars is the increasing difficulty to obtain many of the woods that are traditionally used in the instrument's construction. Export limitations resulting in the skyrocketing prices for Brazilian rosewood are only a preview of what might happen to other species (many insiders predict that mahogany will be the next difficult-to-obtain wood), undoubtedly making it necessary for players and manufacturers to adjust to new options.

Although the spruce and cedar used for most tops grows in both North America and Alpine European regions, the traditional woods for backs and sides often come from endangered rainforest regions, or must be imported from countries far away from where it is ultimately processed. For this reason, many manufacturers have begun experimenting with woods that are easily replenished and don't require shipment from one continent to another. Two kinds of woods that fit this description are walnut and cherry, both of which are seeing an increase of use. Taylor, Martin, and Lowden have all introduced guitars with walnut backs and sides, which are often compared to sounding like a combination of rosewood and mahogany. Godin Guitars has already been relying heavily on cherry for the backs and sides of many of its Seagull and Simon & Patrick guitars, and the company is even beginning to use this wood for the necks of selected models.

Speaking of necks, given how good-quality mahogany (long the primary material for the necks on steel-string flattops) may be on the list of woods that will be increasingly difficult to obtain, several manufacturers are looking for alternatives in this realm. Gibson has been using maple for the necks of many of its models (most notably the J-200) for a long time, and it appears to be a choice that other manufacturers are beginning to utilize. Taylor has been using maple necks on the colored models in its 600 series, and with the exception of a little more weight (which *can* make a guitar heavy at the headstock), the switch has been largely inconsequential. Another possible choice is found in Spanish cedar. Although this has continuously been the wood of choice for classical and flamenco guitars' necks, it's a case of rediscovery for steel-string guitars. Used by Martin and other companies in the 1800s, it was eventually replaced by the stiffer mahogany, which provided a stronger neck in the days before truss rods were invented. With today's advanced truss rods, as well as graphite or metal reinforcements, the stiffness of the actual neck material is much less of an issue. As a result, several smaller manufacturers are using Spanish cedar again, and even Martin is now making the necks for many of its 16 series guitars out of the material. Necks made out of synthetic materials would be another option, but so far, they've had a hard time catching on. Alvarez Yairi offered a Bob Weir signature model with a graphite neck in the early 1990s, but a lack of customer enthusiasm lead to a quick discontinuation.

In some cases, the question is more about where the wood came from and how it was harvested than about what species it is. Martin is the first major manufacturer to offer guitars made completely out of woods that are certified as having been harvested in an environmentally friendly manner and from sustainable sources. Referred to as "Smartwood" models, these instruments are available in dreadnought and 000-sizes. Some luthiers are recycling wood that was previously used for other applications. Examples of this practice include old Alaskan salmon traps made out of old-growth Sitka spruce, and furniture made out of Brazilian rosewood—both of which are excellent candidates for having new lives as musical instruments.

Another recent trend is to cut Brazilian rosewood that from the remaining stumps of trees that were originally felled many years ago. Because this wood would otherwise be dug up and burned as part of land development projects, it is legal to export, even with embargos in place.

Luthier William R. Cumpiano with a seven-string guitar featuring a six-piece back.

How efficiently the wood is used is another issue that most large-scale manufacturers are beginning to look at. Taylor has begun making their necks out of three pieces of wood instead of carving it from one (a practice that is common on nylon-string guitars, but unusual on high-end steel-strings), allowing a greater yield per board-foot. Another example is found in an increasing appearance of tops and backs that are made from four pieces rather than the traditional two, which allows for the use of narrower pieces of wood. With proper gluing techniques, these joints are barely noticeable, and many luthiers find that no tone is lost by using this approach.

The final observation about traditional guitar woods is that we will likely have to get used to the fact that materials of visually lower quality are going to be used on average instruments. This has already manifested itself in the fact that ultra-attractive grain patterns are only found in higher-end models, spruce tops that feature some unevenness, and ebony that has streaks instead of being pitch black. In many cases, these visual "flaws" have little or no impact on a guitar's sound, as they don't impact the wood's actual stiffness-to-weight ratio.

Alternative Materials

Even more radical than the use of woods that aren't traditionally associated with stringed instruments is the introduction of completely alternative materials. Guitars that are made almost completely out of composite materials are already being made by companies such as RainSong, Composite Acoustic, Ovation, and Martin, and it's very likely that more manufacturers will follow. Perhaps on the most radical front, Martin has even introduced a model called the "Alternative X" that has a top made out of aluminum! In many cases, alternative materials will be used in more subtle applications. Fingerboards are a good example of an area where traditional woods have already been replaced with other materials on selected guitars for some time. Ovation began using resin-impregnated fingerboards made out of walnut on its Adamas guitars in the 1970s. Luthier Rick Turner has been using impregnated birch veneer (called "pacowood") for some of his fingerboards, using the material's incredible strength as an added benefit. On a large-scale production level, Martin has switched to using fingerboards made out of Micarta (a dense phenolic material, otherwise used for nuts and saddles) for many of its entry-level models. Looking surprisingly like high-quality ebony, many customers don't even realize that their guitars don't have wooden fingerboards.

Although they are primarily electric instruments (but their piezo pickups enable them to sound like acoustic-electrics on stage), Parker guitars have shown a number of innovations that may find their way into their acoustic counterparts, particularly regarding neck construction. By covering the back of the neck in a thin layer of fiberglass, the company is able to use ultra-lightweight basswood, which otherwise wouldn't offer the strength necessary for the task. A fiberglass and epoxy fretboard further increases the neck's stability, and offers a perfect surface for Parker's radical stainless steel frets. Glued flush to the fretboard, these frets have no tang, and the mounting method allows for tolerances so tight that no further filing, crowning, or adjusting is necessary.

New Finishes

With the exception of instruments made by some small-scale builders, it is very probable that the end of the use of nitrocellulose lacquer is near. While polyester-based finishes used to be a sign of an inexpensive guitar, modern spray techniques and UV-curing has improved its tonal qualities to the point where many high-end makers have already made the switch. Meeting more stringent environmental regulations, offering a drastically reduced drying time, and virtually eliminating the risk of damage through exposure to cold or heat, modern polyester offers a superior finish in many regards.

Moving in the opposite direction, it is noteworthy that shellac-based French polish is seeing an increase in popularity among smaller makers. Always the choice for top-level classicals, the use of this finish was never really adapted by the new generation of American steel-string luthiers that began appearing in the 1960s. While the amount of time it takes to apply will never make this finish feasible in a factory environment, its tonal virtues and ease of restoration and touch-up are being rediscovered by players and luthiers alike. Necessitating almost no equipment to apply, emitting no harmful fumes or waste, and associated with some of the finest guitars of the past, French polish is on its way to become a distinctive option that only high-level luthiers will be able to offer.

Improved Amplification

Having already experienced a gigantic leap forward during the past decade or so, amplification systems for acoustic guitars are certainly going to be improved further. Already a mainstay in electric guitar circles, there is no doubt that digital modeling will also become a force for plugged-in acoustic players. While digital modeling for electric instruments (with units such as Line 6's POD) generally involves the exact reproduction of amplifiers, the ideal acoustic application would be able to choose from a variety of microphones and guitars to be digitally emulated. Yamaha's AG-Stomp already offers a feature that is designed to change the sound of a pickup to that of a microphone, and Line 6 has come out with its Variax Acoustic, an acoustic-electric guitar that digitally imitates a variety of sounds and even tunings. Duncan/Turner has introduced its D-TAR Mama Bear system, which promises similar capabilities. Fishman's Aura also uses advanced digital processing, but instead of modeling a variety of instruments, it seeks to "mirror" the true sound of a specific guitar in an amplified environment.

Yamaha's AG-Stomp

It also doesn't take much to envision how these developments may change the way we record acoustic guitars. While it is unlikely that recording in a great-sounding room with a set of microphones is soon to be replaced at the high end of the spectrum, a digital signal would make interfacing with personal computers a likely next step. For home recording, guitars may have built-in interfaces, allowing them to plug directly into the computer with a special cable, guaranteeing a good sound while cutting tracks no matter what the room conditions are like. With this technology in place, interactive jamming over the Internet would only be a small step away.

While not related to the guitar itself, it is also quite likely that more battery-powered amplifiers will appear on the market. AER and Crate have already started this trend, making it possible for acoustic-electric guitarists to once again be heard without being tied to an electrical outlet.

High-Tech Classicals

Given the conservative history of the classical guitar, it may come as a surprise that this is where many of the most radical new designs are being introduced. On a constant quest for improved tone, volume, and playability, luthiers have not been shy to break with tradition. It was classical players who first embraced guitars made in accordance with Dr. Michael Kasha's scientific bracing design, and it was classical players who were first to call attention to the benefits of carbon-fiber reinforced braces (à la Greg Smallman) and sandwich tops (such as those used by Matthias Damman and Gernot Wagner). While few steel-strings divert much from the X-bracing used by Martin since the middle of the 19th century, many high-end classical builders, including Paul Fisher and Thomas Humphrey, are leaving Torres–style fan bracing behind, using advanced lattice patterns instead.

With more players experimenting in crossover styles, some high-end classical guitars have features that were once only found on steel-strings. Modern players often demand narrower necks, radiused fingerboards, and cutaways, leaving it up to the luthiers to create their instruments accordingly.

Adjustable Neck Angle

Particularly in the field of steel-string flattops, control over the guitar's neck angle is beginning to receive an increase in attention. Realizing that neck-pitch is an important element of a guitar's sound, luthiers are devising ways to make this element of guitar construction adjustable. Taylor has been at the forefront of this development. The company's recently redesigned neck joint (see chapter 2) easily adjusts by using a set of shims that the company supplies. Martin has taken this concept a step further with a limited-edition guitar it introduced in 2001. Designed by Ned Steinberger, the guitar features a neck joint that's adjustable "on the fly" with the help of thumbscrews.

This limited edition Martin features an adjustable neck-joint designed by Ned Steinberger.

Already, Washburn is offering a similar system on its acoustic-electric NV series. Luthier Rick Turner is beginning to make acoustics using a neck design that's based on the obscure late-19th–century Howe-Orme guitar. Almost floating off the body, the neck on these guitars is connected on three small points at its heel, giving it infinite adjustment in all directions. In addition, the design allows for an elevated fingerboard extension (similar to that of an archtop), making it possible to maximize the top's active area.

These types of neck designs can have a drastic impact on how a guitar is set up. For instance, instead of lowering or raising the saddle in order to adjust action, it is now possible to set the height of the strings by shifting the angle of the neck. By keeping the saddle at its ideal height, proper torque of the bridge and a good break-angle of the strings moving over the saddle is guaranteed. Besides optimizing acoustic tone, these factors also affect the performance of under-saddle pickups, increasing consistency of tone from one instrument to the next.

It goes without saying that adjustable neck joints also eliminate the need for complicated and expensive neck resets (see chapter 10). With most flattops needing this procedure eventually as the strings' tension pulls the bridge up and the neck forward, having the flexibility of easy adjustments results in better-sounding instruments.

CNC and the Small Shop

When CNC (Computer Numerical Control) machines were first used in the making of acoustic guitars, they were clearly the domain of a few large factories. With the Fadal-brand machine used by most manufacturers costing several hundred-thousand dollars each, it was the Taylors, Martins, Fenders, and Paul Reed Smiths (of which the latter two pioneered their use in electric guitars) of the guitar world that were able to increase precision and endlessly repeat mundane tasks by way of this technology. While several mid-size manufacturers—including Collings and Santa Cruz—have invested in their own full-sized machines, even the smallest makers don't have to helplessly give in to CNC envy. This is because it is now possible to have parts made to order by one of several companies that specialize in making short runs of necks, bridges, fingerboards, and many other parts exactly to customers' specifications. Eliminating the need for labor-intensive rough shaping of parts, this is a welcome option for many independent luthiers, who easily make up for the cost of having parts manufactured by the time they save. Does this practice diminish the value of an individually made instrument? It probably does to those who insist on a completely "handmade" instrument, but most customers who realize that the luthier will still be able to fine-tune each part will notice that at the worst, there is no difference, and at best, using the machined part offers a level of precision that's virtually impossible to attain by hand.

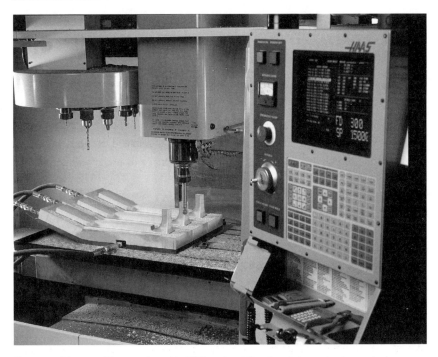

Computer driven machinery such as this CNC router at Garrison is becoming increasingly widespread.

Inlay work has also benefited drastically from the use of CNC. Because it involves much smaller machines than what's needed to carve a neck or other large parts, many small shops have actually invested in their own compact CNC machines. Designing their inlays on the computer, these makers are able to quickly cut their artwork out of abalone, pearl, or other materials, drastically cutting the time—and related cost—for elaborate inlay work, while improving fit and precision.

Although not directly related to CNC technology, another form of computer-aided tooling is found in PLEK's guitar setup machine. Invented by a German team of guitarists and engineers, the machine is able to determine a guitar's ideal setup by precisely measuring the instrument's fingerboard, action, etc. Not only is the PLEK machine able to provide valuable data for proceeding with a manual setup, it is also equipped with a number of tools to automatically file frets, cut nuts, shape saddles, etc. While the machine's expense currently limits it to a small number of locations (mostly in Germany), it is quite imaginable that similar technology will find its way into the manufacturing process at major factories.

Coated Strings

W. L. Gore landed a major coup when they introduced their coated Elixir strings in the mid-1990s. With the marketing budget of a major corporation behind them, the company sent out hundreds of thousands of free samples to guitarists every-where, instantly making a huge impact on the market. With a greatly extended life, the strings were able to live up to the excitement they created; and only a few short years later, coated strings are now offered by every major manufacturer.

While first-generation Elixirs sounded noticeably different from traditional strings, the company's second-generation Nanoweb-coated versions allow for a sound that's practically indistinguishable from non-coated strings. W. L. Gore's patented coating process has prompted other manufacturers to develop their own approaches, with the result that there are now almost as many varieties of coated strings as there are uncoated ones.

Nylon strings appear to be the next frontier. D'Addario is now offering a coated version of its best-selling Pro-Arté strings, and it will be interesting to see which other manufacturers follow suit.

New Factories Opening Up in a Changing Global Economy

With a changed political climate resulting in an increase of foreign investment, the last few years have seen a dramatic increase in guitars made in China. Once the exclusive domain of ultra low-end instruments, Chinese factories are beginning to make the kinds of mid-level instruments previously obtained from plants in Japan, Korea, and Taiwan. Generally made to the specifications of large American or European parent companies, these guitars are reaching a level of quality that would have been unthinkable a few years ago. Following capitalism's constant quest for a descending cost of labor, more and more companies are investing in Chinese production, and the trend is certain to continue.

Not surprisingly, the fall of communism is resulting in similar developments in Eastern Europe. With a rich history of making some of the world's finest bowed instruments, countries such as the Czech Republic are also beginning to also be a force in the world of acoustic guitars. Furch's line of Stanford guitars are already considered by European players to be a high-quality and more affordable alternative to U.S.-made steel strings, and Saga Musical Instruments has offered a line of Czech-made Regal resonator guitars on the U.S. market.

With its proximity to established U.S. manufacturers, and spurred on by recent North American trade agreements, Mexico is another country that is bound to see an increase in the manufacturing of acoustic guitars and accessories. Already, Martin is operating their facility that makes Backpacker travel guitars and many of its strings there, and Taylor has built a case-making plant south of the U.S. border. Fender has moved much of its entry-level electric guitar production to Mexico, and the company also assembles many of its amplifiers in this location.

While the above examples involve major U.S.–based companies taking advantage of Mexico's less costly labor, there are also cases of traditional Mexican luthiers expanding their export potential. This phenomenon is mostly centered around the age-old instrument-making town of Paracho in Central Mexico, with makers such as Cervantes, Montalvo, and Huipe beginning to make an impact on the mid-level nylon-string market.

Decrease in Availability of Vintage Instruments

As we move further away from the days in which today's vintage guitars were manufactured, fewer and fewer of them will be available. Where it was once possible for a player to find a certain vintage guitar with a little ingenuity and patience, we're already seeing the market change to the point where it's becoming increasingly difficult, if not impossible, to find desirable models. The reasons for this are at least two-fold. On one hand, an increased awareness of these instrument has driven prices to the point were someone who is simply looking for a good guitar will question whether a potentially cantankerous old instrument is worth such a large bundle of cash. On the other hand, there are simply fewer instruments to choose from. This may be because their owners aren't interested in selling, but also due to the fact that, every year, more and more vintage guitars will simply have been destroyed, damaged, or otherwise made unplayable. In the case of classical and flamenco guitars, some experts agree that the instruments will simply be "played out" after a certain number of years, making them less desirable than they once were.

Without a doubt, a similar phenomenon will also affect some steel-string guitars, although it may take longer, due to their heavier construction.

So much for that depressing news. The good news is that there are less and less reasons for players to consider vintage guitars. As noted in chapter 11, modern vintage reissues are duplicating the old designs with painstaking detail, often making them better choices than the guitars that inspired them.

Steel-String's Acceptance in Classical Music

Perhaps more than any other factor, the continuing evolution of the acoustic guitar will be determined by the musical styles that it is used in. As we mentioned in the introduction to this book, the instrument has a tendency to show up in musical styles far and beyond what its various designs were originally intended for. Similar to any evolutionary process, luthiers eventually respond to specific players' needs, ultimately creating new designs and genres. There would be no 14-fret necks if it hadn't been for banjo players crossing over, no thin-bodied acoustic-electrics if it hadn't been for acoustic rock music, and no 7-string archtops if it wasn't for jazzers wanting to extend the range of the instrument.

A current trend is found in a cross-pollination of styles. While the classical guitar has already found acceptance in many styles outside its originally intended use (Martin has even made a signature-model classical for pop superstar Sting), an almost reverse development can be observed with the steel-string's entry into the classical world. It is not unusual to see classical guitarists experimenting with the sounds of steel, and world-class players such as David Tanenbaum, Benjamin Verdery, Manuel Barueco, and John Williams have all begun performing and recording in duets and ensembles that include steel-string guitarists. As a result, steel-string players are demanding instruments that feel more like classicals, and offer the latter's complexity and dynamic range.

Final Thoughts

Many of the acoustic guitar's innovations have been spurred by a desire for more volume. Whether it's the development of the dreadnought, the 19-inch archtop, or the high-tech, lattice-braced classical, making the guitar louder has been at the forefront of many luthiers' goals. With few drastic advances having been accomplished in this area over the past 100 years or so, it's difficult to assess whether the potential has been reached: but it is certain that there is no end to further experimentation.

A glimpse into the future? A Martin prototype with built-in PDA for song lists and drum-computer accompaniment.

In some cases, luthiers are coming up with radical solutions to the problems faced by the instruments' players. Noticing the difficulty that players who rely on a variety of alternate tunings face when retuning onstage, California's Steve Klein developed a guitar that tunes itself automatically. Using servos attached to the ends of the strings, the guitar also features a miniature computer that stores hundreds of possible tunings, allowing the player to get from one to another at the push of a button. On a technically less-difficult level, many luthiers are beginning to respond to players' complaints of not being able to hear their guitar as well as their audience does. Soundholes in the side of the instrument appear to provide a solution for many of these players, with luthiers as diverse as Robert Ruck offering

365

this feature on classicals, and John Monteleone incorporating side ports in many of his archtops.

No matter what the future of the acoustic guitar looks like, it can be assured that it is a bright one. Having diversified to the point where it is assured a place in whatever musical styles are yet to come, the instrument is practically extinction-proof. Most people agree that in general, the quality of guitars being built today is at an all-time high, regardless of the model. As such, a good guitar has few rivals when it comes to long-term value.

An experiment by luthier John Kinnard, with the soundhole placed directly under the bridge.

There aren't many things in our consumer-oriented society that are made to give us lifelong enjoyment if properly cared for. While most material goods wear out, break down, or become obsolete within a few short years, guitars will often just start to really open up when that synthesizer, super computer, or motorcycle you bought ends up on the junk pile. With their unique combination of practical utility, beauty of design, and mystery, guitars are a world unto themselves. Whether you play for yourself, your loved ones, or football stadiums full of fans, you should consider yourself lucky to be part of its sound, feel, and culture.

About the Authors

Teja Gerken is a leading authority in all things related to the acoustic guitar. Having begun his journey with the guitar in his native Germany at the age of six, Gerken is now respected as a guitarist, writer, and editor. Currently living in San Francisco, he is an integral part of the Bay Area's acoustic music scene, and his debut CD of original fingerstyle compositions (*On My Way*, LifeRhythm) has received critical international acclaim.

While working on a bachelor's degree in art and society, Gerken spent five months living in Mexico, where he apprenticed luthier Salvador Caro Zalapa in the traditional instrument-making village of Paracho. He also spent five years managing a Northern California guitar shop, and since 1997, has been on the editorial staff of *Acoustic Guitar* magazine. He has also worked as a freelance translator and desktop publisher.

Gerken's journalistic travels have brought him to virtually every major manufacturer of acoustic guitars in the US and Canada, and he has visited and/or interviewed dozens of luthiers throughout the world.

As a musician, Gerken has performed throughout the US and Europe. He has shared the stage with fingerstyle luminaries such as John Renbourn, Alex de Grassi, and Peter Finger, and he has studied with Duck Baker and Peppino D'Agostino. Besides playing solo, he has also written and performed music for San Fransciso's Element Dance theater company, and he frequently collaborates with a variety of vocalists and other instrumentalists. Gerken can be reached on the web at **www.tejagerken.com**.

Michael Simmons is a writer based in northern California. He started playing electric guitar in punk bands as a teenager before being converted to acoustic music by a rabid Django Reinhardt fan. He spent 15 years working at Gryphon Stringed Instruments in Palo Alto, California, where he learned a great deal about the construction and history of guitars, mandolins, and banjos. Simmons is the review editor at *Fiddler Magazine*, co-editor of the *Ukulele Occasional*, and is a frequent contributor to *Acoustic Guitar* magazine and *Guitarmaker*. He contributed entries on the Santa Cruz Guitar Company, Selmer, and Taylor to *Acoustic Guitars: The Illustrated Encyclopedia* and he's the author of *Taylor Guitars: 30 Years of a New American Classic*.

Frank Ford has been working as a professional guitar builder/luthier ever since he and Richard Johnston opened the music store Gryphon Stringed Instruments in 1969. He has written numerous articles on guitar repair for different specialist publications. Moreover, he has been appointed director of the American Association of Stringed Instrument Artisans (ASIA). He regularly gives lectures at the Roberto Venn School of Luthery in Phoenix, Arizona. He has also founded the website www.frets.com, which is the most comprehensive reference for the repair and maintenance of stringed instruments on the web.

Richard Johnston was a luthier and had specialized on the repair of guitars before he—together with Frank Ford—opened the music shop Gryphon Stringed Instruments in Palo Alto, California. He is the co-author of a book on Martin guitars. Since 1990 he has written articles for the specialist magazine *Acoustic Guitar*, for which he has also been a contributing editor since 1995. Richard has written numerous technical articles about different stringed fretted instruments which have appeared in books as well as magazines. At the moment he is working on a book on the history of the Martin Guitar Company.

Bibliography

Anthony Baines
The Oxford Companion to Musical Instruments
Oxford University Press, UK 1992

Julius Bellson
The Gibson Story
Julius Bellson, USA 1973

Robert Benedetto
Making an Archtop Guitar
Centerstream Publishing, USA 1994

Walter Carter
Gibson Guitars: 100 Years of an American Icon
General Publishers Group, USA 1994

Walter Carter
The History of the Ovation Guitar
Hal Leonard, USA 1996

François Charle
The Story of Selmer Maccaferri Guitars
François Charle, France 1999

William R. Cumpiano & Jonathan D. Natelson
Guitarmaking: Tradition and Technology
Chronicle Books, USA 1993

Ralph Deyner
The Guitar Handbook
Knopf, USA 1997

Dan Erlewine
Guitar Player Repair Guide
Miller Freeman, USA 1990

Jim Fisch & L.B Fred
Epiphone: The House of Stathopoulo
Amsco, USA 1996

Nick Freeth and Charles Alexander
The Acoustic Guitar
Running Press Publishers, UK 1999

Alan Greenwood & Gil Hembree
The Official Vintage Guitar Price Guide 2001
Vintage Guitar Books, USA 2001

Stefano Grondona & Luca Waldner
La Chitarra di Luteria: Masterpieces of Guitar Making
L'Officina del Libro, Italy 2001

George Gruhn
Gruhn's Guide to Vintage Guitars, 2nd Edition
Miller Freeman, USA 1999

George Gruhn & Walter Carter
Acoustic Guitars and Other Fretted Instruments: A Photographic History
Miller Freeman, USA 1993

Fredric V. Grunfeld
The Art and Times of the Guitar
Macmillan, USA 1969

John Huber
The Development of the Modern Guitar
The Bold Strummer, USA 1991

Sharon Isbin
Classical Guitar Answer Book
Stringletter Publishing, USA 1999

Franz Jahnel
Manual of Guitar Technology
Verlag Das Musikinstrument, Germany 1981

Hans Moust
The Guild Guitar Book
GuitArchives, The Netherlands 1995

George T. Noe & Daniel L. Most
Chris J. Knutsen: From Harp Guitars to the New Hawaiian Family
Noe Enterprises, USA 1999

José L. Romanillos
Antonio de Torres: Guitar Maker—His Life and Work
Bold Strummer, USA 1995

José Vega Romanillos & Marian Harris Winspear
The Vihuela de Mano and The Spanish Guitar
Sanguino Press, UK 2002

Larry Sandberg
The Acoustic Guitar Guide
A Cappella Books, USA 2000

Paul William Schmidt
Acquired of the Angels: The Lives and Works of Master Guitar Makers John D'Angelico and James L. D'Aquisto, Second Edition
Scarecrow Press, USA 1998

Michael John Simmons
Taylor Guitars: Thirty Years of a New American Classic
PPV Medien, Germany 2003

Various Authors
Acoustic Guitar Owner's Manual
Stringletter Publishing, USA 2000

Various Authors
Acoustic Guitars: An Illustrated Encyclopedia
Thunder Bay Press, USA 2003

Various Authors
The Classical Guitar—A Complete History
Balafon Books, UK 1997

Various Authors
Custom Guitars: A Complete Guide to Contemporary Handcrafted Guitars
String Letter Publishing, USA 2000

Various Authors
Vintage Guitars—The Instruments, the Players, the Music.
Stringletter Publishing USA 2001

Jim Washburn & Richard Johnston
Martin Guitars—An Illustrated Celebration of America's Premier Guitarmaker
Rodale, USA 1997

Tom Wheeler
American Guitars: An Illustrated History
Harper & Row, USA 1982

Tom Wheeler
The Guitar Book: A Handbook for Electric and Acoustic Guitarists
Harper & Row, USA 1974

Eldon Whitford, David Vinopal, & Dan Erlewine
Gibson's Fabulous Flat-Top Guitars—An Illustrated History and Guide
Miller Freeman, USA 1994

Michael Wright
Guitar Stories: Volume One
Vintage Guitar Books, USA 1995

Michael Wright
Guitar Stories: Volume Two
Vintage Guitar Books, USA 2000

Index